Hearing – Feeling – Playi
(Ed. Shirley Salmon)

Hearing – Feeling – Playing

Music and Movement with Hard-of-Hearing and Deaf Children

Edited by Shirley Salmon

forum zeitpunkt
Reichert Verlag Wiesbaden 2008

cover photo: Barbara Asperger

Bibliographic information published by The Deutsche Nationalbibliothek

The Deutsche Nationalbibliothek lists this publication in the Deutsche Nationalbibliografie;
detailed bibliographic data are available in the Internet at
http://dnb.ddb.de.

© zeitpunkt Musik. Forum zeitpunkt
ISBN: 978-3-89500-621-0

Contents

Foreword

Dame Evelyn Glennie

Time and time again I am drawn and inspired by the belief of the highly influential American musical figure Harry Partch, that the individual's path "cannot be retraced, because each of us is an original being". One cannot help but observe the extraordinary challenging task to present a practical and in-depth text on the subject of this book *Hearing – Feeling – Playing* in relation to children with hearing loss.

What does "participation" actually mean when dealing with this fluid art form? Is "sound" music or is "music" sound? How does one attempt to listen to something before hearing it and vice versa? Should we be developing the philosophy of the Italian language by having the same verb for both "to hear" and "to feel"? Surely the art of listening and feeling goes beyond the sound or implied sound, but instead to hearing our own orchestra of internal chatter, our subtle "handing over" and sharing of ideas through physical means such as facial expressions, speed and intensity of movement, depth, texture and dynamic of movement. These are all basic musical ingredients that we *all* participate in whether we realise it or not. The misconception that the only music that exists is what the human ear perceives and if one does not fall into this category of hearing then you hop into another box called the "deaf" box – those who cannot hear the music "conventionally".

When one looks at a notated piece of music it can often make little or no sense to many but as soon as the printed page is transferred to instruments we can virtually immediately create an emotional response. There is no difference in being deaf or hearing – one will always appreciate the subtleties of sound because of the ability to feel things in greater depth to what the ear alone will allow us to hear. We have a choice: either to open our whole body to act as a resonating chamber, or not. Of course, the "orchestra" that each of us creates with our internal chatter, and how that affects how we relate to the external "orchestra" of the world, is much harder for a teacher or guide to control, and indeed to venture into the world of autism may be an intriguing and worthwhile subject of exploration in relation to the complexity of the human mind.

There is no question in my mind that to experience music only through the ears is like eating your food without any indication of what it tastes like. You are satisfied in that it fills you up and keeps you alive, you experience the texture and temperature of the food, but under no circumstances can you say you have truly "experienced" the food and how that relates to your body and mind. Therefore, the admirable task to put into words the ever fluid observations and experience from all contributors to this book must be seen as an ever growing journey of exploration and curiosity.

Our speech is a form of music which overflows with inflection, phrasing, dynamics, rhythm, punctuation, tempo, expression and emotion. Sign language is an even more enhanced form of music because the imagination plays a greater role in the process of direct observation, focus, and extreme concentration; one does not allow external distractions to "visit" the experience but instead the whole body vibrates with infectious exaggerated expression taking the dynamic of "silence" into the heaviest, the loudest, and certainly the most expressive dynamic of all. Silence is the ultimate music but I imagine it is only its experience in death which can enable it to be seen as the pinnacle of life.

Music is our everyday language – there is no such thing as being "unmusical". To play an instrument is but one small aspect, albeit an important one, of what music really is. Each moment of the day presents for us a kaleidoscope of tempo, rhythm, pitch, texture and dynamics which connects everyday living and every living soul. The cross-fertilization of blurring the "boxes" between one activity and another allows us to appreciate the similarities and differences with a much less dismayed and often frightening approach. Perhaps this is why I am keen to say that music is our daily medicine – it is completely accessible to each and every one of us and how we choose to relate to it is something that only we ourselves can control.

For me personally, I have to open up every fibre of my being to be a giver and receiver of sound. This is reiterated in my observations with children through my myriad of percussion instruments. How can I explain the overwhelming physical change of the little deaf boy who was placed lying under the bass end of my marimba? For him to go from a hyper-active state to extreme stillness was something that no one around him had ever seen him do. How could I or his dedicated teachers follow this up? Was it the sound of the marimba, the piece of music being played, was his stillness a display of excitement or was he frightened? His alert face and eager eyes and my gut reaction was an indication that music is something that does not have a place in the exam room, but most definitely has a place as a living, breathing art form whereby we all must open ourselves up to share and learn from each other.

This little boy helped me to "listen" to the journey of the sound – the preparation of the sound, the process of its execution, the giving of the sound, the life of the sound throughout the space, and the death of the sound – he helped me understand the difference between interpretation and translation and, most of all, he helped me to understand that I am the sound. He openly expressed himself in receiving the sound which is something that can be a challenge in a concert hall. He made me realise that no one has possession of the sounds because they are out there for us all to breathe. He was living for the moment which I found extremely infectious because again one can sense a breathing art form that is truly shared and celebrated without any spoken word creating a barrier.

Music Therapy or Sound Therapy (as I prefer to call it) is a recent and exciting field of medicine in development. It comes at a particularly opportune time, in so much as that the mushrooming options for delivery of all music forms and its extreme portability via technological advances allows an inexpensive yet high quality delivery of audio to individuals. Peripatetic and outreach teachers can deliver what might otherwise be financially restricted in these current times of financial cutbacks in curricular music in our schools. However, I am still wary of the fact that reliance on manufactured sound, even if "live" musicians have participated in the recording, causes our listening skills to become one-dimensional. We totally lose the experience of "feeling" the music throughout the body. The reliance is solely on our ears and so we are reverting back to eating without tasting.

This invites the observation that the explosion of audio delivery methods via the internet and technological means has led to a change in all our listening skills. Until possibly the 1960s when the Rock 'n' Roll explosion occurred accompanied by the review of stagecraft and the production of those events, people were content to purely listen. Nowadays, as well as listening they desire all their senses to be stimulated, hence my belief in ridding ourselves of the stifling "boxes" and encourage cross-observation whereby all our senses gel into making the grand sixth sense. It is through the sixth sense that all boundaries, bridges and boxes come tumbling down and we can at last experience a never ending horizon.

Through this book, observations, debates and discoveries will reveal themselves. It gives me hope and satisfaction to know that the sharing of these observations and experiences can only help to make the world a better place for all of us.

Introduction

Shirley Salmon

The idea for this book started to develop a few years ago. I had already spent many years working with children with hearing loss and had become familiar with various approaches concerning the therapeutic use of music and movement and with the work of some teachers and therapists from this field. Looking for technical literature in connection with my practical work, I came across Mimi Scheiblauer, Karl Hofmarksrichter and Claus Bang, who had gained experience in this specific field. I repeatedly studied the works of those "affected" by so-called hearing loss – notably Helen Keller, Emmanuelle Laborit and Evelyn Glennie – those who are the actual experts. This still seems important to me, since we who are able to hear (using our ears) can hardly sense what it means to have or develop a hearing disorder, or respectively what it means to grow up under the conditions of impaired – or the total lack of – auditory information. I am therefore especially pleased that the internationally acclaimed percussionist Dame Evelyn Glennie (who, after developing a hearing disorder in her childhood, learnt to use her own body as a source of resonance in order to actually feel sound) has written the foreword. Here she describes quite distinctly how important and powerful the universal gifts of making music and hearing are to all of us.

When I contacted the English speaking authors Evelyn Glennie, Paul Whittaker, Naomi Benari and Christine Rocca, it was of course necessary to quote the English title of the book[1]. Doing so I came across interesting alternatives: Listening – Feeling – Playing, or respectively Hearing – Sensing – Playing. The title of this book *Hearing – Feeling – Playing* refers to acoustic, vibratory, tactile, emotional and social stimuli as well as to their perception and active realisation. *Hearing* can also involve the conscious, individual activity of listening. *Feeling* can express vibratory, tactile and kinaesthetic stimuli and perceptions on the one hand, or the emotional level of sensing and empathizing on the other. *Playing* not only refers to playing instruments, enacting stories or to playful movement, but also to "play" on the one hand and "games" on the other (cf. *The Importance of Play-Songs in Inclusive Teaching* in this volume).

Some terms of this book need further explanation. "Hearing impaired" refers to people whose (auditory) sense of hearing is impaired. This term is often used comprehensively for slight, moderate and serious hearing disorders as well as for cases

---

1   The book was originally published in German in 2006 entitled *Hören, Spüren, Spielen. Musik und Bewegung mit schwerhörigen und gehörlosen Kindern* by Reichert Verlag, Wiesbaden, Germany.

in which there remain traces of hearing and cases of total hearing loss. "Deaf", on the other hand is used as a category for people who are apparently unable to hear at all. Since we, however, know – also from reports by "deaf" people such as Helen Keller, Emmanuelle Laborit, Evelyn Glennie – that hearing does not only happen via the ears, but also with the whole body, this term merely indicates that the perception does not occur via the ear.

"Hearing impairment", according to the ICF[2] of the World Health Organisation denotes a functional or structural disorder of the body in the sense of a considerable deviation from the norm, or total loss, respectively. The term *hearing disability*, in contrast, does not only refer to the organic impairment, but also implies effects in other domains (activity, participation, full inclusion in our society) as a consequence of the impairment. Generally speaking I prefer the term "children/people with hearing loss", firstly because it includes every degree of hearing impairment and secondly because it does not only focus on the disorder itself. The disadvantage of this term might be that it has a diminishing implication or often causes serious disorders to be taken quite lightly. The expressions "deaf" and "hard-of-hearing" are standard terms used by the people who are "affected" and/or others in the deaf community. Therefore the subheading of this book contains the words "deaf" and "hard-of-hearing" to indicate that the texts contributed present experiences and inspirations for the work with children affected by a varying degree of hearing loss.

The allocation of the various texts contributed was not easy since the logical structure of the book could not allow for age or age groups to be the sole criterion. The beginning consists of accounts describing individual developments and experiences under the conditions of hearing impairment and hearing loss as well as the individual approach to music, its performance and its personal significance. The theoretical principles deal with essential developmental aspects which are relevant to all children, but especially to those with hearing loss. These are supplemented by contributions defining the position of, and offering insights into, the research on the perception of music. The practical principles present approaches which can be relevant to various age groups, whereas the last part offers descriptions of practical work within various environments and with different age groups – ranging from pre-school children and families to school children and teenagers.

In comparison to the USA, where the use of music in education for people with hearing loss has a more than one hundred-year-long tradition, this tradition in German speaking countries is shorter, the use of music far less widespread and its

---

2   ICF (International Classification of Functioning, Disability and Health) serves as a universal language beyond geographic and scientific limits for describing an individual's functional health condition, disability, social impairment and his/her relevant environmental factors, http://www.who.int/icidh, 12/2007 (Ed.).

documentation still incomplete. One of the first pioneers was Mimi Scheiblauer (1891–1968), who as early as 1920 employed rhythmical-musical elements in educating hard-of-hearing and deaf children as well as performing nativity plays with them. Since then several different approaches involving music and movement have been developed, such as those of Karl Hofmarksrichter, Antonius van Uden, Claus Bang, Irmgard Rohloff und Susann Schmid-Giovannini.

While this book intends to introduce the readers to a number of basic principles as well as to a diversity of European approaches, there can be no claim to completeness, since this would be impossible in a single publication. Pedagogic and therapeutic backgrounds and methods are discussed in the various texts contributed, common aspects and differences between pedagogy and therapy, however, are not a central theme of this book. The importance of music and movement for deaf and hard-of-hearing children and the right to receive education, similarly support or therapy with music, movement or dance are central concerns here. The aim of this book is to address, inform and inspire specialists from the educational and therapeutic fields, parents as well as the experts (meaning those "affected") themselves.

The central question in practical settings remains: which approach involving music and/or movement, which methods and which form of participation – be it in education, remedial help and support or therapy – can be of benefit to the children in question?

Thanks go to …
* all authors who were prepared to write about their thoughts and experiences in all their diversity;
* the children at the Förderzentrum des Landes Steiermark für Hör- und Sprachbildung, Graz[3] and its Kindergarten for hearing and hard-of-hearing children and also the children at the Josef Rehrl School in Salzburg, with whom I was able to learn and experience a tremendous amount, as well as to the colleagues who were interested in this work;
* Edda Faes, Karin Schumacher and Sigrid Köck-Hatzmann for their ever-inspiring co-operation, their encouragement and their committed as well as critical exchange;
* the students at the Orff Institute, Mozarteum University, Salzburg who contributed practical and theoretical work in this field;
* Margaret Murray for her invaluable advice;
* Christan Hackl and Jane Bartlmä for their translations;
* Esther Bacher for her interest, skill and dedication in editing the manuscripts.

Shirley Salmon   Grambach, 2008

---

3 County Centre for Hearing and Speech Education in Graz, Austria (Ed.)

Part I: Viva la Musica!

With my Hearing Aids I'm actually quite Normal!

Helga Wilberg

With my hearing aids I am a person with normal hearing. Many people around me thus do not even know that I have a moderate-to-severe degree of hearing impairment (40–60 % loss of hearing) and that without my hearing aids I could not communicate with them at all! The hearing aids are usually well concealed under my long hair. People are not aware of the difficulties that often confront me.

In fact, the initial reaction of people I talk to when they learn of my hearing impairment is usually "How convenient; you can just turn off your hearing aids when it's too noisy for you. That must have its advantages!" – Advantages? I would gladly exchange my hearing aids for two healthy ears and a more stress-free life.

As a toddler I suffered several bouts of middle-ear infection as well as tonsillitis. The doctors suspect that these illnesses caused the hearing problem. So it was that just before I started school aged six I was issued with my first pair of hearing aids. Because my parents put in a lot of effort on my behalf at school and had many discussions with the teachers, I was able to attend mainstream schools throughout my schooling. That was very nice in some ways, but was also a burden because many teachers had difficulty coming to terms with my handicap. At high school level, to my great regret I had to drop out of the *Gymnasium*[1] because I had too much trouble with my hearing there and could not keep up with the necessary remedial study at home. A year after this failed attempt, the audiologist discovered that my hearing aids were too old and were no longer performing properly. This still annoys me, as my life may have turned out differently but for this.

I attended the *Hauptschule* followed by an upgrade to the *Realschule* from where I graduated with a subject-specific university entrance qualification in social sciences. Right through school I felt that I always had to learn and achieve more than my peers. Although some teachers made an effort, I generally had to fight against a lack of understanding. Some never spoke clearly or loudly enough; while others shouted at me, which I found very unpleasant. Despite my parents' numerous

---

1   The German school system has three different tiers of high schools into which students are streamed according to aptitude: the *Gymnasium* (grammar school) prepares students for university, *Realschule* (middle school) for technical professions, and *Hauptschule* (main school) for trades (Ed.).

interventions, I had the most trouble in German classes, since I struggled with my expression and spelling and was two or three years behind my classmates in knowledge and achievements. For instance it was very difficult to make my teachers understand that I was unable to take dictations because I could not lip-read and write all at the same time. I confused letters that sounded similar, and mostly missed the endings altogether. On top of that, the speed of dictations meant that with the best will in the world, I had no time to double-check each word! In other subjects, such as biology, I was also criticised because of my spelling, although my exercises would have been technically correct.

Some teachers helpfully encouraged me to simply put up my hand and ask whenever I had not heard something! Of course that was easier said than done. When I only half heard something and could not work it out for myself, of course I did ask. But when I did not hear it at all, then I had no way of knowing that I had missed something.

After passing my university entrance exams I decided to study Early Childhood Education. But again the hearing disability put obstacles in my way, as I encountered difficulties even with my application for a place in the course. It was assumed that given my hearing problems I would be incapable of taking a group! Yet after a long search I did find a program that was not only prepared to accept me but even showed understanding for people with hearing loss, because there was a centre for the deaf and hearing impaired on the same campus. For the first time in my life I felt happy in my learning environment as the teachers paid real attention to me and checked up on me. In the many training placements I was able to demonstrate that I was very capable of taking a group. Children are not like adults – they treat disabilities in a very open and direct manner. At kindergarten one of the first questions was often "What's that behind your ear?" I would usually compare my hearing aid to a pair of glasses, with which the children were familiar. And that was the end of the matter for them, whereas adults suddenly think they have to talk differently to me, or they feel sorry for me, which I find just as unpleasant.

During my training I discovered my passion for teaching music.

As a child I loved making music and singing, and I learnt to play the flute and then the piano. When I expressed a desire to take up the violin, my violin teacher asked: "Is that really possible with your hearing impairment?" And yet it is the violin that has kept my passion for music alive. The fine tuning, paying attention to the intonation and careful listening suited me. Maybe that irritated my colleagues. You see, my inner ear is very good, since my hearing impairment is situated in my middle ear. I often suffer, in fact, when instruments have not been tuned properly or when people do not sing in tune.

My desire to study music kept growing. So in 1999 I sat the entrance examination for Music and Dance Education at the Orff Institute, Mozarteum University, Salzburg. My violin teacher was behind me all the way – it was she who recommended the course and prepared me for the entrance examination. I frequently fretted about the great unknown – how would I cope with the hearing components, especially the aural dictation, and would I even be able to complete my music studies given my hearing difficulties.

I passed the entrance examination and was over the moon. I could scarcely believe it at the time.

To my great surprise most of the lecturers at the university were much more understanding of my hearing impairment than any of my teachers at school had ever been. Luckily for me, my class was made up of just 16 students and the majority of lectures were given in small groups, which was a great advantage for me. During my studies I was able to spend one semester with the teacher training group at the Institute for the Hearing Impaired in Salzburg. My interactions with the children were exciting as it was quite new for them to have a student with the same problem as them.

It was almost a miracle for me that I was able to complete my studies with distinction, after having left school with only average results despite my huge efforts. Today I work as a music teacher at a secondary school where I teach Years 5 and 6, conduct an instrumental ensemble and the lower school choir, sing with colleagues in the teachers' quartet and play percussion in the teachers' band.

I mentioned at the start that I look like a person with normal hearing when I use my hearing aids. I think I give this impression because I have acquired many tricks and techniques to make up for my loss of hearing.

For example most of my colleagues are not aware that I am heavily reliant on lip-reading. If there is a lot of ambient noise I have to concentrate even harder on the conversation (e. g. in the staffroom, at a restaurant) and tire more quickly than other people. Sometimes it is impossible to follow the conversation. Using the telephone is always an unpleasant experience for me as I cannot lip-read in this situation. This results in frequent misunderstandings that are unpleasant to me. For example I once turned up a day early for an interview because I had misunderstood the date over the phone. Naturally this was very embarrassing for me. I did get the position though, which pleased me.

When I have missed something in the course of a conversation I can often work it out based on what has gone on before.

I usually cannot determine from which direction the sound originates. I often do not even hear quiet sounds or the sounds of nature, or am unable to filter them from background noise, which I sometimes find a shame when I want to observe nature.

In Salzburg I had a go at playing the violin in the orchestra, but I soon had to abandon this because I could not hear myself among the other violins and I could not hold the intonation. It was utterly impossible for me to tune with the orchestra, because I need absolute silence. The positioning of everyone in ensemble play is also important so that I can see all the other players because I do not hear equally well on both ears. It is stressful for me when the positions are suddenly changed for a performance because my hearing ability is dramatically altered and I have to re-adjust in order to play well. This is no problem for someone with normal hearing, so my fellow group members often do not think of me when they make such changes. I have great trouble hearing deep instruments and bass voices. As a child I was always baffled as to why people would play the double bass in an orchestra when it could not even be heard. The tones are like a hum to me which I perceive more as a vibration than as a pitch. Though later on I did accompany a double bass player on the piano, which I enjoyed despite the extra stress of having to listen so intensely.

Situations always arise that remind me how much I depend on my hearing aids. For example when I am forced to improvise when the batteries suddenly run out and I do not have any spares on me. It once happened on an open day at my school – a battery went flat and I could not find a replacement. Since then I have always kept a supply of spare batteries in various locations.

Sometimes I am not able to wear my hearing aid on account of an external ear infection, which means my hearing is much worse. These situations are always a nuisance as my surroundings are not set up for someone whose hearing is actually impaired.

It is obviously a challenge for me to teach music to each class of 30 pupils at the high school where I work, as it is not always particularly quiet! I often have problems hearing my pupils. It can turn into a game of chance when I am asked about the names of notes, if I cannot work out whether the pupil said "c" or "d". But I approach these situations with a sense of humour. It is a simple fact though that I expend more energy and must concentrate harder in each lesson than a teacher with no hearing impairment.

Listening is hard work for me in spite of the hearing aids, but I enjoy teaching and am proud that I have managed to become a music and dance teacher despite my hearing impairment.

As a teacher I have occasionally worked with pupils with hearing loss at our school. I can interact with them in a different way from my colleagues. One such pupil approached me just before the start of a class and showed me her broken hearing aid. She asked me what she should do as she had noticed that I also use hearing aids and assumed that I would be able to help her.

I am constantly reminded of how much my pupils enjoy their music lessons. They leave the class in a happy, joyful mood, especially when the lesson has involved dancing.

Unlike others I see no barrier between having a hearing impairment and actively making music. In spite of my hearing impairment I am a happy person and I blossom when I have the opportunity to make music and dance. It is particularly important and rewarding for me to be able to pass on this joy for music to others.

Every child should be able to attend music lessons, regardless of his or her abilities. Music and dance boost your spirits and enhance your quality of life.

Viva la Musica!

Elke Bartlmä

When I look up the definition of the word music in a Bertelsmann lexicon it reads as follows: "Music (Greek), originally used by the Greeks as a collective concept for musical art, poetry and dance then later, just for the former. The definition of music as the art used to express impressions (19th century) goes back to Aristotle who ascribed ethical value to music. The 20th century has no integral concept of music; it can be divided into diverse groups: 1. according to its aesthetic value; 2. according to content and formal structure; 3. according to its purpose; 4. according to its means of presentation [...]." This clinical description continues without emotion or fervour, almost like reading the operating manual for a DVD player – showing interest for its purpose but with no love for the subject.

My personal definition of music is quite different: Music is the expression of pulsating passion coming from folk groups or individuals. Few other arts are able to express the (well) being of a person as aptly as music with the exception of dance, literature, the language of love and art representation. It is immaterial whether evenings are spent listening avidly to the chords of Chopin emanating from the stereo, singing heartily whilst showering or raving to beat in a disco.

The connotation music is far too comprehensive to reduce it to two columns in a lexicon. Based on such a description somebody who had never come into contact with music would hardly be able to understand its true nature. Rather more we would have to offer this person the opportunity of experiencing music. This is the true answer – the experience of music thrills the soul or lightens the mood, brings on melancholy or ecstasy in its turn. If one took the time and made the effort it would be possible to identify and relive the emotions and worlds of sensitivity expressed by a composer in each of his classical works.

I can no longer remember my first experience of music and I believe that it is not all that important to know when it was made. I can only explain my childhood impressions when my family played music.

I was born into a very musical extended family. Two of my father's brothers were interested musicians. Dieter introduced his four daughters to the art and Günther played himself. In my home town Günther is a well-known bass singer in several choirs and my four cousins are either actively occupied teaching music at academies or enjoy playing privately as a hobby. When the family met on occasions, such as special birthdays or weddings, music was always an important part of the celebrations; Günther played the guitar or contrabass and his four nieces, Barbara, Monika,

Anya and Katya accompanied him on various instruments. A lot of time was spent singing too, Günther with his guitar leading the other members of the family.

As a child I did not appreciate these family musical events as I did not understand the folklore and tradition. It was boring and I also did not realise that the curved object which Günther was strumming was a musical instrument. I chatted with my mother whilst the others were singing but she had to teach me to remain quiet when Günther took out his curved device and began to play, as it was rude not to listen. As I sat there silently, not understanding anything, I had the opportunity to watch the faces of the different family members. Heads were nodded, strange faces were pulled, eyebrows raised and more often than not everyone looked sad.

It was only much later that I realised that the nodding heads were accompanying the rhythm and that there were an overwhelming number of melancholic Carinthian folk songs to which sad expressions were apparently suited.

My sister Nadia started to play this curved instrument at the age of six, this was when I learned that it was called a guitar.

When I was five I started ballet classes and, at the same time, I attended a course for modern dance at that time known as "jazz dance". I knew from my years at nursery school that I could easily copy others so I had no problems with ballet. Our teacher, Sabine, showed us the steps and my colleagues and I just followed suit. At this time I took no notice of the music as I was concentrating solely on the correct order and precision of the required steps. Sabine often drummed on a tambourine and we had to move from one end of the hall to the other to these beats, at times slowly then faster. I followed this cacophony of sound, which was loud enough for me to hear, and placed my steps to the beats. I still did not understand that this was aural training to teach us how to move to a certain beat or rhythm. Ballet productions, which were usually performed in the Renaissance castle in my home town in June each year, also presented no problem; we had all practised the choreography so well by the time the event approached that we were perfect. Sabine stood behind the curtain, hidden from the audience, and showed us each step in case we had forgotten. I still was not aware of the music even though it was accordingly amplified for the theatre: it was of no importance to me.

What I loved about these performances was dressing up in the costumes sewn by our mothers and the enthusiastic applause from the audience, a true reward for our efforts.

In the context of ballet I have an amusing story: once Sabine wanted my group, as well as Nadia's, to practise a Charleston together and to perform the dance in June. The steps were practised; my mother sewed our costumes together with a friend and the great day came closer. To complete the costumes we needed net tights which however were unfortunately not sold in our size. Jane had to buy tights which were at least two numbers too large. Nadia's fitted her more or less as she was older and thus larger than me, mine hung limply on my thin hips and legs but we did not envisage any trouble.

The day arrived. We put on our costumes backstage and awaited our turn. Sabine rushed hectically between stage and wardrobe making sure that all was running smoothly and according to plan. At last the time had come and we tripped onto the stage. The opening chords were struck and we tensed in anticipation. I concentrated especially on Sabine behind the stage who was indicating the start with exaggerated mimicry. The music began, Sabine's order came and we flung ourselves into movement as the Charleston rhythm is fast.

I remembered the steps we had studied for so long and watched the others carefully to make sure I was synchronised (the music was non-existent for me; I used my eyes to keep in step). Suddenly I realised that my tights were slipping; the fast dance was making them lose the little hold they had. There was nothing I could do other than to keep pulling them up into place, a procedure that I intelligently adapted to keep in time with the other dancers. Finally I just kept a desperate hold on my tights and completely left out the arm movements. This must have been a grotesque sight, a six year old girl spending a whole dance trying to keep her tights up. To begin with Sabine wrung her hands in desperation and looked aghast, however as she realised that the audience was genuinely amused and was clapping and laughing enthusiastically she began to relax. The clue was that the audience thought it was a special choreography to parody the Charleston a little.

When I was ten I stopped going to ballet classes as I hated dancing on points but I continued with modern dance.

On my eleventh birthday Nadia gave me a tape with songs by Madonna. I did not really know what to do with it as I had no practice in listening to different types of music. A year later I watched the film *Flash Dance* and was so fascinated that at last I began to take interest in music. Nadia bought the sound track to the film and I began to listen with more awareness. Nadia taught me to listen for beat which at the beginning I could not pick out from the muddle of instruments and song being relayed to my ears. I understood quickly though as we had already practised clapping to beat and rhythm at school. At last I understood the purpose of rhythm and beat; they were there to accompany movement, to dance! At the same time I realised why the other dancers at the ballet classes always knew exactly when to make their steps. Now I began to listen to the music in my dancing lessons and learned how to move feeling the beat. At the same time I made yet another discovery; the "rumbling" that I could feel through my whole body and in my feet was a result of the music which I was physically experiencing. Thus I learned to give in to and follow this "rumbling" which was in reality the vibrations caused by music.

I also began to take active interest in the dances which Sabine was teaching us. My favourite performance was dancing in our musical production of *A Chorus Line*. We danced to the song *One* and it was a resounding success.

When I was thirteen I stopped attending modern dance as I could no longer bear the intrigues within the group. However in the meantime I had broadened my understanding of music and listened to various pop groups, to whose songs I danced. I began to listen just to the music and to move accordingly. I learned to improvise, a talent which was going to be very useful at a later date.

When I was fifteen I went on a skiing course with my form in the upper fifth. As entertainment one evening a disco had been organised. I sat with the other pupils strung out on a bench and none of us dared to step out onto the dance floor. After some time more and more of my colleagues got up and started to dance, I remained where I was and soon was lost in thought. Suddenly a song that I knew came over the loudspeakers. First I hesitated then I became impatient, jumped up and joined the others on the floor. I stayed at the edge and began to dance; I closed my eyes in order to concentrate better on the music. When I had found the right beat and my steps had automatically adapted, I opened my eyes and discovered to my horror that I was alone on the floor. I stopped dancing immediately and wanted to return to my seat but my co-pupils shouted their encouragement so I continued and danced to the end of the song, giving all I had and basking in the attention. This was even better than the ballet performances as this time it was just me in the limelight. Here I must explain that due to my partial hearing I always had problems making friends at school. Through dancing I had at last found a way to gain the attention and respect of my contemporaries. When the song was over I ran to my room and hid. On the one hand I was completely out of breath and no way could I repeat a dance, on the other hand I was afraid of talking to the other pupils. It was not until the next day that I had the courage to face the others and explain to them where I had learned to dance.

A gym teacher had also seen my dance during the skiing week and she asked me if I would have the time and inclination to perform at school events. Surprised and delighted I agreed.

My first important performance was in the gym at our school. Before the event I had practised and produced the choreography with the help of a friend who had also attended ballet and modern dance classes. On this occasion though I felt really stupid as there was a young man sitting in the audience who had caught my eye, he however seemed blithely uninterested in me. This made me think that my dancing was not good enough and when my gym teacher asked me to perform again I refused. She used all her powers of persuasion and eventually I agreed to a further performance. This time it was a great success as I earned enthusiastic applause from the audience. I was proud; I had danced a solo in front of 500 people.

My next significant success was during a school exchange project: In the upper sixth we were sent to stay with Italian families in Pordenone. On our arrival the school organised a welcoming evening including some stage performances. Once again the teacher asked me to dance and so I began in front of an audience of over 1,000. This time I was really nervous and felt I was dancing in a trance when, in the middle of all, I forgot the sequence of my choreography. Immediately I began to improvise and my steps became quite different from those I had originally prac-tised. I was incredibly grateful that I had often improvised at home in my room; it was now serving its purpose. Nobody guessed my predicament, I relaxed and suddenly my choreography fell back into place and I danced as planned to the end. As the audience applauded I heard cheers of approval – it was one of the best mo-ments in my life.

Whilst I was attending the upper high school I also had recorder lessons. As much as I loved dancing, so I hated these lessons. Some years before my cousin Anya had given me private recorder lessons and later my other cousin Katya taught me at the music school. I did my exercises but my heart was not really in it. I used a white lie and told my music professor that I had only been practising for two years (in real-ity it was four). First I felt guilty for not telling the truth, but later I was relieved as the burden of work in other subjects increased and learning took longer and longer. This way I was able to practise the exercises I already knew well just before recorder classes and enough time remained to do justice to the other subjects. After one year on the soprano, I changed to the alto recorder, which has a deeper tone. This was a good decision; I enjoyed the deeper tone much more than the high notes of the soprano, which I found unbearable. I began to take more pleasure in the in-strumental lessons and practised willingly for longer periods in order to master the different finger positions.

I did however have one disagreement with my professor. I was unable to play the trill, especially when I was playing together with a colleague. The usual way of exe-cuting a trill is to alternate rapidly between the note indicated and the note directly above it in the given scale. Attempting these trills made me lose the beat each time and the tone produced sounded like a saw in my ears. I avoided playing trills and I did not practise them. To begin with my professor was tolerant, but gradually she started to get annoyed and once she threatened to give me a lower mark. She then left the room to fetch something. As the door closed I threw my recorder after her, which was luckily made of plastic and did not break when it hit the door. But out-side in the corridor the professor's steps slowed – I could hear her as she was wearing high heels. When she came back into the classroom she did not say a word and I too behaved as if nothing had happened. A week later she asked me, why I did not want to play trills. After I had explained, she understood and no longer asked me to practise them; neither did I get worse marks. Looking back I would like to thank her now for her patience and interest – after listening to my explanation she told me that she had never before taught persons with a hearing impairment and did not realise that partial hearing also implied different acoustic experiences. She then understood that sounds or notes which the hearing world found pleasant could in fact be unbearable for the partially hearing.

Having passed the *Reifeprüfung*[1] at the high school in Spittal/Drau in Austria, I decided to attend teacher training college in order to become a teacher for children with special needs. This wish was not easy to accomplish. With the following letter, which I mailed to all of the most important ministers and politicians in Austria, I would like to demonstrate how difficult it can be in this country to enjoy equal chances if you have a handicap.

18th February 2003

Dear Sirs,

My name is Elke Bartlmä. Since January 1998 I have been working as a support teacher in both primary and secondary schools for children whose hearing is severely impaired. This job is more a vocation for me as I can perfectly understand my pupils' general situation and learning difficulties; since birth I too have been almost completely deaf.

I attended regular schools, naturally I had to work much harder than other pupils to achieve the same standards; in 1994 I passed my *Reifeprüfung* at the high school in Spittal, department for music and educational sciences. From 1994 to 1997 I attended the federal teacher training college in Carinthia.

These years were marked by incredible difficulties: the College requires certain suitability tests for the entrance exam. The physical, spoken and musical suitability of each candidate is examined. I passed the physical and speech tests with flying colours (when I talk my handicap is not apparent), it was the musical tests which were problematical for me. I was unable to sing to the notes played on the piano and my rendering of the Austrian national and Carinthian federal anthem

---

1   The equivalent in England is A-levels, in the USA the high school diploma. A-level is short for 'Advanced Level' – a General Certificate of Education qualification usually taken by students in the sixth form – the final two years of secondary school after they have completed their GCE exams (Ed.).

was not perfect. As a result I was ex-matriculated from the college after one year's attendance.

I was supposed to choose two subjects to study in order to become a secondary school teacher. However, it was my greatest wish to train as a teacher for children with special needs as I already knew that later I wanted to work with partially hearing children. After a wealth of correspondence I was allowed to continue as an extraordinary student but was not permitted to attend the musical tutorials (musical education, choir, instrumental).

I would like to place this decision against the following background:
* Six years recorder instruction (soprano and alto)
* Five years ballet classes and eight years modern dance
* One week modern dance course with the internationally renowned American dancer Bruce Taylor in Vienna
* Two solo performances in front of large audiences
* A finals paper on a musical topic (rhythmic training with partially hearing children) which was awarded an "excellent"
* At the moment a training course for free dance and dance therapy under the direction of Veronika Fritsch in Leibnitz, Austria

Thus I would like to make it clear that for me musical suitability is not confined to singing.

In 1997 I left the teacher training college without having been allowed to sit the final exams. In 1998 I began working as a support teacher with a special contract. In January 2000 I was permitted to sit the written exams for the teacher training diploma and in June 2001 the oral exams, I passed them all successfully. From 1999 to 2001 I attended a teacher training college for the deaf and partially hearing. Here too I was able to pass all exams with very good results.

Now all my documents have been submitted to the examining committee of the Educational Institute in Klagenfurt for further processing – in my case, though, there will be no progress, as there is still no legal arrangement for people like me – I still do not have a teacher training diploma for children with special needs, nor a certificate to qualify as a teacher for the deaf and partially hearing.

Integration is a wonderful word: it works well in primary schools, sometimes it functions in secondary schools but then …? It is sad, but I prepare my pupils in third and fourth forms for the sobering reality that they cannot chose whatever career they wish, in spite of the Right to Equal Education.

A lot must still be done to achieve true integration in the working world!

I would like to request you to kindly consider my situation and inform me as soon as possible of a viable solution.

Yours sincerely,

Elke Bartlmä

The government finally reacted to this missive and in March 2003 I was officially granted the right to receive my teacher training diplomas. In the meantime however the conditions of study at the college had changed and I had to take a number of further examinations. In December 2004 I received my diploma as a teacher for children with special needs and in June 2005 the certificate of further training as a teacher for the deaf and partially hearing. My patience and my battle had paid off! Here I would like to say a heartfelt thank you to my mother. Without her constant support I would not be where I am now.
Thank you Jane – I love you very much.

MatD – Music and the Deaf

Paul Whittaker

When most people see the words *music* and *deaf* in the same sentence they inevitably think of Beethoven, but – of course there are many other deaf people involved in the music business, and countless individuals with hearing loss who cannot imagine a world without music.

I am profoundly deaf myself (from birth) and for the past 17 years have been running "Music and the Deaf" (MatD) a charity based in the UK that helps deaf people – and those who live and work with them – access music and performing arts. Music has always played a huge part in my life: I play the piano and the organ, have trained choirs (quite an interesting challenge for singers when they realise you can't actually hear them!) and also provide sign language interpreted performances for major musical productions both in London and on tour.

I find that, even in 2005, people still find the phrase *deaf musician* something of a paradox, and I think this happens not because they don't understand deafness, but because they don't think about what music *is*. Music tends to surround us from a very early age, and we quickly become conditioned to it: "I know what I like, and I like what I know" is a common statement. But how often do we think about what music *consists* of, why does it move us in the way it does? Is there a difference between noise and music, and is musical ability dependent on being able to hear?

There are thousands of hearing people who profess to be totally unmusical, and – conversely – thousands of deaf people who are very musical. If we take the view that hearing is passive but listening is active then there's no reason why a deaf person should not enjoy music. I would agree that your ears are *useful* when it comes to music, but there's something far more fundamental involved, and that is heart and soul and emotion. Perhaps it would be useful at this point to give you bit more information about myself and my own understanding and perception of music.

I was born in 1964 with a hearing loss and therefore have no full aural memory of music – I could hear certain sounds but these were distorted. Until the age of 7 my hearing loss remained fairly stable, but it deteriorated rapidly over the next 4 years and I have been profoundly deaf since age 11.

Despite my deafness I was aware of a lot of music going on in the home, and at age 5 decided I wanted to play the piano. Two years later I joined the local church choir and through that developed an interest in the organ, which I started to learn when 12. At 14 I took charge of my own choir. Originally I considered a career as a concert pianist or organist, but couldn't really be bothered to practice enough (!) so eventually settled on getting a university degree in music instead. Over a 2-year period I applied to 12 universities and was rejected by all of them because of my deafness, despite already having 3 music diplomas. Eventually I was accepted by Wadham College, Oxford, in 1983 and spent 3 wonderful years there in an environment that couldn't have been more supportive and helpful.

Until I went up to Oxford I never actually considered how I heard and understood music; I had always been deaf and always been a musician, and never considered that what I was doing was unusual in any way. Even now I cannot fully explain my love of music, how I actually *do* it, analyze objectively how I conduct and train a choir, or why I enjoy going to concerts. It is only really when people have questioned me that I've gained more insight into my world of music. For example, I was once asked if it made a difference what clothes I wore when listening to – or more correctly, perceiving – music. I'd never thought about this at all, and I could not at the time give an honest reply; but having thought about it since, the answer must be "yes", because the more heavily clothed I am the less sensitive to vibration I become.

My earliest memory of music is very vague, but I can remember that I have never found it easy to distinguish pitch and intervals by aural means alone. When I first started to play the piano I had partial aural perception of notes up to two octaves above middle C (without hearing aids). Now I can't *hear* a single note on the piano without my hearing aids in, whilst with hearing aids I can *hear* up to 2 octaves above middle C.

So far as *hearing* other instruments is concerned, there is wide variation. A violin is totally inaudible most of the time, the exception being the very lowest notes. A cello on the other hand is an excellent instrument to listen to, partly because of the ease of perception (it has strong vibrations), and partly because its pitch lies within my best residual hearing range. The woodwind family is also, in general, easy to perceive; the clarinet is best because of the clarity of its tone (especially the warmth of its lower register), and the lowest range of the flute is also very appealing. Brass instruments tend to jar on the ear. Percussion instruments are easier to perceive because of being struck, but – with the exception of timpani – most of them are quite difficult to actually hear, often being lost in the mass of sound created by an orchestra. Within an orchestra the horn is easiest for me to hear, its rich tone and attack cutting straight through everything else, while, perhaps surprisingly, the higher pitch of the trumpet puts it out of my hearing range despite its penetrative sound.

Although I am an organist I believe this is one of the hardest instruments for a deaf person to play, because of the way the sound is produced. On a piano you can feel the hammer, hit the string, and the vibrations travel back along your hand and up your arm. With an organ that degree of tactile sensation is largely lost so I need to be much more sensitive and aware of what and how I'm playing. Also I cannot easily tell the difference between the tonal quality of different organs: I have to look at the stop-name and imagine what kind of sound and tone it will have. Thus, I choose stops by association not by sound. For this reason, and for the fact that I cannot judge the acoustics of a building, I always need someone to check my registrations, balance etc. before I do a recital anywhere.

There are certain things which deafness can make difficult or even impossible. Conducting an orchestra or some other group of instrumentalists would be a big challenge, though one I'd happily welcome! On the other hand deafness actually can have advantages, particularly in the understanding of a musical score. When one is forced through circumstances to sit down and read a score rather than mere casual listening of a musical work, the eye does notice many things that the ear misses, so ultimately you gain a much better understanding and appreciation of the piece concerned.

This reliance on the notated score does cut me off from some kinds of music. Electronic and avant-garde music are the major no-go areas, and the use of unconventional notations means that I cannot even get a visual impression of the music. Improvised music also presents difficulties and although I enjoy jazz I really can't access it as I'd like to.

When I'm working in the theatre (giving a sign language interpreted performance) then I have to memorize all the words and music for every character in that show. This is where my score-reading ability and memory really pay off, but – even after 13 years of signed theatre work – I still find spoken dialogue very hard to deal with.

If there is one thing that surprises most people about me it is my ability to train and conduct a choir. Playing the piano or organ is acceptable, but when training a choir I have no physical control over the sound being produced. I teach my choir a piece in very short phrases and then build it up part by part. Obviously, the singers themselves need to be honest about how well they know the piece, and to some extent I rely on them to tell me about issues like tuning and tone quality. I do know when my choir is out of tune because of a clash in the vibrations – a clash between what I see in the score and what I physically feel – but whether they are sharp or flat is harder to determine. I don't have perfect pitch but I do have a very secure sense of it, possibly developed from familiarity with my own piano at home when I was young. Nowadays I find it almost impossible to sing in tune with any piano except my own, because of the very slightly different rates of vibration (tuning). And if someone plays a hymn or song in a different key from the one I'm used to I have to mentally transpose the score of if it before I can even attempt to sing it.

The question of tone quality in some way ties in with a sense of pitch. Again this is difficult to define exactly when the tone quality is wrong. The difficulty in solving this problem is that I cannot tell whether it is an individual voice – or if so, whose – that is at fault, or one whole section of singers or the whole choir. I can detect imbalance in volume however, when one set of vibrations overrides all the others in strength.

Someone once asked me if I could distinguish between different temperaments, and what would happen if I were to play a keyboard tuned to different temperaments. I still don't know the answer to this but suspect that I would be very aware of the difference although it may feel very out of tune. This is an interesting point that I would like to investigate sometime.

Another point – this one purely speculative – is whether I would be a better musician if I could hear. I think that the answer would be both "yes" and "no". As far as musical potential is concerned I would have to say "yes" for then I would be able to do things such as conduct an orchestra and appreciate things like jazz and electronic music. Accompanying would also be much easier if I could hear, and choir rehearsals would be easier because both the learning/teaching and critical processes would be speeded up. On the other hand, if I could hear then my understanding of music may suffer, and my score reading skills would not be as good as they are. If I could hear I wouldn't be "me" and I certainly would not have the fascinating life that I lead!

Enough of me! What about Music and the Deaf and its work? I founded the charity in 1988 and over the last 17 years it's grown from a one-man operation (based in my parents' attic!) to an international one with a staff of 4 and numerous additional freelance workers. We deal with requests on music and deafness from around the world, lead workshops and After School Music Clubs, give talks and lectures, provide signed theatre performances and research and publish a range of books and leaflets.

I should stress that Music and the Deaf is not a Music Therapy organization: using music to develop speech and language, or assist in other ways is not our aim at all. That's not to deny that Music Therapy has its place, but what we're interested in is giving people a creative, social, cultural and emotional skill and outlet that they can begin to explore at a young age and take right the way through life. We do work with all ages and all degrees of hearing loss and the emphasis at all times is on making music and having fun.

I'm the Artistic Director of MatD and we have 2 other deaf musicians here, along with Sue Rosborough, our Administrator. Danny Lane, a graduate in Music and French from Keele University, is our Education and Outreach Projects Manager, and Steven McMahon, a deaf graduate in Performing Arts from the University of Central Lancashire, is our Development Projects Manager.

From the beginning the main thrust of MatD's work has been practical music-making: getting deaf people interested and involved in music, and playing it themselves. Much of this happens in workshops, which take place in a variety of settings, yet the way we begin is always the same – by developing a sense of rhythm, and by exploring instruments.

Fig. 1: Playing together

The foundation of all our music is rhythm, and if you cannot feel and internalize a beat then you'll always have problems. Luckily, rhythm is a very physical and very visual thing, and over the years we've come up with various games and activities that develop rhythmic ability. Having said that, I also think that rhythm is the hardest thing to teach deaf people so you need lots of patience!

Deaf people do need a lot of 'hands-on' experience of musical instruments so that they can develop both a physical and mental 'library' of sounds, pitches and timbre. Admittedly, this is something that a lot of hearing people do not have the chance to do, but it is vital for deaf people. It's also important to emphasize that music is not some abstract noise but can tell a story, give instructions, express emotions and so on. Exploring sound in a creative way could actually be a way of defining music, and the great thing is that there's really no right or wrong way of doing this.

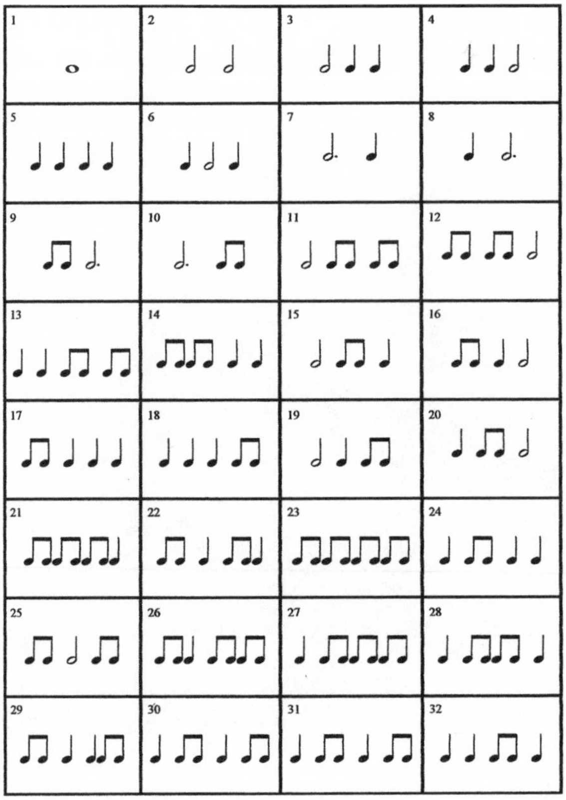

Fig. 2: Rhythms for Bingo, in: Unlocking the National Curriculum: Keys to Music with Deaf Children. *Published by Music and the Deaf (no publishing date).*

We often do collaborative projects with other arts groups, such as opera companies, orchestras, dance groups and so forth. Such events greatly increase the number of resources at our disposal and give other professional musicians and artists a chance to work with a social group they wouldn't normally have contact with. A few years ago we did a project with a regional opera company based on *The Thieving Magpie*. Several of the deaf children involved had never had a music lesson before and had no idea what an opera was, but within 4 days we had created our own mini-opera, based on Rossini's original musical and dramatic ideas. It was a joy to watch the ideas tumbling out of the young people and to see their confidence and self-expression grow.

The biggest project we've done (to date) was *Stories from the Dreamtime* a work for full orchestra, 40 deaf children, narrator and sign language interpreter, that MatD commissioned from David Bedford and performed at the Huddersfield Contemporary Music Festival back in 1992. Based on Aboriginal myths, the children were divided into 8 groups of 5, each working with their own professional musician, and spent almost 6 months preparing their parts. The end result was spectacular, with UK music press praising both the piece and the achievements of the young deaf people involved. One deaf student who took part said it was "the best thing I have ever done, better than football or any sport", whilst one of the school teachers involved wrote afterwards, "it has had a profound effect on all the pupils, and indeed the staff. In over 20 years of working with young people this project has been the highlight for me, with so many unexpected additional experiences and outcomes for the children."

Such events are certainly expensive and time-consuming but show the world at large just what deaf musicians can be capable of.

For many years music within deaf education (in the UK at any rate) was used as a means to an end, (such as to develop speech or language skills in the days when sign language was banned) with the result that very few deaf children actually had any real music experience or knowledge. This has, unfortunately, led to a strong 'anti-music' attitude amongst some older members of the deaf community, but we have led several successful workshops where deaf adults have – for the first time in their lives – been able to really explore and understand what music is about.

With the introduction of the National Curriculum scheme in the UK a few years ago, all children were given the right to a music education up to the age of 14. Regretfully, music education in deaf schools in the UK is still rather 'hit and miss' and even within mainstream schools it has been hard for teachers to successfully include deaf pupils. In response to this MatD has researched and written *Keys to Music: Unlocking the Music National Curriculum for Deaf Pupils*.

Between 2002 and 2004 we created two guides that enable music teachers and deaf pupils to access the music curriculum through adapting existing schemes of work. The first guide covers Primary education (with a small section for nursery and reception age), and the initial print run sold out within seven months. Copies have been sold across the UK, and also in the USA, Canada, Australia and Japan. The second volume, for secondary level education, has also sold well, across the UK and beyond.

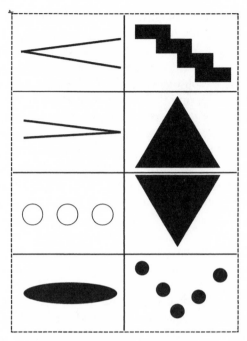

Fig. 3: Cards with graphic notation, in: Unlocking the National Curriculum: Keys to Music with Deaf Children. *Published by Music and the Deaf (no publishing date).*

Keys to Music cannot claim to be exhaustive, but it does cover a very broad curriculum in a way that deaf young people can understand and participate. We have monitored its use, and sought feedback, which will be used to improve future editions of the guide. Such feedback has already led to the research and publishing of two further volumes, one for early years (due in the summer of 2006) and for Music Technology.

Music Technology is one area that presents a particular challenge to deaf people, largely due to the lack of tactile sensation. No matter what sound you may pick on an electric keyboard the 'feel' of it nearly always remains the same. And, of course, if you've never played, felt or heard the acoustic version of the instrument concerned then it's almost impossible to identify what sound you're dealing with. Similarly, with music software programmes you are often dealing with new, strange or unconventional sounds, and the tactile sensation is not profound enough to identify these sounds. For this reason we need to work with equipment manufacturers and music technology specialists and find ways of making this accessible for deaf people. The fact that the technology develops so fast makes this a very challenging project indeed but we believe it is a necessary one.

Although most deaf children and young people have some kind of music education in school today we are always looking to give them further opportunities, one of which has been the development of Hi-Notes After School Music Clubs. Since 2003 we have run these Clubs across West Yorkshire, although our aim is eventually to roll them out across the UK. The Clubs have two aims: one is to give deaf young people greater music opportunities than are afforded in schools, and the second is to bring deaf young people together. With integration being so prevalent it is easy for deaf children to feel incredibly isolated. Sometimes they may be the only deaf child in the school and do not realize that there are other youngsters with the same difficulties, the same communication problems as them, in the locality: the After School Music Clubs therefore have an important social role too.

About 90 young people attend these Clubs every week, which are co-ordinated and led by Danny Lane, along with Steven McMahon and a small team of freelance musicians. The music activities are determined by the participants and regular annual concerts give them a chance to perform to a wider audience. In July 2005 we held a concert at the Alhambra Studio Theatre in Bradford which attracted and audience of 200, plus local TV and press coverage. Over 60 deaf children took part that night, and every single performance was an original composition. Many of the participants have little music experience before joining the Music Clubs, so seeing them write and perform their own music – some only within the space of a few weeks – was a huge thrill.

"Music 4 Ever!" was the comment from one of the deaf teenagers who took part that night, and a parent wrote to us saying, "Thank you for letting my son take part. It means a lot to us." That latter quote is an important one, for parents need to know that, despite being deaf, their child can still lead a 'normal' life and enjoy things like music.

We do plan to publish guide books for running After School Music Clubs so that these valuable activities can be provided to a wider audience. As the After School Clubs develop we aim to include more instrumental teaching. Several students have already expressed a desire to learn an instrument, with guitar and drums being the most popular, and to achieve this we hope to work closely with local authority Music Services. At present very few, if any, Music Services in the UK seem to work with deaf pupils, although there are some isolated cases of peripatetic teachers visiting schools to give instrumental tuition.

The Music Services we have approached admit that they had never actually considered the idea of working with deaf children or adults, an attitude which I think comes largely from ignorance. Admittedly, it can be daunting when suddenly faced with a deaf pupil in a music lesson, and a lot of teachers (in our experience) have grave concerns about how to communicate and how to actually teach. Of course, some instruments are harder to teach than others, and when I was younger I firmly believed that there were some instruments a deaf person simply could not play. I have – happily – been proved wrong in this, and even come across a deaf lady who is having regular singing lessons.

Of all the instruments, the voice has to be the hardest one to teach, because you cannot physically open up your throat and reveal the mechanics of how it's done! The lady I mentioned above struggled to find a singing teacher who was prepared to accept a deaf pupil, but the process of learning has been a real eye-opener for both teacher and pupil. They work by feeling each other's chests and matching the vibrations: it's been a slow but rewarding journey and they both now feel they have an excellent working relationship.

Every one of us learns and works in different ways which is why I firmly believe that one-to-one instrumental teaching is best. With deaf pupils this also aids communication, and it does require a lot of patience on the teacher's part to find an appropriate method. Trial and error is often the only way forward. One must be open-minded, ready to be challenged and – above all – be willing to learn *yourself*, as your own understanding and perception of music will, inevitably be changed.

In any successful instrumental teaching there must always be a degree of willingness from the pupil too. Practically every deaf person I know who plays an instrument to a reasonable level has had to take a certain amount of responsibility to 'fill in the gaps', so to speak. By this, I mean that they have to be prepared to read about music history, musical styles, and so forth: make an effort to read scores and analyse them: work hard at understanding music theory. In short, they need to have a very good 'head knowledge' of music to compensate for the fact that they do not automatically hear, and pick up, musical awareness in the way that hearing people do. This may sound harsh, but if you *are* serious about making it as a musician, you have to put in the effort.

In many ways I have always found it easier to teach deaf children than hearing children. Hearing people become 'culturally conditioned' to music at a very young age – "we know what we like, and we like what we know" – and this often covers quite a narrow musical range. Deaf children, by and large, do not have this same conditioning, and thus have a much greater panorama of sounds to explore.

If you are a deaf child of hearing parents you may well grow up being aware, within the home, that there's this force, this power, that's related to sound and makes people react in very emotional ways. You may not know that this 'thing' is called 'music', yet when you start school you find this sound world has more or less vanished. It's a huge shame, as the arts actually underpin all the other work we learn at school; they're a way of turning facts and figures into something real, that's alive and responsive.

Conversely, if you're a hearing child of deaf parents, or even a deaf child of deaf parents, you may have hardly any exposure to music in the home environment.

Music may be something you discover at a friends' house, or via the TV or a recording of some kind. Music does play a vital role in our early development and it should be actively encouraged in the home.

In the summer of 2005 Music and the Deaf was asked to lead some workshops in the south of England for hearing children and their deaf parents. This is quite the reverse of our usual workshop situation, and we found that the children were incredibly keen to share their joy of music with their parents. Initially the parents were very reluctant indeed to participate but were soon picking up instruments and playing them quite happily. Several of them later said that they didn't realize how much fun music was (they'd never been given the opportunity when they were at school), but one parent expressed a feeling of guilt that – because of her deafness – she had not been able to sing to her child, as other (hearing) parents could. This rather sad situation is something that we aim to overcome through our early years' project.

Alongside the practical work outlined above we deal with daily requests from around the world. These can be from schools and colleges, parents, music teachers, students etc. and we do our best to help them. Because we are only a small organisation (but with a world-wide vision!) creating networks of support and advice is vital. We do have numerous contacts across the UK who can give people more practical help in their own locality, but such ties can always be strengthened and developed. The use of e-mail and internet certainly helps in this but it would be fantastic if we could create a global network where deaf people, musicians and teachers can easily interact and support one another. Maybe one day we'll manage it!

Although our core market is deaf people, it is important to educate hearing people about deafness and the fact that deaf people can enjoy music, so MatD staff often visits groups and societies to speak about our work and our experiences as deaf musicians. Teacher training days and music courses are another valuable way of 'spreading the word' and we've made some very valuable contacts over the years through this area of work.

Our other major area of work is providing sign language theatre performances. This began in 1992 when I did a signed performance of *Joseph and the Amazing Technicolor Dreamcoat* at the London Palladium. In 2005 we had a team of 12 interpreters doing over 170 shows in the UK, which is a huge growth! Our main focus is on musical theatre, (such as *Cats*, *Les Misérables*, *My Fair Lady*, *West Side Story*, *Phantom of the Opera*, *Starlight Express* etc.) but we also cover plays too. Theatre can be a great way of introducing people to music and with some productions we have developed educational work to help deaf patrons gain more from the show. For example, Norwich Theatre Royal has been excellent at providing such opportunities and we have led sessions there on *Joseph*, *Cats* and *Miss Saigon*.

Many large theatres do now have Education and Outreach departments so it is worth contacting your own local theatre to encourage them to work with the deaf community.

Music and the Deaf has achieved a lot since it began in 1988 but there is still much to do. Attitudes and opportunities have improved tremendously over 17 years, as has deaf education in the UK generally. We know, of course, that not every deaf child or adult *will* enjoy music, but then there are thousands of hearing people who do not like music too. What is important is that deaf people are given *a chance* to explore music, preferably at as young an age as possible, but – then again – it's never too late, as our experience with older people has shown.

One of the most wonderful things about making music with deaf people is that you do *not* have to be a music specialist, and you can make this journey of musical discovery together. Our *Keys to Music* volume 1 is aimed at the non-specialist, and you will find many useful ideas in this. Both this and volume 2 are available to buy from Music and the Deaf along with some other publications – see http://www.matd.org.uk for more information – and we are happy to deal with any requests about music and deafness that you may have: e-mail us on info@matd.org.uk.

I would encourage you to explore sound, pitch, rhythm, instruments and all the other wonderful paraphernalia of music with deaf people, and you may be pleasantly surprised at how much your own understanding and preconceptions change. Music, above all, is *fun* and can be enjoyed throughout life.

Happy music-making!

Part II: Theoretical Principles

"All Men will Become Brothers …" –
Time and Rhythm as Basic Processes of Life
and Understanding[1]

Georg Feuser

1. An Orientation

"Because human beings develop, they can be educated.
Because their development is a process of change, it can be influenced.
Since human beings develop over the course of their entire life,
the way they change can always be influenced."

These statements, which may serve as introduction to the following exposition, are taken from the leader to the film *Ursula oder das unwerte Leben* (*Ursula or the Life not Worth Living*), which pays homage to the work of Mimi Scheiblauer in a truly special way that remains of great import today. The EU project "Veronika", dealing with questions of integration in the area of basic schooling, worked towards determining international quality standards for children with special needs aged three to six years, while also aiming at professionalizing integration through methods of music education and through bringing together music, movement and language. My conception of a "general (integrative)[2] pedagogy", derived from "developmentally logical didactics", was the basis for the foundation and extension of integrative basic schooling in Bremen as early as 1981. Today it is probably the farthest reaching conception of an integrative system of basic schooling, education and teaching that has, particularly in the Linz area, found wide and sustainable application in teacher training at the Pädagogische Akademie des Bundes, Upper Austria, as well as in the practice of teaching. The work done in the project "Ve-

---

1   Originally, this contribution formed the basis of a lecture at the occasion of the completion of the international EU project "Veronika", organised by the region Upper Austria in Linz on 6th November 2003. "Veronika" is an EU project for the integration of preschool children with special needs into the general education system. Integration processes are fostered through pedagogical methods in combination with music, movement and language.

2   The attribute "integrative" merely aids communication; a general approach to pedagogy, in the sense that I have put forward, makes the term "integration" redundant, since on principle it embraces neither pedagogical reductionism of education nor is of socially selective and segregating nature.

ronika" has always been an important concern to us and has indeed also been an object of our work.

With view to Mimi Scheiblauer's work, which centred around the elements of music and movement – work in which she approached people with sometimes very serious impairments after many years of hospitalisation and was able to gain their attention, unfold a dialogue and thereby enter communication – a question arises that is now omnipresent in this area of specialisation: is this activity primarily a pedagogical or, after all, a therapeutic activity?

The activity is aimed at reaching the other human being, at maintaining a nearness, and is therefore aimed primarily at the process itself, not at fine-tuning the possibilities of creating music together and perfecting this interplay. This brings music therapy into the picture and gives rise to a question of where to draw the line.

Fig. 1: Mimi Scheiblauer with Ursula ca. 1965, in: Brunner-Danuser 1984, p. 92

There is no need to fear that I might follow this question up, because it is partly contrived, is academically of only limited use and indeed serves only to draw a line between educators and therapists and their respective fields of activity with which they identify and make their living. This is not to endorse a development in education and therapy where everyone practises everything without expertise in a particular field. Quite the opposite: it is especially in the field of integration that we need very specific individual competencies, competencies formed in the different social sciences that become manifest in various professional specialisations. However, in the same respect, we need a highly developed ability for interdisciplinary and multi-professional co-operation, an ability to engage in "competence transfer", as

I called one of the four basic principles in the conception that I developed. A lot of hard work remains to be done to develop both these areas of qualification.

If we turn our attention to working with children with and without disabilities – work that Mimi Scheiblauer practised in her unique way – in order to optimise ways of development for all and if, on top of that, we try to look at the world from their perspective, from the viewpoint of the "inner observer" (Leont'ev), we will immediately recognise the connection of some seemingly disparate circumstances: inspired to movements by music and directed at the other and at a togetherness through its depiction, the "realm of language" (Maturana/Varela 1987, Rödler 2000) manifests itself in the form of fundamental dialogues, which do not require speaking but may lead to it.

A brief scene involving Ms. Scheiblauer and Charlie[3] will show that the musical element is inspiration as well as motivation to open and turn oneself as one human being to another. It likewise shows that it is the medium for dialogue, for communication, and for interaction at the same time. As the child learns to play the instrument better through practice and finds his intentions affirmed through the musical and rhythmical feedback he receives, the desired dialogue not only becomes more intense but the child eventually takes over leading it. Which pedagogical or therapeutic approach could claim to be of higher quality than the one that enables the child, the student or the client in the process of his/her education and rehistorisation to take the leading role? In the overarching context of dialogical co-operation, the traditional differentiations between music education and music therapy dissolve.

I have already pointed far ahead with this. In my further elaborations I would like to, firstly, guide attention to the facts that form the basis of what I have mentioned so far and, secondly, to the question of integration. Then I will bring the two areas back together. Perhaps you would follow me in this?

2. Contemporary Questions

The developments in Bremen on the basis of my conception of integration, as we have brought them about in kindergartens and schools since 1981, have certainly opened doors to a new culture, the culture of an inclusive society from which no

---

3   For the purpose of clarification and to inspire further thought, several short sequences were shown during the talk. Reference is made to the film *Ursula oder das unwerte Leben*, namely to work with the boy Charlie who is lying in a playpen taking claves in his hands. Ms. Scheiblauer gains the child's attention with a rattle, gets him to stand up and a dialogue with the claves that are banged together occurs. Charlie bangs the claves against the side of the playpen, thereby taking the lead in this "dialogue", which Ms. Scheiblauer takes up and follows.

one is excluded on the grounds of the kind or degree of disability and certainly not on the basis of nationality, ethnic background, language or religion. This summer, as part of a symposium on "20 Years of Integrative Education and Basic Schooling in Protestant Daycare Centres in Bremen", we took on the somewhat belated project of analysing the present situation and at finding ways in today's circumstances to continue practising what we discovered to be just and important practice so that we may also see in the future what is to be done. In this respect, I never tire of quoting a statement of warning made by Horst-Eberhard Richter in 1978, which goes as follows: "If in your doing you don't practise what you have come to understand, in the end you will no longer be able to understand what it is you should be doing."[4]

Today, in the third decade of integration, we see ourselves confronted with a very difficult situation due to several societal developments that have taken place. For instance, integration at Bremen schools in its fully regionalised and decentralised form – where the therapeutic needs of children had been integrated into the classroom and a multi-professional team worked very efficiently with the groups on the basis of the "competence transfer" that becomes possible in this kind of setting – was abolished in the second half of the 90s in favour of a co-operation-based model. Under the pretext of exorbitant costs, the integration approach which, when it comes down to it, was not really supported by social and educational policies, was first blocked from spreading further and was then dispensed with entirely. Today, even integration in basic schooling is threatened in its core by deregulation measures, by massive changes to social programmes, health programmes and education as well as by cost-cutting measures and cost-benefit-analyses that inevitably follow in the process of a globalisation that is supported by neo-liberal ideology.

I believe that those who are politically responsible for these social and educational issues are not sufficiently aware of the consequences of their "destruction of good sense", that is, the destruction of parts of an important cultural development for all children and teenagers, when they block or reverse the development of integration. Educational policy does not even attempt any excuses – nor does it have any – in this but instead very clearly points to the immense responsibility that will have to be taken on by those who will be responsible in this matter.

These developments go hand in hand with an unfolding *Zeitgeist* that, as we have been discussing increasingly over the past years, shows tendencies towards segregation more than ever – tendencies which, when it comes to very seriously impaired human life, are connected once again to the "debate over the value of life" and the desire for a new "euthanasia". This must not be underestimated in its negative effect on the idea of integration[5].

---

4   Richter 1978, p. 23
5   Feuser 1994, 1997, 1999

But this also makes all the more clear the need for basic schooling that is integrative and for education in teaching institutions that includes *all* children, because it is people of all ages with very serious developmental problems and disabilities in particular who still constitute the so-called "inner core" that is taken little into consideration even in the integration debate. Even severely disabled children are well able, as we have seen in Bremen, to learn and be adequately encouraged in an integrative teaching and kindergarten setting. Outside of integration, in segregation and hospitalisation, such children in particular will begin to undergo a development that in their adolescence and adulthood will find expression in signs of severe deprivation – for example, in stereotypical behavioural patterns and in severely self-injuring, aggressive and destructive behaviour. As a result, these people will usually be called "beyond therapy", "unable to be rehabilitated", "self-endangering and endangering of others" as well as "unable to live in society". As those "given up" by remedial therapy and special education, they become the clients in our "inpatient" university work[6].

From my many years of working experience in integrative contexts, observing the development of severely disabled children as well as children and adolescents with severe developmental disorders, many of whom I knew from age two or three on, it has become clear that serious conditions, such as those mentioned above, do not necessarily result from a certain kind or degree of a particular disability or a developmental disorder, but are instead – in all the cases I am familiar with – the result of deprivation in education and socialisation, which is to say, such conditions are the result of the way we are dealing with a person.

In particular, it is the time spent in kindergarten in which the quality of schooling and the content being taught is high that forms, in my view, the basis for a level of development that, at the beginning of our integration work, I didn't think possible even considering my positive estimation of a child's developmental possibilities through integration. The prerequisite for the kind of development that we were able to witness, however, is the mastery and application in didactics of relevant basic principles gained from the social sciences!

For this boy[7], who became severely impaired as a result of a mistake in his treatment in hospital when he was kindergarten age (an apallic syndrome, a vegetative state, was diagnosed subsequent to this error), we were at least able to prove his ability to learn and thereby obtain a considerable sum as compensation for pain and suffering, which allowed for his support with sufficient personnel and finances for several years. Prior to this, the court had granted him only a symbolic 5 German

---

6 With my conception in particular, namely Dialogue-Centred, Substitutive, Co-operative Action Therapy (DCSCAT) – a basis therapy – we were able to offer a new life perspective and a high degree of integration to many adolescents and adults with such a history (Feuser 2001, 2002).

7 Scenes from the work with a boy were shown in this context.

marks in compensation, because it was said that his cerebrum was not functioning and thus that there wasn't much that money could do for him. According to the information available to me, he died as an adolescent because an epileptic seizure was noticed too late by the on-call staff person who was in charge of the whole house, following the cutting of proper nightshifts for financial reasons.

Martin Buber says: "[…] and a society may be called human to the degree to which its members acknowledge one another as members."[8]

3. A Matter of Time

Mimi Scheiblauer wrote in 1943: "Music consists of four elements: time, sound, dynamics and form."[9] She emphasises that none of the elements can be taken out of its context and none of them by itself is music, even though each of them, she says, "has a particular educational value in itself and has a particular effect on a person"[10]. She recognises *form* as the structuring principle; *dynamics* as a creative power in the sense of an interaction between time and energy; *sound* as the emotional side; and *rhythm* as relating to time.

In the video sequences shown, these elements were easy to pinpoint, although strictly speaking there was no music being created. The persons in the footage were acting – separately or together – to create a common product which none of them would have been able to realise on their own – and at all times rhythm, emotional dynamics and structure could be observed. Today we call these elements, if I may express it rather figuratively, the elements whose common denominator facilitates the structuring order that allows any living entity to exist: it is time.

With reference to the philosophical as well as scientific – that is, the astro-physical and quantum-mechanical – contexts, time has acquired an entirely new meaning for humankind over the last century and a half and has effected a momentous revolution of our worldview, such as is arguably unparalleled in human history. Slowly – too slowly I believe – are these epistemological concerns reaching the field of pedagogy. Although the profession feeds on the currently dominant idea of man, this idea is intimately connected with the worldview that guides us, and so it is this worldview that gains utmost significance.

Through Albert Einstein, humankind had to acknowledge the relativity of time as subject to position and movement in space and was forced to understand, or at least

---

8 Buber 1975, p. 26
9 Brunner-Danuser 1984, p. 95
10 ibid.

learn to accept, that space and time are not cosmic constants that provide us all with a stable point of orientation, the "secure home" of our existence, but are instead highly dynamically interacting processes beyond which there is no cosmos, no life and no development. If we imagine the cosmos as the space that light, travelling at the "speed limit", has been able to cover since the "Big Bang" marked the beginning of our visible cosmos, then even within this cosmos, we are defining a world line that exists relative to other systems. This means that we are basically dealing with three kinds of time:

- Intra-systemic eigen-time, which is particular to each system thanks to its own dynamics of change and movement
- Time that perceives one system in relation to another. I call this extra-systemic eigen-time.
- Finally, a relational time between two (or more) systems that enables exchange to take place, a dialogue to be led, and makes co-operation possible. It means bringing together the intra-systemic eigen-time of both systems in a superordinate phase space that respects the time-generated identity of each of the systems but nevertheless generates a common time that unites both.

I believe you are beginning to sense that this necessitates a co-ordinating, structuring authority, that is: time which organises time. This is to say that, neurologically speaking, time triggers systems, or that, sociologically speaking, it has a "bandwagon effect" relevant to both systems. In a similar way, you might sense that, preferably, this organising structure could be music and movement. This warrants closer examination.

3.1. Order through Fluctuations

Any living system is *open to its environment,* as Prigogine and his associates[11] show in their fundamental studies and as was confirmed by Maturana and Varela[12] very clearly for the field of biology. It is therefore a dissipative structure, one that can be disturbed – a structure that while being referential to the world continues to create itself in the sense of autopoieisis. Thanks to a central nervous system, it is also able to be self-referential, that is, to organise its bio-psycho-social unity coherently and gain consciousness of it, define itself as "I".

If we go back a long way in evolution and draw on a physics experiment that comes from fractals research, we will be able to define more clearly the indispensable fundamentals of any form of life and at the same time able to recognise that the basic functions and principles we use to define life as such stem from cosmic principles.

---

11 Prigogine 1981, 1985, 1989, 1993
12 Maturana/Varela 1987

They may be described simply by saying that anything that exists originates in interdependencies.

As you can see, this is a video camera and a monitor. The camera is directed at the monitor's screen in such a way that it will record only what is displayed on the screen and the screen will only show what the camera records since the camera feeds directly into the monitor through a cable.

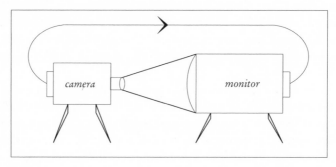

Fig. 2

We are therefore looking at a system that is self-referential but nevertheless open to its environment since the space between the camera's lenses and the screen allows for disturbances to it. If there is no disturbance, you will see nothing on the screen, despite the fact that much is happening because billions of photons – light particles – are racing through the system. The system is in a symmetrical state inasmuch as at any given time it assumes any and all conceivable states that it is able to assume; put in the simplest terms possible, it is chaotic. A lighter held in front of the monitor which sends forth photons, that is, light (warmth cannot be detected by the system) disturbs the symmetry, breaks it. A visible order – although one that at the same time continuously changes its form and tests its own stability – is established[13]. It is the expression of the system's integration of the disturbance using that system's own means that allows it – despite the disturbance experienced – to ensure its stability in a new way. Jean Piaget[14] describes this kind of process in his genetic epistemology and developmental psychology (using the term "equilibration"). The visible product of such a process is generated by the system itself but is not developed by it alone. As a system that is open to its environment, it needs to restructure itself since, considering the ever necessary exchange with the world, it would not

---

13 This refers to an experiment conducted by Prof. Dr. Peitgen, University Bremen, on fractal geometry, which I used here for the purpose of developing these ideas. It was published in: *Spektrum Videothek: Fraktale-Schönheit im Chaos*, VHS. Immediately after taking the lighter away from the monitor, rotating structures that appeared as stripes continued to be visible on the left and right sides of the screen.

14 Piaget 1969, 1973, 1980, 1983

be able to exist with its own identity were it not to integrate disturbances. Such processes of self-organisation – which, triggered by external events, are capable of changing the state of the central nervous system – are thus innervated, are characterised by the construction of the world as it is experienced and therefore by the coming into being of our world within ourselves and by our knowledge about the world. This can lead to a new understanding of what a human being is and what we call a "disability". If we take a giant leap of billions of years from the beginning of life to the state of human beings today, we could say: "Disability can be understood as the product of a developmental logic, of the integration of internal and external system disturbances into the system with the means of the system – disturbances that accumulate in the biography of an individual and are seen as both starting conditions and general circumstances."

This is also to say that: a disability is a person's expression of her ability to lead a human life under her initial circumstances and general constraints.

3.2. Limit Cycles

Let us return to time. Its relevance to our subject is easily shown. We know from work experience that persons with severe mental disabilities or autism, who otherwise appear to be characterised by an inability to enter into or sustain a dialogue, become quite awake and oriented when we play music and engage them in rhythmical movements. They then become more approachable and partake more actively in a common activity. It is not so rare that they modify or omit stereotypical or even self-injuring behaviour. This sheds light on the causes of such seemingly "pathological" behaviour. External rhythm synchronises the respectively individual intra-systemic eigen-time of teachers or therapists with that of the children or students. A common phase space develops in whose "field" we then lead a dialogue, interact, communicate and co-operate. Consequently, what is important here are not particular individual talents that a child has, as is often claimed in the literature of the field, but rather, are the events that through their rhythmical structuring can be perceived and processed even under very impaired conditions. The exterior rhythmical structures synchronise the internal time emitters, determine their pace, stabilise them and in this way improve the ability to perceive, to think, and to act.

If a person, due to a high degree of internal and/or external isolation, remains without quantitatively and qualitatively sufficient exchange processes, she will need to compensate for the growing informational and social deprivation, to generate her own intra-systemic eigen-time by taking recourse to her own (rhythmically structured) activities, that is, by making herself the object of the exchange – through rocking movements, beating herself, yelling – in order to hear herself. This leads to dissociative psychological states and to an unravelling of the person's physical self-image, as has been amply documented by René Spitz[15] for hospitalised infants whose problem was not overcoming internal isolation but facing being deprived of their primary attachment figures, of the relationship and bonding necessary for life.

In order to maintain the system's inner structure, at least as much as is necessary for survival, structuring time has to be created by the system itself – an ingenious response available in any life situation – through rhythmically structuring movements that generate information in the system, trigger it and thereby stabilise it, resulting in positive emotions. The threat of chaos is reduced and thereby anxiety as well. Subjectively, this makes "sense" and serves as the basis upon which the person in question attributes meaning to her stereotypical, self-injuring or aggressive and destructive actions.

Movement in space creates 'time', which, as a structuring process that represents extraordinarily complex and dynamic events, generates several elements and functions that are communicated as an integrated whole, namely:

1. That of an *internaloperator* who is in charge of organising the system, which we may see as connection patterns of the internally running processes, which in turn explains the structuring aspect
2. That of a *relationsoperator*, who constitutes common super-individual phase spaces, enabling exchange with other systems
3. That of *attractors*, which determine the direction and speed at which the system 'drifts', its line of development
4. That of operators which bring about *processes of transformation* meaning that through the exchange processes structural changes become possible and development manifests itself. We could also say that learning (exchange) sets off development (structuring).

It is these circumstances which allow those actions that, when seen from the outside, are evaluated as "pathological", to be characterised as "developmentally logical". These actions are secured on the level of "biological significance". Time is – we can already conclude – the crucial factor that generates the unity of an evolving system, the unity through which a system (in the sense of energetically and informationally synergetic processes) is able to relate to other systems[16] and, with respect to its own evolution following exchange processes, is able to follow its world line, that is, to preserve itself.

With respect to our species, we can acknowledge a species-specific phase space, in which, through a process of ontogenesis, we are able to realise our individual exist-

---

15 Spitz 1956
16 Haken/Wunderlin 1991; Haken/Haken-Krell 1992

ence as part of the cosmos in accord with the phylogenesis of humankind. The model of the "limit cyclic phase space" clarifies this. If a living system crosses a certain border area, within which it is able to realise its species-specific life and thus exchange processes, it must, as we have seen, take recourse to time-generating forms of compensation so as not to drift into a kind of 'chaos' where the system is in a symmetrical state that does not generate time, leading to the system's death, or else to prevent growing rigid in a single state of existence in which all movement "freezes", also without being able to generate system-structuring time and likewise leading to the system's death. There is no escaping from these limit cyclic states using only one's own means. Pedagogical-therapeutic measures become necessary to enter again into a relationship where exchange, that is, 'dialogue' and co-operation, are possible. What better way to achieve this could there be than through creating music together?

4. All Men will Become Brothers …

In summary, we can conclude: evolution is always co-evolution, as any individual development can only be understood in the sense of the co-ontogenesis of systems. "The human being through You becomes I", says Martin Buber – he/she becomes the I whose You we are to him/her! – a consequence that is hardly ever taken into account. With this conclusion at hand we cannot help but recognise that any limitation of an individual's exchange with his/her environment – exchange that is necessary for both the individual and the entire species of which he/she is a member and includes culture-specific schooling as well as social exchange – will also limit his/her development and not just modify it. Segregation and special labelling of people who are disabled, who display behavioural problems or whose mental health is impaired basically reflects sheer cynicism with respect to the learning and development of this group. It is neither academically reasonable with view to pedagogical goals nor is it ethically justifiable. The above only very briefly compiled insights into what gives rise to life and constitutes life and its development can only lead to the conclusion that persons who are classified as disabled need to be integrated into heterogeneous schooling, education and teaching systems but also into all other areas of life. They must be offered comprehensive opportunities to experience the world, relationships and co-operation, because: a human being gains access to things through human beings and accesses human beings by way of things.

As far as human development is concerned, we have to understand that for any one person, it is primarily dependent on the degree of complexity of the respective other, whereas the means and abilities of the individual system always come in second place. Primarily we are concerned with what a person can become according to her possibilities, while what a person is at a particular moment, once again is of only secondary importance.

Learning that sets off development, necessitates a developmentally logical didactical approach, one that lays out a general (integrative) pedagogy which is concerned with educating all children and youth without social segregation or confinement to, for example, areas of special education and without reductionist and parcelled-off education and learning opportunities. Foster, educate and teach. Mimi Scheiblauer writes: "Concerning children with seeing, hearing and speaking impairments, they should, whenever possible, be included in a regular classroom. So the damaged senses experience regular training, instead of the remaining 'rest' being left to atrophy. People with physical problems should neither be pitied nor singled out. Both lead to isolation. Only in an acceptance that is taken for granted can the greatest possible independence develop."[17]

Today, this statement is valid without qualification for people with all kinds and degrees of impairment.

Let us conclude by directing our thoughts back to where we started. When we consider the consequences of social segregation and reductionist and parcelled-off pedagogical-therapeutic approaches, as they are represented by our entire educational system and especially the schools, and do so taking into account the insights and the experience that we have available today, we realise that the practice of integration should long be the norm. Understood as co-operation in a society constituted of members of equal value and with equal rights, which is what probably characterises them best, the line "All men will become brothers ..."[18] from Schiller's *Ode to Joy*, which I have chosen as the title for my elaborations and would like to use to conclude it, takes on a deep meaning. Set to the music of Beethoven's Symphony No. 9, this statement comes to symbolise the meanings that we attribute to music and movement for the creation and shaping of human society today. In and through society alone is the human being able to evolve according to her possibilities, which she in turn owes society in large part. Trends determined by some *Zeitgeist*, as for example, self-realisation as an egomaniacal act that is disconnected from any social obligations and responsibility, should provoke serious pedagogical misgivings at all stages of education, socialisation and enculturation. That all men will become brothers and all women sisters describes a central concern of integration. In the context of a "general (integrative) pedagogy", I therefore define schooling and education as follows:
Schooling means *bringing out the desire of persons for other persons* and on this basis the structuring of the individual's activity with the goal of achieving the greatest possible control over reality; whereas

---

17 Brunner-Danuser 1984, p. 137f.
18 Schiller (no publishing date), p. 394

Education means the *entirety of a person's competences related to perception, thinking and acting*, in the sense of her active self-organisation, found condensed in her biography.

Integration, in basic schooling as well, as has been shown in our work experience over the last 22 years, is primarily a question of using the appropriate didactics and not a question of any particular child's abilities or what we call disabilities. If we do not take this into account, we will ultimately keep practising educational, social and societal segregation, even if we hang the word "integration" over our work. The future of a humane and democratic basic schooling and educational system does not lie in the plurality of educational systems that select and segregate but in the unity of a basic schooling and educational system that fosters a nearly infinite diversity of human developmental possibilities and modes of existence.

Literature

Ballmer, Thomas T./Weizsäcker, Ernst von: *Biogenese und Selbstorganisation.* In: Weizsäcker, Ernst von (Ed.) (1974): *Offene Systeme I: Beiträge zur Zeitstruktur von Information, Entropie und Evolution.* Stuttgart, 229–264.

Brunner-Danuser, Fida (1984): *Mimi Scheiblauer – Musik und Bewegung.* Zurich.

Buber, Martin (1975): *Urdistanz und Beziehung.* Heidelberg.

Calder, Nigel (1979): *Einstein's Universe.*

Ciompi, Luc (1988): *Außenwelt – Innenwelt. Die Entstehung von Zeit, Raum und psychischen Strukturen.* Göttingen.

Ciompi, Luc (1999²): *Die emotionalen Grundlagen des Denkens. Entwurf einer fraktalen Affektlogik.* Göttingen.

Eigen, Manfred (1992²): *Stufen zum Leben.* Munich/Zurich.

Einstein, Albert (1955): *Mein Weltbild.* Frankfurt/Main.

Feuser, Georg (1987³): *Gemeinsame Erziehung behinderter und nichtbehinderter Kinder im Kindertagesheim – Ein Zwischenbericht.* Selbstverlag Diak. Werk e. V. Bremen.

Feuser, Georg: *Allgemeine integrative Pädagogik und entwicklungslogische Didaktik.* In: *Behindertenpädagogik* 28 (1989)1, 4–48.

Feuser, Georg: *Möglichkeit und Notwendigkeit der Integration autistischer Menschen.* In: *Behinderte in Familie, Schule und Gesellschaft* 15 (1992)1, 5–18.

Feuser, Georg: *Vom Weltbild zum Menschenbild. Aspekte eines neuen Verständnisses von Behinderung und einer Ethik wider die "Neue Euthanasie".* In: Merz, Hans-Peter/Frei, Eugen X. (Ed.) (1994): *Behinderung – verhindertes Menschenbild?* Edition Schweizer Zentralstelle für Heilpädagogik [SZH]. Lucerne, 93–174.

Feuser, Georg (1995): *Behinderte Kinder und Jugendliche. – Zwischen Integration und Aussonderung.* Darmstadt.

Feuser, Georg (1997²): *Wider die Unvernunft der Euthanasie. Grundlagen einer Ethik in der Heil- und Sonderpädagogik.* Edition Schweizer Zentralstelle für Heilpädagogik [SZH]. Lucerne.

Feuser, Georg: *Gemeinsames Lernen am gemeinsamen Gegenstand. Didaktisches Fundamentum einer Allgemeinen (integrativen) Pädagogik.* In: Hildeschmidt, Anne/Schnell, Irmtraud (Ed.) (1998): *Integrationspädagogik. Auf dem Weg zu einer Schule für alle.* Weinheim/Munich, 19–35.

Feuser, Georg: *„Die Würde des Menschen ist antastbar."* In: *Gemeinsam Leben. Zeitschrift für integrative Erziehung* 7(1999)1, 35–40.

Feuser, Georg: *Grundlagen einer integrativen Lehrerbildung.* In: Feyerer, Ewald/Prammer, Wilfried (Ed.) (2000): *10 Jahre Integration in Oberösterreich. Ein Grund zum Feiern? Beiträge zum 5. Praktikerforum.* Linz.

Feuser, Georg: *Zum Verhältnis von Sonder- und Integrationspädagogik – eine Paradigmendiskussion? Zur Inflation eines Begriffes, der bislang ein Wort geblieben ist.* In: Albrecht, Friedrich/Hinz, Andreas/Moser, Vera (Ed.) (2000): *Perspektiven der Sonderpädagogik. Disziplin und professionsbezogene Standortbestimmung.* Berlin, 20–44.

Feuser, Georg: *Ich bin, also denke ich! Allgemeine und fallbezogene Hinweise zur Arbeit im Konzept der SDKHT.* In: *Behindertenpädagogik* 40(2001)3, 268–350.

Feuser, Georg: *Qualitätsmerkmale integrativen Unterrichts.* In: *Behinderte in Familie, Schule und Gesellschaft* 25 (2002)2/3, 67–84.

Feuser, Georg: *Die "Substituierend Dialogisch-Kooperative Handlungs-Therapie (SDKHT)" – eine Basistherapie.* In: Feuser, Georg/Berger, Ernst (Ed.) (2000): *Erkennen und Handeln. Momente einer kulturhistorischen (Behinderten-)Pädagogik und Therapie.* Berlin, 349–378.

Feuser, Georg/Meyer, Heike (1987): *Integrativer Unterricht in der Grundschule – Ein Zwischenbericht.* Solms-Oberbiel.

Fraser, Julius T. (1966): *The voices of time.*

Haken, Hermann/Haken-Krell, Maria (1992): *Erfolgsgeheimnisse der Wahrnehmung. Synergetik als Schlüssel zum Gehirn.* Stuttgart.

Haken, Hermann/Wunderlin, Arne (1991): *Selbststrukturierung der Materie. Synergetik in der unbelebten Welt.* Braunschweig.

Hawking, Stephen W. (1988): *A brief history of time.*

Jantsch, Erich (1980): *Self Organizing Universe.*

Jantzen, Wolfgang (1987/1990): *Allgemeine Behindertenpädagogik.* Vol. I and II. Weinheim/Basel.

Latash, Mark L. (1993): *Control of Human Movement.* Champaign IL.

Leont'ev, Aleksej N. (1973): *Probleme der Entwicklung des Psychischen.* Frankfurt/Main.

Leont'ev, Aleksej N. (1982): *Tätigkeit, Bewusstsein, Persönlichkeit.* Cologne.

Mantell, Peter (1991): *René Spitz 1887-1974. Leben und Werk im Spiegel seiner Filme.* Cologne.

Maturana, Humberto R./Varela, Francisco J. (1987/1998): *Tree of Knowledge: The Biological Roots of Human Understanding.* Boston.

Peitgen, Heinz-Otto/Jürgens, Hartmut/Saupe, Dietmar (1992): *Bausteine des Chaos.* Berlin/Heidelberg/Stuttgart.

Piaget, Jean (1969): *Das Erwachen der Intelligenz beim Kinde.* Stuttgart.

Piaget, Jean (1973): *Einführung in die genetische Erkenntnistheorie.* Frankfurt/Main.

Piaget, Jean (1980): *Das Verhalten – Triebkraft der Evolution.* Salzburg.

Piaget, Jean (1983): *Biologie und Erkenntnis.* Frankfurt/Main.

Prigogine, Ilya (1981): *From Being to Becoming.*

Prigogine, Ilya/Nicolis, Grégoire (1989): *Exploring Complexity.*

Prigogine, Ilya/Stengers, Isabelle (1985): *Order Out of Chaos: Man's New Dialogue with Nature.*

Prigogine, Ilya/Stengers, Isabelle (1993): *Das Paradox der Zeit. Zeit, Chaos und Quanten.* Munich/Zurich.

Richter, Horst-Eberhard (1978): *Engagierte Analysen.* Reinbek bei Hamburg.

Rödler, Peter (2000[2]): *"geistig behindert": Menschen, lebenslang auf Hilfe anderer angewiesen?* Neuwied/Kriftel/Berlin.

Salmon, Shirley/Schumacher, Karin (Ed.) (2001): *Symposion Musikalische Lebenshilfe. Die Bedeutung des Orff-Schulwerks für Musiktherapie, Sozial- und Integrationspädagogik.* Hamburg.

Salmon, Shirley (2001): *Wege zum Dialog: Erfahrungen mit hörgeschädigten Kindern in integrativen Gruppen.* In: Salmon, Shirley/Schumacher, Karin (Ed.) (2001): *Symposion Musikalische Lebenshilfe. Die Bedeutung des Orff-Schulwerks für Musiktherapie, Sozial- und Integrationspädagogik.* Hamburg, 71–92.

Schiller, Friedrich: *An die Freude.* In: Schiller, Friedrich: *Gesammelte Werke*, Vol. III. Gütersloh (no publishing date), 394–397.

Sinz, Rainer (1978): *Zeitstrukturen und organismische Regulation.* Berlin/DDR.

Spangler, Gottfried/Zimmermann, Peter (Ed.) (1999[3]): *Die Bindungstheorie: Grundlagen, Forschung und Anwendung.* Stuttgart.

Spitz, René (1956): *The First Year of Life.*

Spitz, René (1957): *No and Yes. On the Genesis of Human Communications.*

Spitz, René (1959): *Genetic Field Theory of Ego Formations: Its Implications for Pathology.*

Spitz, René (1984): *Dialogues from Infancy.*

Vygotskij, Lev S. (1974): *Denken und Sprechen.* Berlin.

Vygotskij, Lev S.: *Ausgewählte Schriften.* Vol. I, 1985; Vol. II, 1987. Cologne.

Wheeler, John A. (1999): *A Journey into Gravity and Spacetime.*

Winfree, Arthur T. (1987): *Timing of Biological Clocks.*

Development. On Realities that Open up Possibilities – on Possibilities that Create Realities

Sigrid Köck-Hatzmann

When I meet a "disabled" person,
and look at him thinking what he might be like,
I am describing myself – my perception of the other person.
Whether I make use of this chance to recognise myself,
is a different story …!

(Feuser 1996)

Introduction and Outline Sketch

This opening statement taken from Georg Feuser's lecture titled *The Relation between the View of the Human Being and Inclusive Education – "There Are No Mentally Handicapped!"*, held at the Vienna parliament in October 1996, asks us to consider what the developmental possibilities of a human being depend on.

Since the concept of the world and the human being greatly influence the possibilities of development and learning, I shall start off by outlining the classic-scientific paradigm and then place it in opposition with the basic assumptions of a post-relativistic epistemology. After defining the term "reality", I will illustrate the developmental possibilities of persons who were, respectively still are, considered incapable of developing and learning. I will speak about the so-called "deaf-blind". These are people who, due to a loss of hearing combined with blindness, have no access to information gained via the long-range functioning senses of hearing and vision. In connection with this I shall focus on the work of Marie Elisabeth Scheiblauer (1891–1968) and Anne Sullivan (1866–1936), who as early as not quite a century ago both offered the deaf-blind possibilities of development, so that access to schools and universities and thus to academic degrees became a reality to them[1].

The shared concern of the teachers and scientists mentioned above can be summarised as follows:
- Development can become a reality, providing we open up the required possibilities.
- What can *become* of a person is of significance, not what she currently *is*.
- Orientation according to the competences and not the deficits.

---

1   cf. Keller 1961

Concept of the World and the Human Being

The mechanistic Cartesian concept of the world, dominant in the sciences since the 17th century, was strongly influenced by Galileo, Descartes and Newton. Galileo demanded that the sciences should be limited to the examination of the measurable and quantifiable qualities of objects. All subjective matter was to be excluded from scientific research. Descartes postulated the essential separation of body and mind making the distinction between the two basic forms of reality: the world of awareness (*res cogitans*) and the mechanistically explicable world (*res extensa*)[2]. According to Newtonian mechanics all physical phenomena could be reduced to the movement of material particles in space, caused by the mutually attractive forces, i. e. by gravity. Time to Newton was an absolute entity, a steady flow from the past through the present to the future.

Newton's examinations were not concerned with the *why*, but with the *how*. Quoting Newton: "It is irrelevant that I cannot explain gravity. I can measure it, observe it and make predictions based on it – this is the sole aim of science."[3] Newton designed the image of a stable, reversible world, functioning, as it were, like a piece of machinery or clockwork. He even proposed that, in principle, one could make this clockwork run backwards.

The characteristic factors of this approach are:
• Causality
• Calculability
• Objectivity
• Reversibility
• Predictability (determinism)

The turn of the 19th to the 20th century marked the onset of a new development which led to a radical change in all disciplines of scientific learning. The knowledge that observations were not absolute, but relative to the observer's location (in the co-ordinate system – cf. Einstein's Theory of Relativity, 1905) and that observations influenced the matter observed (Heisenberg's Uncertainty Principle) was irreconcilable with the laws of traditional physics.

"The laws of the macrocosm were not applicable in the microcosm, for objects from the microcosm are not diminutive versions of those from the macrocosm, but much rather represent systems, which are subject to totally different measuring modes. The process of measuring (observing) always involves interfering with the condition of a system while at the same time changing it."[4]

---

2   cf. Kriz et al. 1990, p. 207
3   adapted from Berman 1985, p. 44
4   March 1958, p. 120

These discoveries "have initiated a change of perspective which not only provides a new basis for our concept of the world, but also for concepts of exploring human development"[5].

Since the early sixties yet another scientific paradigm shift has been taking place, which is summarised under the collective term of 'self-organisation'. The following concepts, which in their initial phase developed independently of each other, are indicative of this process:

The theory of dissipative structures (Ilya Prigogine), the theory of synergetics (Hermann Haken), the theory of autocatalytic hypercycles (Manfred Eigen), chaos theories (Edward Lorenz, Benoit Mandelbrot), system theoretic-cybernetic concepts (Heinz von Foerster), autopoiesis and self-reference (Humberto Maturana, Francisco Varela) and the theory of the adaptive ecological system.

The core theories and model concepts of the various disciplines up to the seventies were only very loosely related to each other, with the exception of the co-operations at the "Biological Computer Laboratory" (BCL)[6], which had been founded by Heinz von Foerster at the University of Urbana (Illinois). But it was also in the seventies that a more coherent research programme started to develop from its once quite heterogeneous origins, resulting in a new science of the complex.

---

5 Lüpke/Voß 1994, p. 1
6 The BCL was founded in 1957. Heinz von Foerster, who was actually a mathematician and physicist, worked at the Massachusetts Institute of Technology (MIT) together with Warren McCulloch and Norbert Wiener in addition to being involved in research studies at the Mexico laboratory with the neurobiologist Arturo Rosenblueth. Fascinated by these possibilities to conduct research, he founded the BCL, which consisted of a group of interdisciplinary researchers working on various systemic theoretical approaches. There was no strict separation between the humanities and the sciences. The philosopher Lars Löfgren worked on a concept for a self-referential logic (autologic), the dolphin researcher John Lilly studied the sound patterns of dolphins, the structure of their phonemes and the quality of their hearing, the neurobiologists Humberto Maturana and Francisco Varela produced significant work examining the concept of autopoiesis, Ludwig Bertalanffy worked on an approach to a general system theory, Ross Ashby, a psychiatrist, and Norbert Wiener carried out research in the field of cybernetics, von Neumann and Turing were involved in the development of an automata theory. Open conferences were regularly held, at which the latest research findings were discussed. Thus, a conference focussing on "The Principles of Self-organisation" took place in 1960, to which almost 40 researchers followed von Foerster's invitation. Another result of the work at the BCL were significant developments such as the world's first parallel computer (cf. Foerster 1998, p. 147ff.).

It would be going too far, within the framework of this exposition, to discuss in further detail the various concepts of self-organisation. I will therefore focus on two significant features:

- The openness of the system to a material and energetic exchange with the environment
- The operational loop

The openness of a system enables it to be in constant exchange with its environment, i. e. free energy can be continuously imported, respectively entropy can be exported. This, in turn, prevents the system from assuming the condition of a thermodynamic equilibrium. In an open system there is much rather a dynamic equilibrium, a so-called "flowing equilibrium", which adapts another state of order whenever instabilities occur. Thus instabilities can be regarded as the motor of system change.

The operational loop characterises the organisational interaction principle of autonomous systems with their environment. Contrary to the concept of a system as a complex machine reacting to stimuli from its environment, this system now operates with recursive functions, i. e. the reaction becomes the new stimulus – the effect the new cause[7].

Paslack[8] recapitulates the theoretical "shifts" in the perception and evaluation of phenomena as follows:
- From reversibility to irreversibility
- From linearity to nonlinearity
- From periodic occurrences to recursive processes
- From continuous (linear) development to dividing processes (bifurcation)
- From successive functional chains to networks of correlation
- From a static to a dynamic equilibrium (respectively fluctuations, oscillations etc.)
- From closed to open systems
- From strong to weak causality, respectively
- From the ideal of universal predictability to the acknowledgement of the basically unforeseeable
- From searching for universal laws of nature to revaluating unusual fringe conditions and individual solutions
- From reducing the complex to the simple to acknowledging the complexity (also of the simple), respectively
- From methodic reductionism to the acceptance of the holistic organisation of entities (autonomous systems)
- From the concept of an ahistorical universe to an evolutionary perception

---

7   cf. Krohn et al. 1987, p. 446f.
8   Paslack 1991, p. 89

From this follows that "the biological evolution can only occur in accordance with the general laws of physical and chemical evolution which precedes and engenders it, and hence, also, the attempt to analyse and understand it. – Complex processes such as perceiving, thinking and becoming aware can only take place with an understanding of these laws."[9]

The human being in this context is seen as a *bio-psycho-social* entity, the respective lower levels of the organisational system being pre-conditions of the higher ones, which, in turn, have a feedback effect on the lower ones and restructure them.

Reality

Reality is:[10]
- "The realness which divides itself up in various domains of the real and reveals itself under different aspects"
- "Everything real in contrast to the possible and the apparent […]"
- "No longer to be understood as a constant, autonomously existing order as was the case in classic antiquity, since findings in modern physics give evidence that observing an object is a process which interferes with it and thus changes it"

From the host of all the other existing definitions of reality I want to select just a few that are relevant to my further expositions.
- "Reality and thus experience, awareness, perception, imagination, memory etc. are – we might speculate – an 'invention' of our brain, integrating multi-sensory information processed with the aid of experience stored in our memory, finally enabling it to produce modes of procedure."[11]
- Reality as a network of terms which in the experience of life hitherto have proved appropriate, useful and viable by repeatedly leading to a successful overcoming of obstacles or by terminologically assimilating experiential complexes[12].
- Reality, a construction? "The environment we perceive is our invention."[13]

Responding to the opinion that *reality* can be depicted with the help of technical devices, Heinz von Foerster comes up with a little joke: "A wealthy American traveller with enough money to buy famous paintings visits Picasso at his palais;

---

9 Feuser 1995, p. 85
10 according to Brockhaus 2001, p. 266
11 Roth 1997, p. 328
12 Glasersfeld 1997, p. 47
13 Foerster 1985, p. 25

Picasso is delighted and guides him around, showing the visitor his paintings. Finally the American inquires: 'My dear Mr. Picasso, why don't you paint people as they really are?' And Picasso answers: 'How should I do that? How could it be done? What are people like? Can you give me an example?' The American pulls out his wallet, produces a small photograph and says: 'Here you can see my wife as she really is.' Picasso is fascinated and takes the photo in his hand, turning it around several times while commenting: 'I see, so this is your wife. How small and flat she is!'"[14]

Representatives of constructivism assume that reality is not discovered, but invented by us. They hold the belief that the true insight of an absolute reality is not accessible to human beings.

I would now like to just briefly tell Virgil's story, which in my lecture was enhanced by the complementary screening of a video. In his book *An Anthropologist on Mars* (1995) Oliver Sacks described in great detail his experiences with Virgil and supplemented them with diary entries written by Virgil's bride, Amy. Virgil, at the time, was fifty years of age and had a permanent position as a trained physiotherapist at the YMCA[15]. He had turned blind in his early childhood due to a severe opacity of his ocular lenses, diagnosed as Retinopathia pigmentosa. Amy, who as a diabetic had to undergo regular examinations of the eyes, took Virgil along to her eye specialist, who after learning about the course of the illness was doubtful as to the diagnosis which had been made. Since an operation of the ocular lenses was fairly straightforward procedure and there was little to lose on the one hand, but possibly a lot to be gained on the other, the operation was carried out. Virgil was able to see again, but he did not see what he and others had expected to see. Now what could Virgil actually see after the surgical dressing had been removed?

"[…] at the first moment he couldn't grasp what he was seeing. He was able to perceive light, movement and colours, a blurred, meaningless blend of impressions. It wasn't until a voice inquiring 'Well?' emanated from this confusion that he realised this chaos of light and shade was a face – the surgeon's face. […]"

To us who are born with the gift of vision such utter confusion seems unimaginable. Since we are endowed with all senses and are able to place them in relation to each other, we from the very first moment create a world of vision, a world of visual objects, concepts and meanings. When we open our eyes in the morning, a world presents itself to us visually that we have *learnt* to see for a whole lifetime. This world is not given to us: We are constantly building it up, resorting to our experiences and our abilities of categorisation, memorisation and association. When

---

14 Foerster 1998, p. 103
15 Young Men's Christian Association

Virgil however first opened his eyes after living in blindness for 45 years, there were no visual memories to support his perception; no world of experience and purpose was awaiting him. Virgil was indeed able to see, but what he saw, lacked coherence. His retina and optic nerve were sending impulses, but his brain was incapable of providing them with any meaning; Virgil was suffering from what neurologists call "agnosia"[16].

Virgil could distinguish between a wide range of colours and classify them, some of them, however, he gave the wrong names. Sacks believes that it was not a matter of colour agnosia in Virgil's case, but much rather that previously established allocations from the past had been forgotten again. "Such allocations and the initially weak neural connections underlying them had been disrupted in his brain, not on account of any injury or disease, but due to a lack of practice."[17]

Virgil could also perceive movement, but he could not associate his visual impressions with what he had already literally "grasped" with his hands. He did not recognise what he was seeing[18]. On a visit to the zoo with Oliver Sacks, a gorilla aroused Virgil's interest. He insisted on touching the animal, in order to better see it. Since this was not permitted, Sacks led him to life-size bronze statue of a gorilla standing nearby, so that he could touch the model.

"Gently and very thoroughly he explored it with his hands, displaying a confidence which had never been apparent when he was scanning something with his eyes. It became clear to me [...] how skilful and independent he had been as a blind person, with what ease and natural grace he had experienced his world with his hands, and to what extent we were now imposing something upon him which was against his nature. [...] His face seemed to shine with recognition as his fingers felt the statue."[19]

This is a spectacular example of how feeling an object can enable a person to see it.

---

16 Sacks 1995, p. 167f.
17 ibid., p. 183. Compare Scheiblauer's statement in reference to Ursula: "She would have to become dumb for lack of impressions."
18 People who were born deaf or lost their hearing at an early age and have had a cochlear implant inserted, are confronted with difficulties similar to Virgil's. To them the phenomenon of sound waves at first is meaningless.
19 Sacks 1995, p. 191f.

Development under Special Conditions

In a post-relativistic science and epistemology processes of change and development are no longer considered to be linear in their organisation and deducible in their causality. The *current* condition of a system (the human being) is no longer of focal interest, but much rather the possibilities what can *become* of a system (the human being).

Feuser[20] sees *development* "in general as a process-like, dynamic, organised change of system aiming at greater complexity and diversification." This process of *development* depends primarily on the complexity and diversity of the environment and only secondly on the abilities of the system itself. In reference to human development this means that it first and foremost depends on processes of co-operative exchange, i. e. the possibilities of dialogue, communication and exchange.

Point of view and perspective are extremely important for what a person can perceive, i. e. *"hold to be true"*, respectively for what a person can deem possible for herself and/or others.

Dialogue

Dialogue can be regarded:
* "As the most general, basic and fundamental form of exchange"[21]
* "As a mutual feedback process within the dual relationship between mother and child in which the emotional component plays a special role"[22]
* "As the interplay with the partner(s), aiming to achieve results together, which are unpredictable and frequently surprising to the participants themselves"[23]
* "As inseparable with life – this already applies to the evolutionary level of micro-organisms"[24]
* To Heinz von Foerster a game is also a form of dialogue and thus a matter of cybernetics. A gives to B, B returns to A. "Circularity of interaction, this is the essence of cybernetics."[25]

"There is no development that is not self-organised and actively acquired on the one hand, and on the other hand there is no development – regardless of the level

---

20 Feuser 1996, p. 8
21 Feuser 1996
22 Spitz 1972, 1976
23 Milani Comparetti 1995
24 cf. Jantzen 1994
25 Foerster 1985

and hierarchy of its system – that is not co-evolutional, respectively that is not mediated socially via dialogue, interaction and communication."[26]

Many people with a "disability" are excluded from and denied this chance, space and dream to develop and unfold. The respective people's "observable features" become their "qualities". We describe them based on our perception and make statements as to what he/she *is* like. We limit their potential to develop by excluding them from regular life's context, respectively by isolating them in systems which significantly reduce their possibilities of exchange. So these people gradually become what we expect them to be.

The developmental possibilities of a human being do not so much depend on a fully functional neocortex, but rather on the possibilities of dialogue and exchange this person benefit from. Both, the neurologist Andreas Zieger as well as the music and movement teacher Mimi Scheiblauer repeatedly refer to the importance of dialogue in their studies.

Marie Elisabeth Scheiblauer

In the film *Ursula oder das unwerte Leben*[27] (*Ursula or the Life not Worth Living*) Mimi Scheiblauer's approach to her work is impressively revealed. Her principle working method of *Experiencing – Recognising – Naming* meanwhile is almost 80 years old. Some of her statements correspond almost literally with those made by Zieger. Selected quotations taken from the film might illustrate this more vividly:

> *"Because human beings develop, they can be educated.*
> *Because their development is a process of change,*
> *it can be influenced.*
> *Since human beings develop over the course of their entire life,*
> *the way they change can always be influenced."*

> *"Whoever is capable*
> *of co-ordinating their eyes with the movement of an object,*
> *is not incapable of learning.*
> *A relationship to the environment is established with/through the object."*

> *"What does a person need to develop?*
> *Devotion, acceptance, recognition,*
> *meaningful occupation and love."*

---

26 Feuser 1996, p. 104
27 Mertens/Marti 1966

"At institutions no work is attempted with the so-called uneducable.
They are nursed, attended to, kept clean.
But young children are irrevocably condemned not to develop,
because they are stigmatised as incapable of development.
All they ever see is their equals,
they never hear a meaningful sound,
and bore themselves to death!"

"From feeling to realising,
from touching to grasping,
from acting to understanding."[28]

When Scheiblauer first met the eight-year-old Ursula at the "institution", the doctors claimed that she was blind, deaf, imbecile and epileptic. At the time Ursula did not weigh more than a mere 10 kg and measured about a metre in size. She could neither sit nor walk and was fed with a bottle. Scheiblauer did not go by Ursula's deficits, but instead searched for possibilities to make Ursula aware of the world. She was convinced that there was no such thing as an uneducable person and that every person carried in them the ability to act creatively.

"If Ursula is deaf, one has to convey the world of sound to her, like with hard-of-hearing people; elemental rhythms and terms that are normally perceived via the sense of hearing with children whose hearing is intact. If Ursula, however, is also blind, she will have to learn how to move in the space of a room, in order to be able to imagine this spatial dimension."[29]

Since therapeutic work with the so-called "uneducable" was unheard of in institutions, Scheiblauer sought a place with a foster parent for Ursula. Ms. Utzinger, an educator for deaf-blind children, put Ursula up at her home. In the following years an intensive form of co-operation developed between Ms. Utzinger and Mimi Scheiblauer. Ursula made great progress. "If a child's mother were not constantly trying to communicate the surrounding world to her infant, thus successively extending the baby's experiential scope, this child would grow dumb for lack of impressions. After Ursula had experienced the wind at the seaside, she was able to learn how to use her breath to blow out air."[30] The variations of dialogue that Scheiblauer offered were diverse. She worked with rhythms which she expressed instrumentally, vocally, in sound gestures or in movements. Verbal dialogue is of no importance here. Instead, "It is a dialogue of action and reaction, taking place in a circular pattern [...] as a continued, mutually stimulating feedback circuit."[31]

28　Scheiblauer quoted in: Mertens/Marti 1966
29　ibid.
30　ibid.
31　Spitz 1988, p. 14

And it was Scheiblauer's belief that all people – even the weakest – carry in them the ability to act creatively and that this creative ability will always prosper providing it is allowed to[32]. This means that only the children that are not educated are uneducable.

Alternatively, one could quote from René Spitz' study *Vom Dialog*[33]: "The person who is denied dialogue as an infant, becomes an empty shell, dumbed down intellectually, a candidate for institutionalisation. Life in the human(e) sense of the word cannot be anti-social, it must be social. Life in our sense is created through dialogue."

Scheiblauer developed no theoretical concept or she did not record it in writing. But her working methods are impressively illustrated in film documentaries. Her basic assumption that no person is uneducable and that every person has the potential to be creative, providing there is the necessary opportunity to engage in dialogue, enabled even severely impaired persons to develop.

The film *Ursula oder das unwerte Leben* was shown in many countries and later also broadcast on TV. It was furthermore highly acclaimed among remedial teachers, and yet to this day nobody has contacted either Ursula or Ms. Utzinger to find out how they fared later in their lives.

Anne Sullivan

Anne Sullivan fulfilled two conditions to be regarded as an expert teacher for Helen Keller:
- for one thing, she had very little eyesight herself when she entered the Perkins Institution for the Blind[34],
- and for the other, she had lived together with Laura Bridgman at this institution for six years.

Laura Bridgman had already entered the Perkins Institution in 1837, when she was eight years old. She had lost her hearing and eyesight at the age of two. Laura's teacher was the doctor and pedagogue, Samuel Gridley Howe, who had founded and also ran the Perkins Institution. He developed special books with raised types and had them printed as textbooks for his school. Laura Bridgman was the first child that we know of, unable to see, hear, or speak who was educated.

---

32 Mertens/Marti 1966
33 Spitz 1988, p. 23
34 "In 1833 Thomas Handasyd Perkins (1764–1854) donated his Boston residence to the New England Asylum for the Blind, which in 1839 was renamed in his honour: 'Perkins Institution for the Blind'." (Mescerjakov 2001, p. 25)

Helen Keller (1880–1968) lost her hearing and eyesight after a severe illness at the age of eighteen months. After the disease she had also completely lost her sense of orientation and thus was unable to walk. Unlike Ursula who had lived in an institution, or rather had been pushed off from one institution to the next, leading to total isolation from the outside world, Helen Keller had been able to gain experience at her mother's apron strings in their house and its surrounding environment. She was familiar with many objects and could handle them. By imitating her mother's activities, which Helen followed with her hands, she developed her first gestures to communicate. In addition she spent a lot of time with Martha Washington, the family cook's daughter, who spent the whole day working outside in the yard, the kitchen, the horse stables and the cowshed. Martha taught Helen to help her with certain tasks. Helen Keller describes this period of her childhood in her autobiography "The Story of My Life". Unfortunately there is no detailed description of the sign language, which nevertheless must have been quite comprehensive. For Helen could communicate in gestures that she wanted to search the grass for eggs laid by their guinea fowl. Martha, in turn, never permitted Helen to carry these eggs back to the house for fear that she might fall and break them on the way.

When Anne Sullivan began to work with Helen, she was able to orient herself in the house, the yard, the garden and the immediate neighbourhood. She was familiar with household appliances and knew how to use them. She could make herself understood to Martha with the help of gestures and to a certain extent could also communicate with her mother.

Anne Sullivan promptly started teaching Helen words with the help of finger spelling. However this process of "translating familiar terms into language" was not an immediate success, since Helen was not used to working with adults and everybody so far had submitted to her tyranny[35].

At the beginning this kind of work very often resembled a battle in the true sense of the word, but Sullivan persistently kept on searching for the right method. One of her diary entries reads: "I wonder how children with intact senses learn to speak? The answer is simple: by imitating. [...] They see, how others do certain things and try to do them alike. [...] Long before they utter their first words they understand what people are saying to them. [...] These considerations will guide me and show me the right way to teach Helen how to speak. I must speak into the palm of her hand, much like we do when speaking into a young child's ear. I assume she has the same abilities to assimilate and imitate as any other child. I shall speak to her in full sentences, explaining the meaning, when necessary, in gestures and her own descriptive signs."[36]

---

35 cf. Mescerjakov 2001, p. 43ff.
36 Mescerjakov 2001, p. 47

The successful training and education of Laura Bridgman and Helen Keller did not only gain fame through the writings and lectures by Charles Dickens and Helen Keller herself. It was also scientists who became involved in this topic. Thus as early as 1905 the psychologist William Stern wrote a study titled: *Helen Keller. The Development and Training of a Deaf-blind Person from a Psychological, Pedagogical and Language-theoretical Perspective*. This, however, did not lead to a general acknowledgement and acceptance of the basic educational potential with deaf-blind people. Helen Keller was much rather regarded as a unique genius or miracle, who was only able to acquire knowledge due to her extraordinary talent[37].

Sullivan realised "that the essence of the matter is not the word, but the existence of a psychological image. Words can only be completely acquired, when they refer to 'what has truly been experienced', [...] it is then that the word becomes fully linked to its concept. Words acquired for their own sake have no meaning; they gain meaning when the immediate knowledge associated with them is based on 'true experience'."[38] I believe there quite clearly are parallels here to Mimi Scheiblauer's working principles.

As we know Sullivan's efforts turned out to be extremely successful. Helen was later able to attend school and went on to study at Radcliffe College, from which she graduated with honours in 1904. She travelled to all continents with the exception of South Africa and met up with many celebrities of her time. Unfortunately I cannot discuss in detail here her remarkable career. May it suffice to add that in 1955 – at the age of 75 and as the first woman in history – Helen Keller was awarded the Havard University Honorary Degree.

"In order for human beings to develop, they need communication, human relationships, socially inspiring living conditions, hope and meaningful perspectives in their lives. Humans are basically open to their environment, as well as eager to know and to make contact. The denial of acceptance and communication triggers a process of 'emotional starvation', leading to hospitalism, sensory deprivation, stress, physical as well as mental deterioration, conditioned helplessness, a lack of purpose in life, disease and death."[39]

It is up to us to open up possibilities
so that development can become reality.

---

37 The general attitude that it was impossible for the deaf-blind to develop and to be trained and educated, remained and was supported by studies such as the one written by Henri Lemoine for his postdoctoral thesis in 1913: "The deaf-blind are degenerated by birth, much like idiots, incapable of any normal psychological development. No matter what the nature of the pedagogical intervention might be, they will stay utterly underdeveloped and all one can do is feel sorry for them." (Mescerjakov 2001, p. 30)
38 Mescerjakov 2001, p. 48f.
39 Zieger 1996, p. 73

Literature

Bauby, Jean-Dominique (2002): *The Diving-bell and the Butterfly.* London.

Berman, Morris (1985): *Wiederverzauberung der Welt. Am Ende des Newtonschen Zeitalters.* Reinbek bei Hamburg.

Berman, Morris (1981): *Reenchantment of the world.* Cornell.

Brockhaus (2001): *Die Enzyklopädie.* Study edition. Vol. XXIII. Leipzig.

Ethymologisches Wörterbuch des Deutschen (2000⁵). Munich.

Feuser, Georg (1995): *Behinderte Kinder und Jugendliche. – Zwischen Integration und Aussonderung.* Darmstadt.

Feuser, Georg (1996): *The Relation between the View of the Human Being and Inclusive Education. "There Are No Mentally Handicapped!"* Speech to the members of Nationalrat in the Austrian Parliament on the 29th Oct. 1996 in Vienna. In: *http://bidok.uibk.ac.at/library/feuser-humanbeing.html,* 01/2008.

Foerster, Heinz von (1985): *Entdecken oder Erfinden.* In: Gumin, Heinz/Mohler, Armin (Ed.): *Einführung in den Konstruktivismus.* Munich.

Foerster, Heinz von (1985a): *Sicht und Einsicht.* Braunschweig.

Foerster, Heinz von (1998): *Wahrheit ist der Erfindung eines Lügners: Gespräche für Skeptiker.* Heidelberg.

Glasersfeld, Ernst von (1997): *Wege des Wissens.* Heidelberg.

Jantzen, Wolfgang (1994): *Zur Naturgeschichte, Psychologie und Philosophien von Tätigkeit, Sinn und Dialog.* Marburg.

Keller, Helen (1961): *The Story of My Life.*

Kriz, Jürgen/Lück, Helmut/Heidbrink, Horst (1990): *Wissenschafts- und Erkenntnistheorie.* Opladen.

Krohn, Wolfgang/Küppers, Günter/Paslack, Rainer (1987): *Selbstorganisation – Zur Genese und Entwicklung einer wissenschaftlichen Revolution.* In: Schmidt, Siegfried J. (Ed.): *Der Diskurs des radikalen Konstruktivismus.* Frankfurt, 441–465.

Lüpke, Hans von/Voß, Reinhard (Ed.) (1994): *Entwicklung im Netzwerk. Systemisches Denken und professionsübergreifendes Handeln in der Entwicklungsförderung.* Pfaffenweiler.

March, Arthur (1958): *Das neue Denken der modernen Physik.* Göttingen.

Mertens, Reni/Marti, Walter (1966): *Ursula oder das unwerte Leben.* (VHS video cassette, 87 min.) Bundesverband Rhythmische Erziehung e.V. Zurich.

Mescerjakov, Alexander (2001): *Helen Keller war nicht allein. Taubblindheit und die Entwicklung der menschlichen Psyche.* Berlin.

Milani Comparetti, Adriano: *Von der "Medizin der Krankheit" zu einer "Medizin der Gesundheit".* In: Janssen, Edda/Lüpke, Hans, von (1995): *Von der Behandlung der*

Krankheit zur Sorge um Gesundheit. Konzept einer am Kind orientierten Gesundheits-förderung von Prof. Adriano Milani Comparetti. Frankfurt/Main.

Paslack, Rainer (1991): *Urgeschichte der Selbstorganisation.* Wiesbaden.

Pearce, Joseph Chilton (1994): *Der nächste Schritt der Menschheit. Die Entfaltung des menschlichen Potentials aus neurobiologischer Sicht.* Freiamt.

Pearce, Joseph Chilton (1992): *Evolution's End. Claiming the Potential of Our Intelligence.*

Pschyrembel, Willibald (1998): *Pschyrembel Klinisches Wörterbuch.* Berlin.

Ramachandran, Vilaynur/Blakeslee, Sandra (2001): *Die blinde Frau, die sehen konnte. Rätselhafte Phänomene unseres Bewußtseins.* Reinbek bei Hamburg.

Roth, Gerhard (1997): *Das Gehirn und seine Wirklichkeit. Kognitive Neurobiologie und ihre philosophischen Konsequenzen.* Frankfurt/Main.

Sacks, Oliver (1998): *The Man Who Mistook His Wife For A Hat: And Other Clinical Tales.*

Sacks, Oliver (1995): *Eine Anthropologin auf dem Mars. Sieben paradoxe Geschichten.* Reinbek bei Hamburg.

Sacks, Oliver (1995a): *An Anthropologist On Mars: Seven Paradoxical Tales.*

Spitz, René A. (1972): *Eine genetische Feldtheorie der Ichbildung.* Frankfurt/Main.

Spitz, René A. (1959): *A Genetic Field Theory of Ego Formation. Its Implications for Pathology.*

Spitz, René A. (1988): *Vom Dialog. Studien über den Ursprung der menschlichen Kommunikation und ihrer Rollen in der Persönlichkeitsbildung.* Munich.

Zieger, Andreas: *Grenzbereiche der Wahrnehmung.* In: *Behinderte in Familie, Schule und Gesellschaft: Bewusstsein und Bewusstheit* 6/1998. Graz.

Zieger, Andreas (1996): *Wieviel Gehirn braucht der Mensch?* In: Doering, Waltraud/Doering, Winfried/Dose, Gude/Stadelmann, Mario (Ed.): *Sinn und Sinne im Dialog.* Dortmund.

Rhythmic Musical Education – a Basic Instrument to Support Development in Educational Work[1]

Helga Neira Zugasti

During my work as a teacher for children and young people in school groups with different cognitive and physical handicaps and as a rhythmic teacher I have used Rhythmic Musical Education as a basic procedure in daily work. Through experiences I have made, I find increasingly that we should discover the principle qualities that developmentally orientated educational systems in their entire, inclusive approach have in common.

In general, educational work seems to me too specialized nowadays. We work too much in single sectors without taking into account the integral view of social, ethical, administrative and political consequences. (We could begin thinking about pre-natal diagnostics and the consequences for education and for society as a whole.) This specialisation causes decisions where judgements about one area of a child's development are applied to the entire complex of developmental and educational challenges. This does not support harmonious development of our children. Developmentally supportive work with children is only possible with an integral approach.

The search for common principle qualities in integral educational procedures is a constant challenge and was started by our own famous rhythmic-teachers and shining examples like Jaques-Dalcroze, as well as Feudel, Erdmann, Höllering and Frohne. Today we are again trying to take a small step in this direction.

In my opinion there is only one legitimate educational aim: the support of individual development of the child within the society of youths, adults and persons with or without handicaps. Educational situations, methods and procedures can be beneficially furthered by this basic position. Thus, on the one hand we have to look for and improve practical ways to find situations, general conditions and materials to offer these educational impulses. On the other hand we have to look for the theoretical background which in its turn reflects the holistic educational process – not focussing on selection but on the inclusion of all functions a person mobilises in educational processes. The complete person, not partial aspects, has to be the centre of reflection.

I believe that for practical access the most effective and basic instrument to support the balanced and holistic development of a person is Rhythmic Musical Education.

---

1   Paper for the International Rhythmic Congress, Trossingen, Germany, 11/16/2006

In Vienna, for the purpose of theoretical reflection, we can now apply a system for observation, analysis and statistical documentation based on the theory of cognitive development and offering a detailed itemised survey on the essential developmental steps a person uses in any single situation.

I would like to offer two themes:
1. A specific view on the term rhythm and its different qualities
2. The connection of rhythm with developmental educational processes

It may be that I am repeating a lot of facts we all already know, but it seems a good thing to put them in a new context and thus to create the chance of finding new conclusions.

Rhythm: what are we really talking about?
What do we mean by rhythm?

Rhythm is the basis of the procedure Rhythmic Musical Education. Up to now I have encountered this term in practical work and in literature as standardised. However this is not true, rhythm is a complex concept.
Rhythm results from a number of different qualities and conditions which are not constituted by each single quality alone. Only the combined effect of all of them generates rhythm, e. g. water is liquid. But each component of water – oxygen and hydrogen are gasses. Only the specific combination of these elements generates the liquid quality of water.
This is my understanding of what we mean by rhythm. Here I refer to rhythm in the general meaning of processes in living structures, not only the musical rhythm of a sequence of notes in the bars of a piece of music, because Rhythmic Musical Education supports and helps to balance the development of a person as a whole in his active capabilities.

Up to now I have found 13 qualities and conditions that give rise to rhythm. The idea is really fascinating. If one of these qualities is lacking, there will be no rhythmical process. First I would like to discuss the overall meaning of these qualities in life procedures in general.

- Synchronisation
- Entirety
- Continuity
- Repetition
- Polarity
- Structure
- Activity
- Interdependence

- Variation
- Subject Bonding
- Intention Orientation
- Irreversibility
- Periodicity

Rhythm is generated by **synchronisation**. Each living structure consists of an uncountable number of elements which need different periods of time, space and dynamics for their activities. To generate a rhythmical process all the elements of this organism have to be synchronized. If they do not work together the process is not harmonious, the organism cannot develop in a positive, healthy, forward-looking way. This is relevant for the structure of each tiniest cell as equally for the extensive rhythmical phases of the seasons with their influence on the growth of all the plants in a region. Certain butterflies for example synchronize their reproductive cycle to the flowering time of certain plants.

Rhythm is activated by the **integral combination** of all elements of the structure. This means that all elements of this particular organism are included and affected. If my sleeping rhythm is balanced it gives me a good start to the morning, all my energy reserves are available and many other psychophysical systems equally benefit and induce a feeling of well-being. The activity and the influence of all these constitutional elements are of different intensity, but they are all integrally involved.

Rhythm depends on **continuity**. Without the continuous flow of integral elements of a structure rhythm cannot surge. I will mention only one aspect on the topic: If our neuronal system did not continually associate incoming impulses and adapt the inner pictures then, without continuity, every alteration of exterior requirements would involve a new organisation of each structure. How could then an organism create stable structures? Exterior influences are permanently existent. However the organism has to stabilize its functions, each living being needs stable patterns to manage the continuous process of renovation, and representation of patterns. This is only possible through continuity of the essential elements of the structure.

Rhythm results through **repetition** of the essential substance of a form (Gestalt). For example the diagram of single systole-diastole frequency of my heart is not sufficient evidence for the cardiologist. He needs a certain number of continuously repeated results to find out if the heart frequency is okay. The essentials of the rhythmical structure can only be observed by repeated sequences.

Polarity is a main quality of rhythm. Each organic movement has a fixed oscillation between the two extreme points of the possible movement available. Within this field it organizes changes, this means it is able to introduce development, e. g. a baby learns how far it can shift its balance forward by hundreds of trial and error processes. We know the amplitude of our steps and can adapt the rhythm of our walking steps to the required speed and we can balance the extreme points in the numerous bipolar processes in different parts of the body that lead to a single step. This means rhythm is in accordance with the homoeostatic principle, a principle that continuously causes the equilibration process between two poles which are mutually dependent. This is one of the qualities we have to adapt to during our whole life – the equilibration between large numbers of bipolar processes that keep us alive.

Rhythm is **organized**. Rhythm consists of structured time, structured space and structured dynamics. The resulting forms (Gestalten) are sizeable and understandable. They can be compared to past sequences and allow planning for following sequences. This organization is one of the most important prerequisites for the development of living structures.

Rhythm can only be produced by **activity**. It is always a dynamic process. Without activity there is no rhythm. We are not always aware of the many different rhythms that are part of our reality, they are either too infinitesimal or too extensive but their activity affects us.

Rhythm is **interdependent**. Each sequence is determined by the previous sequence and determines the following sequence. Thus the relationship is interdependent and provides the continuous flow of developmental processes.

Rhythm depends on **variation**. This does not mean repetition of the same, but repetition of essential elements and the slight deviations due to life processes. The quality of variation forms the basis for changes to new processes. The slight differences offer the possibility of experiencing new ways without losing the acquainted structure. This takes place in every developmental process; the microscopic processes in our brain as well as macroscopic processes in galactic systems or the evolution of new species of animals and plants. Each new phenomenon has a long development process of many varied experiences until a new creation emerges.

Rhythm has to be produced by a **subject**. Rudolf Bode says that rhythm is not divisible, it is individual. It is not divisible from time, space and from the producer. Rhythm is bound to the specific organism, to the subject. It cannot be transferred. For example even if we identically copy a movement we have to recreate it with our own neuronal system. Therefore we have planning neurons, action neurons and the recently discovered mirror neurons (*Spiegelneuronen*), which copy emotional impressions and create and represent their inner picture. In no way is rhythm transferable.

Rhythm is **intention-orientated**. Rhythmical processes are the opposite of goal orientated processes. Purpose or aim orientated processes reduce intention and exclude impulses in order to reach certain, preconceived results. The direction towards which the activity of a rhythmical process moves is determined mainly by the inner structure of an organism, by its immanent capacities to cope with exterior influences. Here there is an important connection to the theses of Jean Piaget: Accommodation, assimilation and adaptation are goal orientated processes.

Rhythm is **irreversible.** This means that rhythmical process cannot be turned back. The patterns caused by a rhythmical process are facts bound to the time and the space in which they happened. If we want to re-present, to reactivate stored information we cause a new active process.

Rhythm has a **periodical** structure in developmental dynamic processes. Through the new possibilities, which arise through continuous flow, variation, and all the other qualities we had a short look at, refinement, extension, deepening, networking and consolidation of the developmental processes result. The basic elements of the structure appear after a certain time in a differentiated and more complex form in the next loop of the developmental spiral.

These are the qualities and conditions on which rhythm depends that I have discovered so far. If one of these items is lacking a rhythmical process cannot be generated. Simply: life would not work.

But there is one much more fascinating and important fact: **All these items constitute active guiding principles of developmental supportive educational situations.** The various progressive educational approaches and methods in the last century, as well as new scientific knowledge in the fields of Neuro Education and Neuropsychology, demand these qualities for successful educational work which supports development and is child-centred[2].

This is yet more proof that Rhythmic Musical Education plays a fundamental role in educational work in general. Our pedagogical intentions in general, not only in rhythmic musical tasks, have to respect and implement these qualities if we are aiming at sensible support in learning and development processes. Of course other qualities not concerning the rhythmical principle such as empathic relationships, competent didactical knowledge and child-orientated conditions must also be included.

We are aware of the effectiveness of Rhythmic Musical Education through experiences we have made; however for generally comprehensible articulation and reflection it is not enough. I feel it is very necessary to demonstrate these experiences in theory and to produce scientific evidence for their validity. It is not a new theory

---

2   cf. Hüther 2004 and Spitzer 2008

of rhythm which is necessary, rather more the affirmation of what we daily experience as operative structures. To substantiate, confirm and thus combine this by applying valid knowledge from other scientific fields is a challenge which has been neglected for too long.

Before we go on to practical work, I would like to emphasize that each task usually includes all qualities, but I have looked for examples that emphasize the one or the other quality in particular.

Practical Example 1[3]

Let us stand up and shift our weight from one leg to the other until we achieve a gentle swinging, placing our legs then farther apart. The movement continues to the accompaniment of a bass xylophone that plays a crescendo but without altering the speed. Automatically (or if necessary with the help of the teacher) the movement of all the participants has a uniform direction. Then we start self-accompaniment using voice, language, humming as the bass xylophone gradually fades out. Participants are asked to put their hands or arms on the shoulders of both neighbours, the xylophone joins in again increasing and decreasing in volume several times leading slowly to the end of the process.

In an overview of the single qualities it becomes clear that in this exercise *synchronisation* was the most significant factor. Each of us started with an individual time structure and ended in a common time structure. We achieved a collective energy field. Improvised accompaniment, humming, singing, touching each other harmonized the different time structures to result in a joint time structure of the group.

This experience of shared tension and relaxation in a group is very supportive, satisfying and stabilizing. Especially in groups with children who express their difficulties with conspicuous behaviour, this can be changed if they frequently experience such situations over a longer period of time. They learn that they are equal parts of a whole, that they can work as active, constructive members of the group and that they too can contribute to coping with a task. Acceptance occurs through individual, physical activity and direct experience, not only by talking about it. Here I refer to the results of research on the effect of music by Hans G. Bastian. I placed emphasis only on one aspect of the educational significance of synchronisation.

Practical Example 2: An imitation task

A simple, predetermined rhythm is clapped (| ⌐⌐ | ⌐⌐ | | | –) and repeated until it can be copied. Everyone stands up. The task is altered: the rhythm is played

---

3   These examples were experienced practically by participants at the lecture.

on the arms of the chairs, stamped on the floor, then the short notes are left out once. In the next sequence, which is played on the body, they are changed to the next beat and, at the end, clapped again in this altered dynamic ($|$ $|$ $|$ $|$ $\lceil\rceil$ $\lceil\rceil$ $|$ $-$). The sequence is repeated many times at different speeds until it either slowly comes to an end or finishes in a climax reaching either a maximum in volume or speed.

In this task the emphasis is on variation. The main element – the ratio of double tempo – is maintained but the parts of the body, the sensory input and the dynamic expression are altered in that the same elements are played in some of the many different possible ways. The main structural component – the doubled speed – is maintained, can be stabilized and consolidated.

What is the importance of variation for learning processes?

It is indeed the small differences in an activity that stimulate concentration, curiosity and attention. These facts can be found in the works of Gerald Hüther and Manfred Spitzer. They state that repeating the same thing is tiring and that the neuronal coding system shuts down because our brain works very effectively. However, if the information is too differentiated it cannot be absorbed because impulse transmission cannot find access to existing, stored data and the thus non-representational information seeps away.

The last point can be repeatedly found in children with cognitive limitations. They have a high knowledge of detail available and can acquire a good figure and skeletal structure. However, in order to apply this knowledge in independent use in differing situations they would need many more situations in which they could construct their own, stable, generalised inner picture of information through variation of the significant elements of content. To this purpose contemporary learning support and learning programmes (= content orientated not development orientated curricula) offer far too little opportunity. This is one of the most important aspects for the seriously increasing number of children with slight cerebral dysfunctions, children who suffer an attention deficit due to the current social dynamics: maintaining the significance of a structure and at the same time incorporating variation, small alterations and short units in order to be able to develop competence for concentration, perseverance, orientation towards the group, collective dynamics and many more factors through one's own, active experiences.

These are two exemplary instances which precisely demonstrate the deep connection between the qualities of rhythm and learning i.e. development processes.

The connection between the qualities (that have been recognized up till now) and the conditions are presented in the following list. Let us take these thoughts one step further and find out the meaning of these qualities in connection with developmental processes and the process of active learning.

Synchronisation refers to the agreement of differing time, space and dynamic structures within one's self (intrapersonal) and with processes from the environment (interpersonal).
This quality permits recognition of own activity as a meaningful part of the common composition of processes. One of the basic requirements of a person is that her way of expression or of manner is accepted per se. For personal development reinforcement of others' acceptance is the result and with reference to own reactions reinforcement of self esteem in the community. This encourages *empowerment* – the acceptance of the person, of her way of expression within the community. This acceptance is one of the basic human needs.

Entirety refers to the multi-functional activation of abilities and leads to the *combined storing of data.*
Activation of various functions at the same time causes more intensive networking between the different cerebral centres and a broad representation of the information. In every activity, with more or less intensity, all eight functions that we possess are activated in order for us to enter into an exchange with ourselves and our environment. These functions are: motion, perception/sensation, thought, speech, social-emotional activity, wanting, intuition/creativity and memory/remembrance. In the research project of the Institute for Music and Movement 2004[4] in co-operation with the Institute for Educational Science in Vienna, scientific proof was presented that in each and every action all functions are activated in differing intensity and also which correlations and subsequent significance arise from the evaluation of data from different variables. In this way the networking of information in neural fields is intensified.

Continuity stabilizes memory content especially during sensitive learning periods in so-called "learning windows" and leads to *tuning of the networking process.*
The representation processes of stored data increase their speed through continual use of the conductors, the neuronal pathways become stronger (myelinisation of the nerve tracts), the capacity to reactivate knowledge increases with respect to durance and quantity.

Repetition allows differentiation, refinement and consolidation of memory content and thus the choice of more effective expressive possibilities as well as the grasp of the most important points of information transfer by leaving out unimportant details and concentrating on significant ones.

---

4   Institut für Musik- und Bewegungserziehung sowie Musiktherapie, University of Music and Performing Arts Vienna, Austria

This is the *basis for feedback* (comparison and safeguarding of data) and *anticipation* (looking forward, expecting).

Polarity in the equilibration of tension is a *condition for developmental effective learning.*
The interchange of the homeostatic principle aims at the equalisation between two reciprocal provisory poles. Action in good emotional conditions, with balanced feelings, means that our neuronal systems produce positive transmitters, action under stress causes the production of transmitters which block neuronal activity and the flow of the networking process (which constitutes 80 % of our cerebral tracts according to Spitzer) between the single cerebral areas is constricted. Balanced psychophysical stress conditions are a prerequisite for developmental, dynamic and effective learning.

Structure is necessary for safety and self-competence and is a *basic requirement for self-organized learning.*
If there is sufficient overview of the main elements of a structure, energies can be effectively organised, proper decisions made alone and one's own solution strategies found. Self-organized learning needs the commitment of one's own competences.

Activity: Cross-linking activity of the cortex fields is mainly determined by self-controlled and active confrontations with inner and exterior impulses.
Learning by doing is solely through self-motivated, creative confrontations with processes and is self-controlled access to solutions by trial and error.

Interdependency: Logical connection of contents leads to *mutual dependency of data.*
Georg Feuser explains very clearly that each individual possesses his own developmental, logical structure; this means not only the didactical structure of our lessons has to adhere to the principle of interdependency; but also the entire developmental support in our educational work has to respect this personal development logic as a positive basic structure. All data, with which the brain controls activities, interrelate in continuous reciprocity. Information has a reciprocal function; it alters the map already stored in our brain and, at the same time, establishes the amount and intensity of the renewed assimilation of data. Here it is important for the individual to be able to process the information according to his developmental logic.

Variation: collecting and extending new experiences → *condition for generalisation.*
By maintaining the most significant elements of a structure the important processes of differentiation, intensification and enhancement of basic experiences can be achieved. Finally an increasingly complex package of organised single data becomes available for the solution of problems. This is a prerequisite for generalisation of memory content.

Subject bonding means that the individual alone copes with information, this *increases autonomy and individual competences*.
The main aim of our educational work should be to encourage solution of problems with own ideas and offer adequate competences. However this can only be learned by self determined decision processes and the phasing out of supportive accompaniment. This leads to an increase of self competence and finally to the development of an autonomous world view.

Intention orientation: individual approach to solutions → *focus on capacities, not on deficits*.
The interest of accompaniment and observance lies in the process not in the result. It is interesting to see how solutions are found, which actions in a child's repertoire are activated and which elements of a task have importance for the child in this specific situation. Nobody works with his deficits everybody employs his capabilities and advantages for process solution. Capabilities not deficits are important. Through individual participation in a process arrangement, individual development goals are attained. These are the basis for balanced personality development.

Irreversibility: respecting each act as the best possible for the moment → *future orientation*.
Georg Feuser explains that each act has to be understood as a future orientated act, even regressive, or self destructive acts have this future orientated meaning (attitude) and have to be respected as the momentary basis for the best strategy. Developmental meaningful options can only result from this positive view; we must communicate understanding and find supportive speech in even the most difficult situations. Rhythmical processes with their space-time relativity are always future-orientated, thus repeatedly a positive access to development is achieved.

Periodicity: maturing of complex patterns → *developmental loops*.
We should meet after a while and reflect which changes have taken place by combining this knowledge with our practical work, with our personal life. The development from simple to complex demands, the periodical recurrence of the most significant elements in the shape of (sensorimotor) cycles so that the maturing of complex development patterns both towards differentiation as also intensification is possible.

Each of these qualities or conditions is important for the structures necessary for development and learning. In rhythmic-musical tasks each person reacts with the whole palette of capabilities at her disposal at that moment in time. Each individual decides freely – consciously or unconsciously – which effect, which impulse from the many ideas within a task is important. Here I find a very important difference between therapeutic intentions and the intention of rhythmic-musical tasks. Therapeutic intentions have to be based on a specific diagnosis, have to elaborate defined methods and have to achieve predetermined results. A process distinguishing the basic demands of both procedures (therapeutic or educational work), meaningful overlapping and unclear, goal-orientated mixing is very necessary.

We can see that the basic qualities of rhythm have a very direct and intensive connection and influence on developmentally orientated learning. Therefore we need to establish Rhythmic Musical Education as a basic element in all educational training, because if taught well this procedure is the basis of the main qualities that developmentally supported learning needs.

Since the beginning of the last century the purpose of Rhythmic Musical Education has been the support of the development of the personal skills and capabilities in an integral way. The qualities of this procedure are most effective in inclusive educational situations. The term "inclusive" is holistic in two ways: it refers firstly to work in heterogeneous groups of children with and without disabilities and secondly to the development of the different abilities and functions of the single person. Inclusion has a personal as well as a social aspect.

It is one of my deepest desires to contribute to the realization of participative, shared learning and living of handicapped and non-handicapped children in heterogeneous groups; that diversity is recognized as an enrichment and that the process of selection is seen as an impoverishment of society's potential. Rhythmic Musical Education can offer a creative and forward-looking procedure to take on this challenge.

Literature

Bastian, Hans G. (2001⁴): *Kinder optimal fördern – mit Musik.* Zurich.

Bühler, Ariane/Thaler, Alice (2001): *Selber denken macht klug.* Edition Schweizer Zentralstelle für Heilpädagogik [SZH], Series HPS, Nr. 17, 43f. Lucerne.

Erdmann, Alice (1982): *Humanitas rhythmica. Rhythmisch strukturierte Sinnesphänomene – eine Orientierungshilfe für die Ausbildung des Menschlichen?* Bonn.

Feuser, Georg (1995): *Behinderte Kinder und Jugendliche. – Zwischen Integration und Aussonderung.* Darmstadt.

Garnitschnig, Karl: *Integration – Postulate und Bedingungen ihrer Verwirklichung.* In: *Erziehung und Unterricht* 1994, Nr. 6, 339–350.

Garnitschnig, Karl (1999): *Förderung von Kindern im Alter von 10 bis 14 Jahren mit besonderen Bedürfnissen in der Lernwerkstatt durch offenes und aktives Lernen.* Vienna.

Garnitschnig, Karl: *Eine Theorie, innovative Ideen praktisch werden zu lassen. Orientierungen und Kriterien guter Schulen.* In: *Erziehung und Unterricht* 1997, Nr. 1, 4–22.

Held, Martin/Geißler, Karlheinz (1995): *Von Rhythmen und Eigenzeiten.* Stuttgart.

Hüther, Gerald (2004): *Die Macht der inneren Bilder.* Göttingen.

Kegan, Robert (1982): *The Evolving Self: Problem and Process in Human Development.* Cambridge.

Maturana, Humberto R./Varela, Francisco J. (1987/1998): *Tree of Knowledge: The Biological Roots of Human Understanding.* Boston.

Neira Zugasti, Helga (1987): *Rhythmik als Unterrichtshilfe bei behinderten Kindern.* Vienna.

Neira Zugasti, Helga (2002): *Was passiert im Unterricht wirklich?* In: *Rhythmik – Zeitschrift des Berufsverbands Rhythmik Schweiz*, Nr. 1, 6–16.

Spitzer, Manfred (2008): *Learning: The Human Brain and the School of Life.* Amsterdam.

Stengel Rutkowsky, Sabine (1998): *Kinder mit Down Syndrom.* Stuttgart.

Between Music Pedagogy and the Natural Sciences – Perspectives on Researching Music Perception (in People with Hearing Loss)

Ulrike Stelzhammer-Reichhardt

"All men will become brothers ... "[1]

Did you know that our European anthem was composed by a deaf man? Ludwig von Beethoven (1770–1827) started to suffer from hearing loss at the age of 28. Tinnitus (ringing in the ears), loss of listening comprehension, hyperacusis (oversensitivity to environmental sound) and loss of high frequencies lead to complete deafness in 1819. The composer and conductor Beethoven withdrew from the world of music and gives expression to thoughts of suicide in his letters. Only his music saved him. Even though he could no longer hear, it was still as alive for him as it was before. Exquisite compositions such as *Missa solemnis* (Op. 123) or the Ninth Symphony *"Choral"* (Op. 125) were composed following Beethoven going deaf[2].

But also less prominent people who suffer from hearing loss or impairment – be it inborn or acquired – do not wish to do without music in their lives. Since the end of the 19th century records detail music instruction for deaf and hard-of-hearing individuals. The deaf and blind Helen Keller described how she recognized and appreciated music through her tactile senses[3]. Other deaf or hard-of-hearing people repeatedly report of their particular approach to music. Thereby the entire human body plays a large role as an instrument for hearing music.

"Hearing is basically a specialized form of touch. Sound is simply vibrating air which the ear picks up and converts to electrical signals, which are then interpreted by the brain. The sense of hearing is not the only sense that can do this, touch can do this too."[4]

---

1 Schiller, Friedrich: *An die Freude.* In: Schiller, Friedrich: *Gesammelte Werke*, Vol. III. Gütersloh (no publishing date), p. 394
2 cf. Zenner 2002
3 cf. Katz/Révész 1926, p. 291ff.
4 Glennie 2005

About Hearing ...

Following the reception of a sound wave/music by the functional outer-, mid- and inner ear, the sound information passes from the acoustic nerve to the brain at various switching stations. There the signals are filtered, patterns recognized and the point of origin gauged through the time discrepancy between the two ears. In one part of the brain – the thalamus – sound information is purposefully passed on or suppressed. This so-called "gating-effect" enables selective attention, for example when listening to one instrument in an orchestra. On the way from the acoustic nerve to the brain, the acoustic signals are not only analyzed and processed sequentially, but also simultaneously and parallel. "Different areas of the brain process the same information [...] under diverse aspects."[5] Thereby the information is compared with available patterns, familiarity and musical sensibility. The musical pattern is comprised of different structures such as:

• Structure of Melody
• Structure of Time
• Vertical Harmony Structure
• Dynamic Structure[6]

Incoming impressions create new neural connections, old connections dissipate. Hearing is not the same as listening. Whereas hearing is the purely physical process of recognizing sound by the acoustic nerve, listening is the processing of this information that requires the co-operation of the brain. The brain researcher Hellmuth Petsche speaks therefore of a "highly creative process" during the processing of music[7].

Apart from the analytical processing of music there is also its emotional processing. By analyzing and storing music, the limbic system and thus emotional reactions are involved. The elements of emotion are created through the discovery of symmetries and regularities, but also through surprise effects, such as a sudden transition away from the familiar musical pattern. The resulting emotional patterns are: relaxation, excitement, tension, relief, relaxation[8]. Decisive thereby is the listening experience. Studies involving musicians and non-musicians revealed different emotional reactions to a change of key. "Musical events such as the change of key are heard by them [non-musicians] but not interpreted, and thus evoke no emotional reaction."[9] The individual processing of sound events is not directly related to the pure-tone audiogram. This means that individuals with similar hearing ranges of-

---

5   Altenmüller 2002, p. 21
6   cf. Altenmüller 2002, p. 20; Carter 1999, p. 19
7   Petsche 1989
8   cf. Carter 1999, p. 147
9   Roederer 2000, p. 225

ten demonstrate variations in hearing capabilities in everyday situations. The music therapists Robbins and Robbins perceive "hearing" and "listening" as very different skills that also play an important role in the musical sphere. Musicality is more a task and skill of the brain than hearing.

"To me, musicality is the ability to retain, recognize and produce sound patterns and to associate them with emotions and with other aspects of experience. It certainly isn't something that resides in the ear. It resides in the brain."[10]

... and the Inability to Hear Music

Before a sound wave can reach our brain, it runs through the exceptionally complex process of transformation from a mechanical stimulus to an electrical stimulus. The mechanical stimulus of the ear drum by a sound wave passes through the middle ear into the cortical organ in the inner cochlea, on whose switching point – the hearing cells – this mechanical stimulus is transformed into an electric impulse and thus capable of being transferred over the acoustic nerve into the brain. The sensitive elements of the ear can be damaged at birth or during the lifetime of the afflicted individual.

Mild hearing loss dulls the perception of very fine sounds. Beginning hearing loss in old age is often noticeable first through the inability to hear natural sounds, such as swirling leaves or the song of birds. Although the individual suffers from no deficits in a normal conversation, many small details have already been lost.

With moderate hearing loss it is difficult to follow a normal conversation without a hearing aid. Especially when background noises (such as traffic through an open window) are present.

Severe (between 71 and 90 dB) and profound (90 dB or greater) hearing loss render understanding conversation without a hearing aid impossible. The ability to perceive speech with a hearing loss of 90 dB, even with a hearing aid, is so limited that teachers speak of deafness at this stage[11].

The range of music perception is detailed in the so-called "hearing range" of the hearing individual; in the frequencies within which our hearing achieves conscious recognition. Normally this range lies between 20 and 20,000 Hz. in the volume range of 0 to 120 dB.

---

10 Robbins/Robbins 1980, p. 22
11 cf. Prause 2001, p. 31

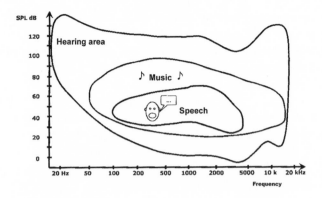

Fig. 1: Büchler 2005

Hearing is specialized in the realm of speech. Approximately 200 to 550 Hz indicates the sensitivity to speech. The range of speech however is only a small portion of our hearing range. The range of music is much larger in comparison. The sound wave of music is both in the range of frequency as well as intensity much greater than the sound wave produced by speech. Even if a hearing impairment is present that hinders the perception of speech, music is still capable of being perceived – although in a somewhat restricted manner.

A hearing impairment does not however simply mean a displaced hearing threshold. The losses and disruptions are not equally distributed across the range of frequencies, resulting in the afflicted often having a distorted or fragmentary perception of what is heard. A depiction of such distortion can be visualized in the following image of the world 'hearing'.

HEARING

For individuals with a hearing impairment contracted later in life this is often a frustrating aspect of listening to music because the distorted notes sound "wrong" compared to what they used to sound like. This is because our brain, as described above, analyzes, compares and evaluates the input from our senses. If the hearing suddenly changes or provides distorted signals, it results in at least irritation or discomfort, just as an out-of-tune guitar irritates. For individuals born with a hearing loss this aspect is less problematic because the impression they receive from their impaired hearing is stored in the brain as "correct".

Helping to Hear?

The technical possibilities to treat hearing loss have advanced enormously over the last ten to fifteen years. This is due in part to the further development of the conventional hearing aid with the assistance of computer technology as well as the development of cochlear implants (CI – a hearing aid that is implanted in the bones of the skull behind the auricle that transforms sound waves into electrical impulses with the assistance of a speech processor and passes these signals directly into the cochlea and the acoustic nerve). Both, however, concentrate on the improvement of speech perception. Music has its own physical properties that are frequently paid insufficient attention, thus hearing aids are not always of assistance in the perception of music.

Music and Cochlear Implants

The current standard strategy of coding the so-called "speech processor" of the cochlear implants is designed and geared towards providing an optimal comprehension of the spoken word. Music and language do have very similar parameters in that they are both highly organized combinations of pitches, timbre, accents and rhythms that follow certain rules. The importance of the individual parameters can however be different for perception and language.

"Speech for example can still be understood when the pitch is incorrectly represented; in any case, the melody of speech (the prosody) might not be correctly communicated. Then, for example, it becomes unclear if a sentence is intended as a question, statement or request, or if the speaker is a male or female. If the pitch is incorrectly produced in music however, the melody is corroded to a great extent and is hardly any longer a pleasure to the listener."[12] Naturally, speech should also sound pleasant. For the encoding of the speech processor, which prepares the sound waves for the implant, music, though, presents a larger challenge.

The encoding strategy of the CI processes three of the most important musical parameters:
• Loudness
• Timbre
• Pitch

Under loudness is to be understood encodings of beat, rhythm and pauses. These are already sufficiently transferred by the CI. For this reason, many CI wearers prefer musical pieces that have a pronounced rhythmic structure. It is different however with the dynamic range (from very quiet to very loud): "The dynamic

---

12 Büchler 2005

range of the gauge in the CI is optimized for language (approx. 40 dB), whereas by comparison a much greater range of differences is possible in a classical concert (up to 60 dB), which is approximately 10 times that of speech."[13]

A signal of such great dynamics cannot be processed linearly due to technical reasons. The signals have to be compressed by the speech processor: "The CI thus compromises the signal, that means the loud parts are quietened and the quiet parts are made louder – a process that is typical with conventional hearing aids, but also in radio and television. In such cases the range is restricted through the broadcasting process. With a CI, this can result in both loud and quiet sounds being perceived as of equal volume and this results in a sort of 'sound porridge'."[14]

With timbre we distinguish between instruments and voices. The variations in timbre depend on the number and intensity of the overtones, as well as their pace while being played and the fading away of a note. Every instrument, every voice has a specific spectrum profile. The reproduction of this specific profile is however restricted by the limited number of electrodes that are available to the CI to stimulate the acoustic nerve.

Similar problems are present in the transfer of pitch. Overtones also play an important role here. Because they always demonstrate a harmonic relationship with the fundamental, the harmonic structure is corroded by the limited frequency processing of the CI. In extreme cases this can result in two different overtones stimulating the same electrode[15].

---

13 Büchler 2005
14 ibid.
15 cf. Büchler 2005

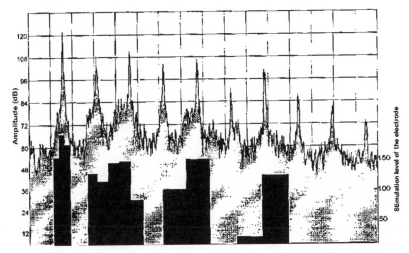

Fig. 2: The frequency spectrum (grey) of the tone "G" of a recorder. The recognizable spikes in the spectrum represent the fundamental and the harmonic overtones. The electrodes of the CI (black) are stimulated by the fundamental (in this case at 784 Hz) and approximately the range of the first four overtones. In: Büchler 2005

"Through the limited number of electrodes the frequency resolution is greatly decreased and is insufficient to maintain the harmonic structure of the note, which has effects on the perceived pitch and timbre."[16]

Especially CI-wearers whose hearing loss developed later in life must struggle with the insufficient transfer of music by the CI, this is due primarily to their experience before hearing loss and their remembrance of musical patterns that are dissimilar to the impressions that the CI provides.

Music and Hearing Aids

Hearing aids were the only possibility prior to the development of the cochlear implant. Hearing aids boosted the sound waves that were received by a microphone, and amplified specific frequencies according to the individual's threshold of hearing. This means that a hearing aid was matched to the individual variety of hearing loss and boosted only the frequencies that were not – or only insufficiently – transferred to the acoustic nerve. Apart from hearing loss in regard to sound-perception and sound-transfer, numerous hard-of-hearing people (75 %) are also affected by 'recruitment'. This means that quiet levels are heard less well than loud levels. Modern hearing aids compensate for this, resulting in a compres-

16 Büchler 2005

sion of the arriving sound waves much as by the CI. As described in regards to cochlear implants earlier, this effect limits the music perception of those who wear a hearing aid.

The percussionist Evelyn Glennie (who gradually lost her hearing as a child and learned to use her whole body to hear sounds and music) reports in an interview about her experiences with hearing aids, which she wore from the age of 9 until her late teens: "But as I was drawn more and more into music, the hearing aids increased primarily the volume too much and the quality of the sound not enough. I needed however pure notes and not volume. [...] For that reason I slowly set the hearing aid aside and concentrated on listening as I now understand it. I discovered my own body as a resonance chamber, akin to an organ pipe, over a longer period of time."[17]

Research to Date – Approaches and Interests of Science

Manuela-Carmen Prause worked intensively on the beginnings and development of the phenomenon of music and deafness in her dissertation. Therein she also compares the development of the Anglo-American and German speaking realms, between which there exist small discrepancies[18].

Publications in relevant journals are mostly descriptive articles and case studies until the 1970s. The article *Musikgenuss bei Gehörlosen* (Musical Enjoyment for the Deaf) by David Katz and Géza Révész in the 1926 *Zeitschrift für Psychologie* (Journal for Psychology) is one such example. Katz describes the musical preferences and capabilities of Eugen Sutermeisters, who went deaf at the age of four. Empirical and experimental studies did not begin before the 1980s.

The research to date often treats the perception of rhythm, less frequently the ability to perceive melodies – but the possibilities of perceiving and processing vibrations have also been studied. Most however relate research to performance that can be achieved by various hearing aid devices. The question as to how the hearing organ can be supported or even replaced is focussed upon again and again by the research field. This is often done with the intent of improving speech instruction for deaf and hard-of-hearing children as well as to ease and/or improve language comprehension. Prause orders the research interests into three thematic areas[19]:
- *Therapeutic approaches*: An early example of speech therapy or rehabilitation in the German speaking realm after the acquisition of a hearing aid can be found

---

17 Profit 2000, p. 43
18 cf. Prause 2001, p. 20ff.
19 ibid., p. 21

in the work of the Swiss music and movement teacher Mimi Scheiblauer[20]. Also worth mentioning is the work of the music therapist Claus Bang and his use of bass tone bars who substantially influenced speech therapy for deaf children[21].

- *Curricular approaches (concerning the syllabus)*: These can be found in the empirical long-term studies undertaken by Robbins and Robbins at a school in New York, out of which a teaching plan for playing instruments with deaf children was developed. Their research indicates that children are at first interested in instruments they know from their environment such as a piano or guitar. The instruments with which Robbins and Robbins began their research were clarinets, bass clarinets and trumpets. They provide a list of common instruments that they recommend for use in music instruction for hard-of-hearing individuals[22].

- *Musical skills of the hard-of-hearing individual*: Studies treating this topic are found primarily in the Anglo-American sphere of influence[23]. Most of this research however focusses on the results that can be achieved with modern hearing aids. The CI and its capabilities receive the most attention. Sandra Trehub, for example, studied the possibility of melody and song recognition by CI recipients who were deaf or deafened prior to language acquisition (prelinguals)[24].

Recent research increasingly makes use of the methods employed in the field of general brain research. With the help of functional MRI (Magnetic Resonance Imaging), MEG (Magnetoencephalography) or EEG (Electroencephalography), the workflow and processing strategy of the brain is investigated in an attempt to better understand how the brain works. With this development of events, another field of research received increased attention.

Multi-Sensory Approaches in the Study of Music Perception

Music, as a complicated sensory event, entails the use of all of the applicable senses. The following diagram schematically depicts all of the possible senses involved in music perception.

---

20 cf. Salmon 2003
21 cf. Bang 1984, p. 44
22 cf. Robbins/Robbins 1980, p. 399
23 cf. Prause 2001, p. 21ff.
24 cf. Trehub 2004

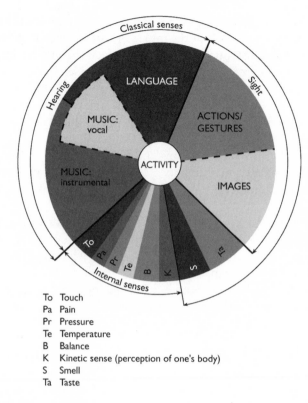

To Touch
Pa Pain
Pr Pressure
Te Temperature
B   Balance
K   Kinetic sense (perception of one's body)
S   Smell
Ta Taste

Fig. 3: Schematic depiction of the senses involved in music perception, adapted from: Wicke 2006, p. 10

The possibility of multi-sensory music experience has been recognized and described in practical work with deaf and hard-of-hearing children since the end of the 19th century. Whereas the deaf and blind Helen Keller describes how she primarily senses music by placing her hand on an instrument, Eugen Sutermeister who was deafened at four years of age, describes his music perception in terms of resonance vibrations in his body[25].

Later, these two forms of perception were defined as 'contact-perception' (via direct contact to the sound source) and 'resonance-perception' (transmission of vibrations through the air) by van Uden and presented as alternative possibilities for music perception by deaf individuals. Other authors include indirect vibration reception, i.e. direct contact with vibrating object such as balloons or drums[26].

25 cf. Katz/Révész 1926
26 cf. Uden 1982; Plath 1991; Prause 2001

The physical foundation of these perception possibilities is the ability of the skin to register pressure, touch and vibration – in short, the tactile sense. This capability is present both on the body's surface as well as inside the body (surface sensitivity and proprioceptive sensibility). The Pacinian corpuscles are specialized to register vibration.

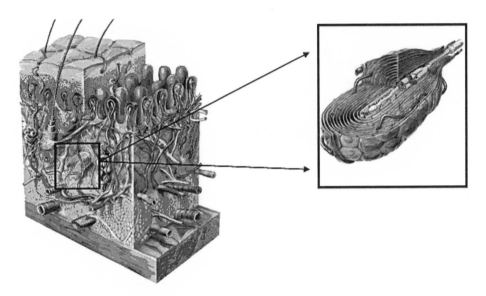

Fig. 4: Schematic depiction of the skin layers with an enlarged cross section of a Pacinian corpuscle, in: Leonhardt 1990, p. 343

The Pacinian corpuscles (named after its discoverer, the Italian anatomist Filippo Pacini) are the largest lamella corpuscles of the skin's nerve endings. They are constructed like an onion skin and can reach 4 millimetres in length and 2 millimetres in width. They react to vibrations and convey these as a proportional impulse frequency to the transferring nerve fibres. Such 'acceleration detectors' are also to be found in the tendons, muscles and joints. They play an important role in proprioceptive sensibility[27].

There have been investigations into the processing strategies of vibratory sensations of the deaf since 1998[28]. Studies of deaf and hearing individuals have shown that vibrations are processed in both groups in a certain part of the brain. In addition to this region, vibrations are processed in deaf test subjects in the section of the brain that is normally activated solely for the processing of hearing sensations.

---

27 cf. Leonhardt 1990
28 cf. Levanen 1998; Shibata 2001

"These findings illustrate how altered experience can affect brain organization. It was once thought that brains were just hard-wired at birth, and particular areas of the brain always did one function, no matter what else happened. It turns out that, fortunately, our genes do not directly dictate the wiring of our brains. Our genes do provide a developmental strategy – all the parts of the brain will be used to maximal efficiency."[29]

The importance of visual impressions while listening to music were slowly recognized only after the invention of hearing aids. Until that point, visual and audio information were practically always linked. Observations of deaf individuals, such as the musician Sutermeister mentioned above, called attention to this point relatively early.

"The eye assists in my music perception in so far as the movement of the conductor and the musicians, particularly the pianists, helps me prepare for the coming music in a manner that is both simpler and quicker than when I do not watch."[30]

In reception research, the study of the interconnections of various sensory events has been advanced through improved techniques and methods. The research group surrounding Altenmüller, for example, has pursued this important aspect of music processing and has confirmed the observations made by Sutermeister. Not only the sound, the auditory stimulus, evokes music inside of us. Observing a musician during a concert (that is using the visual sense) influences our perception of the music just as do the vibrations that are felt, for example during loud passages. When one plays an instrument, we perceive music as a sequence of fingering patterns – as a form of sensorimotor information. With sufficient practice, the mere sight of notes, while studying a score for example (a purely visual event), evokes music inside of the individual. We are capable of remembering and representing music in all of these modalities[31].

Other research investigates the meaning of sound events that occur outside of hearing range. Studies by a Japanese research group[32] were able to prove that music whose ultrasound frequency remains unfiltered (as is usually the case in recordings due to technical reasons) increased brain activity in comparison with filtered music, and was perceived as more pleasant by test subjects.

As early as 1870, the physiologist and physicist Helmholtz (1870) recognized the importance of overtones for the perception of pitch, and the composer Hindemith

---

29 Shibata et al. 2001
30 Katz/Révész 1926, p. 302
31 cf. Altenmüller 2002, p. 24
32 cf. Oohashi 2005

(1984) established overtones as the basis of musical composition. Musicologists such as Fricke have investigated the acoustic phenomena of beat tones in the range of the highest audible tones and the neighbouring ultrasound in musical hearing[33].

The insight of diverse disciplines has been utilized again and again to research and consolidate findings on ultrasound perception. The most recent study investigates ultrasound perception and its importance for the deaf and those with severe hearing loss. During the study, rhythmic ultrasound tones were projected into a sound proof chamber and the unconscious reaction of the test subjects were measured using an electroencephalogram. The results demonstrated a considerably higher sensitivity to ultrasound tone by deaf test subjects in comparison with their hearing counterparts[34]. Together with the multi-sensory research presented above, the conclusions show that deaf and hard-of-hearing individuals can find alternative means to experience music.

Closing Thoughts

Ludwig van Beethoven included an urgent request to his doctor in his last will and testament of 1802: "As soon as I am dead, […] ask him in my name that he describe my illness, […] so that as much of the world as possible will be reconciled with me after my death."[35]

Beethoven sought for an explanation for his hearing loss. He wanted to understand, yet knew at the same time that there was no explanation during his lifetime. But he asked his doctor to look into hearing – with himself as a subject – so that those who followed him would experience improved conditions.

The examination of the functional mechanisms and the factors influencing music perception serve as the foundation for music education and music therapy. Through the co-operation of music education with the natural sciences, valuable synergies have resulted that contribute to discussion and assist the respective fields to develop further.

Deaf individuals demonstrate their own individual approach to music. The complex phenomenon of hearing music requires diverse methods for research. The analysis of what it means to not be able to hear enables us to better understand what it means to hear, and leads ultimately to a greater sensibility both of our selves

---

33 cf. Fricke 1960
34 cf. Stelzhammer-Reichhardt 2007
35 quoted in Zenner 2002

and others. Experiencing music with all of our senses is the basis for a comprehensive understanding of music. Or as Joseph Beuys (1921–1986) said: "Art is thinking with the entire body." In keeping with this sentiment, music as an artistic medium means that "music is thinking with the entire body".

Literature

Altenmüller, Eckart: *Musik im Kopf.* In: *Gehirn* & *Geist* 2002, Vol. I, 18–25.

Bang, Claus (1984): *Eine Welt von Klang* & *Musik.* In: *Hörgeschädigtenpädagogik*, Nr. 2. Heidelberg.

Büchler, Michael (2005): *Musik hören mit dem Cochlea-Implantat – Lust oder Frust.* In: *http://www.sprachheilschule.ch/images/stories/01_Sprachheilschule/05_Referate/PDF/ CI_Forum%2004/Musik%20hoeren%20mit%20CI.pdf*, 12/2007.

Carter, Rita (1999): *Atlas Gehirn: Entdeckungsreisen durch unser Unterbewusstsein.* Munich.

Carter, Rita (2000): *Mapping the Mind.*

Carter, Rita (2004): *Exploring Consciousness.*

Fricke, Jobst (1960): *Über subjektive Differenztöne höchster hörbarer Töne und des angrenzenden Ultraschalls im musikalischen Hören.* In: *Kölner Beitrag zur Musikforschung*, Vol. XVI. Regensburg.

Glennie, Evelyn (2005): *Hearing Essay.* In: *http://www.evelyn.co.uk/live/hearing_essay.htm*, 11/2007.

Helmholtz, Hermann van (1870/2005): *On The Sensations Of Tone As A Physiological Basis For The Theory Of Music.*

Hindemith, Paul (1984): *The Craft of Musical Composition: Theoretical Part – Book 1.*

Katz, David/Révész, Geza: *Musikgenuss bei Gehörlosen (Ein Beitrag zur Theorie des musikalischen Genusses).* In: *Zeitschrift für Psychologie* 1926, Nr. 99, 289–323.

Leonhardt, Helmut (1977): *Human histology, cytology, and microanatomy.* Stuttgart.

Leonhardt, Helmut (1990): *Histologie, Zytologie und Mikroanatomie des Menschen.* Stuttgart, 343–350.

Levanen, S. /Jousmaki, V./Hari, R. (1998): *Vibration-induced auditory-cortex activation in a congenital deaf adult.* In: *Current Biology*, 1998, Vol. VIII, Issue 15, 869–872.

Oohashi, Tsutomu et al.: *Inaudible high-frequency sounds affect brain activity: hypersonic effect.* In: *Journal of Neurophysiology* 2005, Vol. 83, 3548–3558.

Petsche, Hellmuth et al. (1989): *Die Bedeutung des EEG für die Musikpsychologie.* In: Petsche, Hellmuth (Ed.): *Musik – Gehirn – Spiel. Beiträge zum vierten Herbert von Karajan-Symposium.* Basle/Boston/Berlin, 111–134.

Plath, Peter (1991): *Allgemeine Grundlagen des Hörens und seiner Störungen*. In: Jussen, Heribert/Claussen W. Hartwig (Ed.): *Chancen für Hörgeschädigte: Hilfen aus internationaler Perspektive*. Munich, 31–44.

Prause, Manuela-Carmen: *Musik und Gehörlosigkeit. Therapeutische und pädagogische Aspekte der Verwendung von Musik bei gehörlosen Menschen unter besonderer Berücksichtigung des anglo-amerikanischen Forschungsgebietes*. In: Piel, Walter (Ed.) (2001): *Kölner Studien zur Musik in Erziehung und Therapie*, Vol. V. Cologne/Reinkassel.

Profit, Karl-Ludwig: *Evelyn Glennie – im Gespräch mit der Weltklasse-Percussionistin*. In: *Hörgeschädigtenpädagogik* 2000, Nr. 1, 40–45.

Robbins, Carol/Robbins, Clive (1980): *Music for the hearing impaired & other special groups. A resource manual and curriculum guide*. Saint-Louis MO, USA.

Roederer, Juan G. (2000): *Physikalische und psychoakustische Grundlagen der Musik*. Berlin.

Roederer, Juan G. (2001³): *The Physics and Psychophysics of Music: An Introduction*. Berlin.

Salmon, Shirley (2003): *Spiellieder in der multi-sensorischen Förderung von Kindern mit Hörbeeinträchtigungen*. In: *http://bidok.uibk.ac.at/library/salmon-dipl-hoerbeeintraechtigung.html*, 11/2007.

Shibata, Dean et al. (2001): *Brains of deaf people rewire to "hear" music*. In: *http://www.uwnews.org/article.asp?articleID=2730&Search=shibata*, 11/2007.

Stelzhammer-Reichhardt, Ulrike (2007): *Möglichkeiten der Musikwahrnehmung bei Gehörlosigkeit und hochgradiger Schwerhörigkeit – Studien zur Ultraschallwahrnehmung*. Dissertation zur Erlangung des Doktorates der Naturwissenschaft an der Universität Mozarteum, Salzburg.

Trehub, Sandra E. (2004): *Music recognition by children with cochlear implants*. In: *http://www.utm.utoronto.ca/~w3psygs/Vongpaisal2004.pdf*, 11/2007.

Uden, Antonius van (1982): *Rhythmisch-musikalische Erziehung*. In: Jussen, Heribert/Kröhnert, Otto (Ed.): *Handbuch der Sonderpädagogik. Band 3. Pädagogik der Schwerhörigen und Gehörlosen*. Berlin, 320–330.

Wicke, Peter (Ed.) (2006): *Musik Lehrbuch S II, Gymnasiale Oberstufe*. Berlin.

Zenner, Hans-Peter: *Beethovens Taubheit: "Wie ein Verbannter muß ich leben"*. In: *Deutsches Ärzteblatt* 99, 2002, Nr. 42, A–2762–2766.

Part III: Practical Principles

Music as a Form of Dialogue for Children with Hearing Loss[1]

Shirley Salmon

"Everyone is elementally endowed with the basic powers of the arts,
with that of drawing, for instance, or of music; these powers have to be developed,
and in education of the whole person is to be built up on them
as on the natural activity of the self."

(Martin Buber[2])

What can music mean to children with hearing loss? In Greek antiquity there was no single term for "music" itself. Speaking, making music and dancing were closely related to each other and referred to as "musiké". Carl Orff realised that rhythm, being the original form of human expression, was their "unifying force".

The significance of music becomes clearer when we understand it as elemental music: "Elemental music is never music alone but forms a unity with movement, dance and speech. It is music that one makes oneself, in which one takes part not as a listener but as a participant. It is unsophisticated, uses no big forms, is near the earth, natural, physical, within the range of everyone to learn it and to experience it, and suitable for the child."[3] Although the music-pedagogical ideas of Carl Orff and Gunild Keetman were not conceptualised especially for children with disabilities, their importance to children and adults of all ages and with various disorders was recognised and they served as the basis for the further development of several new approaches[4]. In Germany of the 50s the educational model of Orff-Schulwerk and the so-called "Orff instruments" were used by Karl Hofmarksrichter within the education of deaf and hard-of-hearing children. "Elemental music" was perceived and performed as "the realisation of an original, central musical force with which every human being is endowed"[5].

---

1   Revised lecture held on 13th May 2002 at the Herbert von Karajan Centrum in Vienna. During the lecture short video sequences were played which for obvious reasons have to be omitted in the written form.
2   Buber, Martin (1955): *Between Man and Man*. Boston, p. 84
3   Orff, Carl: *Orff-Schulwerk: Past and Future*. Speech given on 25th October 1963 at the opening of the Orff Institute in Salzburg. *Orff-Institut Jahrbuch* 1963. Translation: Margaret Murray.
4   cf. Hofmarksrichter 1963; Bang, Claus 1978 and 1984; Keller 1996; Salmon, Shirley/ Schumacher, Karin (Ed.) (2001): *Symposion Musikalische Lebenshilfe*. Hamburg
5   Keller 1984

Is it possible to imagine what a hearing disability is like? Manipulated recordings simulating various degrees of impaired auditory perception may give us an idea of the impairment in question. Such examples, however, are purely artificial products that cannot take into account other parameters necessary for a genuine understanding. These are the condition of the central auditory canal, fields of association, intelligence and hearing experience. For a complete communicative setting gesture, facial expression, posture etc. would also have to be taken into consideration as well as vibrations, which are especially perceptible in lower-range frequencies. These recordings can help us to gain an impression, of how people with slight hearing disorders perceive, what it would be like to have slightly impaired hearing. I doubt, however, whether it is possible to develop a true understanding of how people with severe or total loss of auditory perception hear.

We should be aware of our knowledge as well as our lack of knowledge concerning the perception of people with hearing loss. For when working with children who can hear, we have our own previous experiences and perceptions and have our own memories. On the other hand when working with children who have impaired hearing, we can only learn in practice from and with the children as well as from the contact and exchange with adults who have hearing loss themselves. A certain modesty is required, for I must ask myself: "What relevance can my experiences with hearing, playing, dancing and playing music have for these children? How can we get into contact and above all: How can we initiate dialogue?"

Since it is impossible for teachers and therapists with intact auditory perception to even have the vaguest idea of deafness and human development under such conditions, it is not only interesting, but absolutely crucial in educational and therapeutic work to initiate a dialogue with the children and adults entrusted to us so that we may learn together. Furthermore it should be our aim to not only get to know the work of experienced teachers and therapists, but also to learn about the experiences of those "affected", the deaf and hard-of-hearing themselves[6].

What can music mean to children with hearing disabilities? Here are three hypotheses:

1. Children with hearing loss may often find it difficult to develop a competence for dialogue.

This is on the one hand due to their hearing loss and the reduced auditory ability caused by it. On the other hand the environment of the children – above of all their

---

6   e. g. Emmanuelle Laborit, the French actress who was born deaf; Helen Keller (1880–1968), who at the age of 18 months went deaf and blind after an illness and the world-famous percussionist Evelyn Glennie, who, after developing a hearing disorder in her childhood between the ages of 8 and 12, learnt to use her own body as a source of resonance in order to actually feel sound

immediate persons of reference – is also influenced and challenged by the hearing difference. Impaired hearing does not only mean a diminished or altered ability to hear, but can influence a person's perception, their development of language, communication, social learning and their development of identity.

2. Every person, including the deaf or hard-of-hearing person, needs dialogue in order to develop progressively.

Especially with children suffering from hearing loss dialogue must include pre-verbal as well as non-verbal dialogue. Children with impaired hearing need to be supported particularly well in their development of dialogue ability.

3. A multi-sensory approach can support the development of dialogue ability and thus development in general.

A multi-sensory approach with music and movement as in Orff-Schulwerk encourages and supports the playful interaction and establishment of relations between music, movement, language and materials. The main aim here is always active communication, whether it concerns an individual, a couple, a small or a large group. The access via more than one sense (especially the senses of touch and vibration) allows for the most diverse variations of experience and expression and can thus support the development of dialogue and individual expression.

Preliminary Considerations

Dialogue and emotional exchange with others are decisive criteria for human development. To Georg Feuser (1996) dialogue is "the most general, basic and fundamental form of exchange". René Spitz (1988) sees non-verbal dialogue within the dual relationship between mother and child as a cyclic, a mutually stimulating feedback process in which the emotional dimension plays a special role. The most distinct definition and representation to my mind comes from Adriano Milani Comparetti (1975), who defines dialogue as "the interplay with the partner(s), aiming to achieve results together, which are unpredictable and frequently surprising to the participants themselves". Milani Comparetti's diagram is a representation of true dialogue with its creative content. The difference between this genuine form of dialogue in comparison to pre-studied question and answer-games, often described as dialogue, becomes very clear here. This interpretation of dialogue can apply to a pre-verbal as well as a verbal (in the form of phonetic or sign language) exchange, but also to non-verbal media such as music, dance and movement. When establishing a dialogue with these media, improvisation plays an important role.

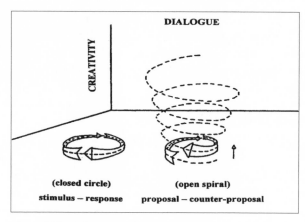

Fig. 1: Milani Comparetti 1998

Communication is influenced by limited auditory perception. The possibilities for children with impaired hearing to develop their dialogue competence depend largely on their environment and the available forms of communication. The pre-verbal dialogue between the child and the person closest to it can also be negative-ly influenced by the child's disability and the adult's psychic reaction to it. Early mother-child games are multi-sensory and offer the children proprioceptive (phys-ical), tactile, acoustic and visual perceptions and sensations in a co-ordinated form. They are effective due to the adult's emotional participation and can be seen "as the biological foundation of physical, personal and social awareness"[7]. This decides whether a common basis of communication can at all be found.

Sir Karl Popper regards human speech as an instrument, a "Darwinist product of evolution" – a tool. He defines three functions of human language: the function of expression, of communication and, most important of all, of representation[8].

Children do not only learn language by listening (in the case of sign language by watching), but also by making active attempts to speak. Having fun, when play-ing together, is an important factor. Encouraging and supporting speech does not mean practising words and language, but creating fun when playing with vocabu-lary (rhythm, intensity and form) that both players understand[9]. Active attempts to speak are practically a re-creation of language by each child. Active attempts, bringing forth new creations with music, dancing and materials are also ways of getting to know the "language" of the medium, of handling and using it.

---

7   Verden-Zöller in: Maturana/Verden-Zöller 1994[2]
8   Popper/Lorenz 1985, p. 95
9   cf. Schumacher 2001, p. 21

Perception

Perception and movement have an interactive relationship and their significance evolves from this interaction. The cycle of movement and perception is known as sensorimotor response. In the sensorimotor phase (according to Piaget) the sensorimotor intelligence develops, which represents the basis of human thinking. The pre-condition for this is the balance between perception and movement. "Motor and sensory response normally correspond like lock and key: Movement makes perception possible. Perception induces movement."[10] If the child can adequately react to sensory perceptions and successfully integrate sensory and motor response, he experiences satisfaction, joy and fun.

Children with hearing loss, like children with "normal" hearing, discover the world and themselves in an active confrontation of their perceptions received on various levels. "There is an interactive relationship between hearing and moving: On the one hand sound always originates from movement. On the other hand auditory perceptions (in the form of speech, music, rhythm or certain signals) often have a movement and activity inducing function."[11]

Due to a hearing disability auditory perception is altered or reduced. Here it is often the case that other forms of perception, such as the tactile, visual or kinaesthetic senses are developed on a higher level in order to compensate for the lacking or reduced auditory sense. Movement and perception, motor and sensory response are linked to one another. They form a superior entity, the effect of which can unfold from their interaction. If other senses cannot compensate for the lacking auditory perception, the general development of the child is possibly influenced.

Perception of Music

"Listening is intrinsically active. It demands your full attention and employs all senses – hearing, seeing, feeling. To a musician the sense of touch is the most important of all senses."[12] When talking about music in reference to people with hearing disabilities, the distinction between *feeling music* and *hearing music* is made. With people suffering from a severe hearing disability tactile perception plays an important role. With people who are deaf "feeling music" consists firstly of the sensation of contact (e. g. body contact with the ground, loudspeakers, balloons or drums)[13];

---

10 cf. Marbacher Widmer 1991, p. 19
11 Marbacher Widmer 1991, p. 23
12 Glennie 2004
13 "I enjoy the music of the piano most when I touch the instrument. If I keep my hand on the piano-case, I detect tiny quavers, returns of melody, and the hush that follows." (Keller 2004, p. 36f.)

secondly of the sensation of resonance, which enables the feeling of vibrations in the hollow parts of the body (e. g. chest or belly). Mimi Scheiblauer (1891–1968) made use of the piano, balloons and drums in order to train and sensitise the children's perception of vibration.

When perceiving music the entire body is involved. Evelyn Glennie reports of wearing hearing aids for nine years during her teenage years. These devices, however, were more inclined to improve on the volume, but not the quality of the sound. For her music-making and her percussion-studies she needed clear and very distinct sounds. Therefore she gradually gave up wearing hearing aids and concentrated on hearing as she could then perceive it. "Over a longer period of time I discovered my body as a resonating instrument, much like an organ-pipe. I literally tried to distinguish the various tones and sounds with my whole body instead of solely with my ears."[14] In Thomas Riedelsheimer's film *Touch the Sound. A sound journey with Evelyn Glennie* this is impressively demonstrated – in visual as well as acoustic terms[15].

Perceiving music and listening to it is something hard-of-hearing children can enjoy just as much, providing certain frequency ranges are amplified and the vibrations are enhanced with suitable devices or certain aspects of the music, such as rhythm, timbre and pitch, are visualised. With a total loss of auditory perception, certain deep tones can still be perceived, but not so much the harmony and tonality of a piece of music. Rhythms in deep frequencies are well perceptible. With those who are hard-of-hearing the acoustic perception of harmony depends on the degree and the form of hearing loss. Vibrations play a less important role in the perception of music, which is primarily auditory, but not necessarily equivalent to the perception of those with non-impaired hearing. Perceiving is an individual process[16]. Various forms of sensory perception can correspond, support and enforce each other. This integrated mode of perceiving happens via various sensorial channels, making the perception of music not only an auditory, but also a visual, kinaesthetic and tactile experience[17].

The Multi-Sensory Approach

In order to employ music as a form of dialogue a multi-sensory approach (as in Orff-Schulwerk) is necessary. This approach has to be development-oriented, inte-

---

14 Glennie 2000, p. 42f.

15 *http://www.touch-the-sound.com*, 01/2008

16 Evelyn Glennie points out that every person hears, perceives differently cf. *http://www. evelyn.co.uk/live/hearing_essay.htm*, 01/2008

17 cf. Prause 1995

grative and dialogical. It is not a learning programme, but offers various activities meeting the child's abilities and needs. A multi-sensory approach with music and movement provides for and encourages the inter-play between sound, movement, language and materials. The active confrontation of the individual on her own, in pairs, small or large groups always remains the essential idea. The multi-sensory access creates a wide potential for experience and expression, it encourages every form of dialogue, thus contributing to the general development of the child. A broad range of perceptual possibilities can be offered while there are myriad ways of playfully discovering and developing how to encounter music, movement and language as well as various materials in a communicative setting. Similarly, this applies also to the individual creative expression within the group.

The choice of *instruments*, found objects and materials depends on the children's individual abilities of perception, their level of development and their interests. Their own body instruments are enhanced by other instruments and found objects:

Rhythm Instruments
- All kinds of membranophones: tympanums, bass drums, bongos, congas, bombos, djembes
- Latin percussion: claves, maracas, afuché, guiro, castanets, agogo-bell, cowbell
- Idiophones: wooden blocks, cymbals, gongs, triangles, rainmakers, boomwhackers
- Effect instruments: vibraslap, spring drum, whirled friction drum, instruments for imitating animal voices e. g. occarinas, duck whistle
- Various materials, e. g. wooden sticks, metal spoons

Melody Instruments
- Melodica, kazoo, recorders, various flutes, kalimba, sansula, slit drum, mallet instruments such as xylophones, metallophones, glockenspiels, resonator bells, tone bars
- String instruments: veeh harp, bowed psaltery, kantele, lyre

Harmony Instruments
- Piano, accordion, keyboard, guitar

Mallet instruments (resonator bells, glockenspiels, xylophones, metallophones) and rhythm instruments are especially suitable for making music with deaf or hard-of-hearing children. On the one hand the playing technique, metre and rhythm are easy to follow, on the other hand deep sounding drums, large wooden resonator bells, wooden slit drums and bass xylophones are well perceivable on account of the strong vibrations in the low frequency range. Furthermore some instruments enable one to simultaneously play and move so that it is possible to accompany oneself. When playing rhythmically in an ensemble, a conductor is effective only to a limited degree. Since the children all perceive the vibrations of the lower frequencies, the metre is more effectively played on a bass resonator bar or a tympanum. Actively and, most of all, creatively dealing with the instrument, as when experimenting and improvising on it, is an essential aspect[18].

The use of a wide range of *materials* (as e. g. Japanese paper balls, spinning tops, scarves, newspapers and balloons) in combination with music and movement contributes to the support of the children in question and inspires their creative potential. With new materials new sensory experiences can be made, the materials' essential qualities, their potential and limits can be explored and different ways of handling and treating them can be developed. By playing with these materials various abilities, such as sensory and spatial perception, memory, reaction and physical skill as well as an understanding for shapes and forms are trained. Communication and interaction are supported while creativity and imagination are inspired.

Children discover, explore and develop the creative potential of materials in combination with music, movement and voice. They become creative and improvise on their own, with a partner or in a group. Expressive and creative abilities as well as the joy over one's own solutions are supported as is respect for the solutions of others. Being creative involves spontaneous solutions and improvisation as well as planned and trained forms of expression.

Building instruments[19] has a special significance with children that are deaf or hard-of-hearing. Not only does it enable them to consciously experience the making of a tone, but it also motivates them to experiment, compare, play and create. The discovery of sound as a resonating vibration can be interesting to all children and is especially important to hard-of-hearing children. Making and designing one's own instrument does not only influence one's relationship to the instrument itself, but also to sound and to music. When building an instrument one embarks on a journey which starts off with handling and experimenting with the basic materials and leads to the design, production and the finishing touches of one's own instrument.

The following instruments were built with great enthusiasm in several instrument making projects for hearing as well as for deaf and hard-of-hearing children: flowerpot xylophone, tin xylophone, wind chimes with nails, cardboard tube guitar,

---

18 Evelyn Glennie comments on this: "So imagination is something that simply cannot be taught. You have to nurture it. You're not going to find that in a study book. You're not necessarily going to find a teacher who has the time to do that. But if it's just poked at then, if the pupil or student just realizes 'Wow, I can do anything with this instrument' then they will take that off themselves." (Glennie 2004, p. 62, Interview with Shirley Salmon 22.2.2003)

19 for inspirations and ideas cf. Kreusch-Jacob 2003², Martini 2001⁹, Widmer 1997

glass marble chimes, tin rattle, yoghurt cup rattle, rainmaker, friction drum, pluck-
ing cup, kazoo, flowerpot drum, nutshell castanets, nutshell rattle, nutshell drum,
light bulb rattle. By using instruments playfully in various activities, contact via
sound was established, which made communication independent of language possible.

Instruments are here to discover, to invent and to make music – they are here to
accompany songs, to play musical stories, to improvise, to encourage and motivate
movement, to accompany and many things more. However, they can also take over
other functions.

Gertrud Orff sees instruments additionally as carriers of meaning since they can be
viewed therapeutically "from three starting points: tactile, visual and acoustic. The
combination of these three sense categories makes a three-fold therapeutic effect
possible. It also means that where a sense is defective or non-existent it can be com-
pensated or stimulated by another." Instruments can also be associated with an object, activity or story thereby extending the sensorial capacity and communication.
"The child is confronted with the instrumentarium, his senses are engaged, and he
reacts in three ways: seeing, hearing and doing. With our material we can complete
the circle between these human senses."[20] The use of the senses and the connections
between them are especially important with deaf and hard-of-hearing children.

In education and therapy instruments and certain materials activate, encourage and
motivate. They are an *activating medium* bridging the gap between the individual's
internal and the external world. Not only do they convey sensorial impressions,
but they also provide a means for individual expression.

Instruments can support the establishment of contact (to oneself, to the object and
to others) as well as enhance the encounter and, most of all, the non-verbal communication with others. Instruments inspire our imagination and provide new possibilities for creating and playing.

Movement and physical experience are essential principles when working with deaf
and hard-of-hearing children. Some of these children develop excellent abilities in
dancing and pantomime. Due to their impairment and missing or lacking experience with movement some children do not have a particularly good relationship
to their bodies, resulting in a poorly developed physical awareness. According to
Marianne Frostig physical awareness is closely related to self-identity and a crucial
pre-condition for a normal emotional and physical development. "From within the
body", "from the internal movement", "with the internal rhythm" are significant
clues concerning educational and therapeutic work.

---

20 Orff 1980, p. 28

In this context I find the late Veronica Sherborne's work *Developmental Movement*[21] very inspiring. Sherborne paid great attention to the development of physical awareness. Children should get the feeling of being "at home" in their own bodies. On the other hand the establishment of relationships – to oneself and to others – is another aim pursued via body-work (without music). The activities focus on different priorities: *for each other, together with each other and against each other*. I find this approach very helpful for many children, since it does not concentrate on hearing (and speaking). This way children can make fundamental experiences in integrative groups.

When it comes to *dancing*, there are limits to the use of music. The function and type of music ought to be thoroughly questioned, and the music itself should not be selected for those with unimpaired hearing, but for dancing children with hearing differences. Naomi Benari has studied the concept of "Inner Rhythm". Benari wants to make these children more aware of the rhythms within their bodies so that they can more easily perceive the rhythm, dynamics and phrasing of each movement in a dance. The dance need not develop from artificial, pre-played music, but much rather from the inner rhythm. Unified breathing is a pre-condition for synchronised movements. Sound (vibration) and movement can be experienced as a unity, e. g. when children are moving around in the room, simultaneously playing instruments. Dialogue can also exist in movement and dance.

Activities involving the *voice* are by no means limited to singing. When playfully using rhythmical elements, children can discover myriads of ways to express themselves and to communicate with their voice, in language, with their whole body as well as in gestures and pantomime. It is essential that breathing becomes a conscious experience which can be controlled and that children discover and use the quality of resonance within their own bodies. Games and experiments involving language and voice seem an obvious option here[22].

Some activities are developed from mother-child games and finger games. Rhymes, poems and songs (old and new songs as well as songs taken from the children's own experience such as songs involving movement) are used under consideration of the hearing and speaking abilities as well as the developmental level of the individual children in question. The main aim is for the children to actively participate and to become creative.

Children with hearing loss enjoy singing. They can acquire the rhythm of a song as well as the melody, respectively the "up and down"-movement of the melody.

---

21 Sherborne, Veronica (1990): *Developmental Movement for Children. Mainstream, special needs and pre-school.* Cambridge.
22 as described e. g. in Stöcklin-Meier 1980, Schafer 1972 or Keller 2002

Children with no auditory perception usually find it difficult to monitor the pitch of their own voice. They cannot distinguish if they are singing the same pitches as others or as a particular instrument. When they sing in a group, it often sounds like a cluster which, according to the melody, moves up and down rhythmically in pitch. Verses or songs with a refrain are particularly suitable and once the children have "got" the rhythm, they are usually highly motivated to invent their own stanzas and thus create "their own song".

The *objectives* of this multi-sensory approach are:

1. Sensitization
- Perceiving and processing tactile/vibratory, auditory or visual stimuli
- Perceiving and experiencing music as 'hearing music' or 'feeling music'
- Supporting the physical perception and awareness of one's own body
- Supporting the perception of oneself and others
- Orientation by establishing an order in space and time
- Training of various abilities by using a diversity of materials

2. Developing personality, e. g.
- Perception of oneself and others, adapting to others
- Integrating, subordinating, superordinating
- Supporting one's self-confidence, independence and self-esteem
- Discovering and developing one's creativity and expressive potential
- Contributing one's own ideas
- Solving tasks together

3. Supporting vocal language and communication, e. g.
- Meeting the pre-conditions for the use of the voice by exercising the breathing technique as well as the whole body
- Experiencing the phenomenon of resonance within one's own body
- Developing and supporting the joy to communicate, sign, speak and sing
- Creating verses, rhymes, poems and songs (in spoken or sign language)

4. Developing competences in music and dance, e. g.
- Gaining experience with body instruments and other creators of sound
- Gaining experience with different tapes of movement, becoming familiar with different types of dance
- Becoming familiar with the use of a diversity of instruments
- Encountering, consciously experiencing and creating forms of expression and presentation in music and dance

Music and Dialogue

Various activities (with and without speech) offer the element of dialogue in their attitude and possibilities of creative realisation. How the tasks and their rules are conveyed depends on the communicative potential of the children in question. It is essential that the tasks are communicated in such a way that all children are able to understand everything and that none of them suffer a disadvantage on account of their hearing difference. In some groups spoken language will be appropriate for all children, in others it might be signs in addition to or supportive of spoken language or the relevant sign language itself. In some groups it will be necessary to use several forms of communication, possibly in combination with visual aids (such as pictures, charts, graphic notation).

The use of musical dialogue with deaf and hard-of-hearing children is elemental and should address their original creative instinct. "Elemental" here is to be understood as "the force that brings forth the genuinely original, as the autonomously active and effective, the self-organising and self-renewing and as an event which autonomously sets itself in scene."[23] With this potential, taking into consideration individual strengths and abilities, suitable themes can be discovered and developed for the particular child in question or for the entire group. The focus should be aimed at modes of playing which enable the child to contribute his creative input and gain his *own experiences*.

Musical dialogue can be encouraged when working with individuals, but also in groups. In integrative projects involving children with different levels of hearing I was able to experience how musical dialogue could initiate certain processes, how it could lead to encounters and to individual as well as collective creativity and how it ultimately was a benefit to all children. Especially for children with hearing differences the use of music and movement should be an integral part of every curriculum. Musical dialogue is as much aim and result as it is the driving force.

---

23 Jungmair 1992, p. 136

Literature

Bang, Claus (1978). *Ein Weg zum vollen Erlebnis und zur Selbstverwirklichung für gehörlose Kinder*. In: Wolfgart, Hans (Ed.): *Das Orff-Schulwerk im Dienste der Erziehung und Therapie behinderter Kinder*. Berlin.

Bang, Claus (1984). *Eine Welt von Klang und Musik*. Special reproduction of *Hörgeschädigten Pädagogik*, Vol. 38, April 1984. Heidelberg.

Bang, Claus: *A World of Sound and Music. Music Therapy and Musical Speech Therapy with Deaf, Hearing-Impaired and Multi-Handicapped Children*. In: *Nordic Journal of Music Therapy*, 7(2), 154–163.

Benari, Naomi (1995): *Inner Rhythm – Dance Training for the Deaf*. Chur.

Brunner-Danuser, Fida (1984): *Mimi Scheiblauer – Musik und Bewegung*. Zurich.

Feuser, Georg (1996). *Zum Verhältnis von Menschenbild und Integration – "Geistigbehinderte gibt es nicht!"* Lecture held at the Austrian parliament in Vienna on the 29th October 1996. In: *http://bidok.uibk.ac.at/library/feuser-geistigbehinderte.html*, 11/2007.

Feuser, Georg (1996) *The Relation between the View of the Human Being and Inclusive Education – "There Are No Mentally Handicapped!"* Speech to the members of Nationalrat in the Austrian Parliament on the 29th October 1996 in Vienna. In: *http://bidok.uibk.ac.at/library/feuser-humanbeing.html*, 12/2007.

Frostig, Marianne (1992): *Bewegungserziehung. Neue Wege der Heilpädagogik*. Munich.

Frostig, Marianne (1970): *Movement Education: Theory and Practice*. Follet Educational Corporation.

Glennie, Evelyn (2000): Interview. In: *Hörgeschädigten Pädagogik*. Heidelberg.

Glennie, Evelyn (2004): Interview. In: *Orff-Schulwerk Informationen*, Nr. 73. Edited by: Hochschule für Musik und Darstellende Kunst "Mozarteum" in Salzburg, "Orff-Institut" and Orff-Schulwerk Forum Salzburg; Salzburg; *http://www.orff-schulwerk-forum-salzburg.org/deutsch/orff_schulwerk_informationen/pdf/Heft_Nr_73.pdf*, 12/2007.

Hofmarksrichter, Karl (1963): *Orff-Schulwerk bei Gehörlosen*. In: *Orff-Schulwerk yearbook 1963*. Mainz 1964.

Jungmair, Ulrike (1992): *Das Elementare. Zur Musik- und Bewegungserziehung im Sinne Carl Orffs. Theorie und Praxis*. Mainz.

Keller, Helen (2004): *The world I live in*. In: Shattuck, Roger (Ed.): *New York Review Books Classic*. New York.

Keller, Wilhelm (1984): *Elementare Musik von und mit Behinderten*. In: *Musik und Bildung*, Nr. 12. Mainz.

Keller, Wilhelm (1996): *Musikalische Lebenshilfe. Ausgewählte Berichte über sozial- und heilpädagogische Versuche mit dem Orff-Schulwerk*. Mainz.

Keller, Wilhelm (2002): *Ludi Musici Band 3 – Sprachspiele für die Früh- bis Späterziehung in der Vor-, Zwischen-, und Nachschulzeit*. Revised edition incl. CD. Boppard/Rhine.

Kreusch-Jacob, Dorothée (2003²): *Klangwerkstatt für Kinder. Miteinander Instrumente bauen und Musik machen.* Munich.

Laborit, Emmanuelle (1999): *The Cry of the Gull.*

Marbacher Widmer, Pia (1991): *Bewegen und Malen. Zusammenhänge – Psychomotorik – Urformen – Körper- und Raumerfahrung.* Great Britain.

Martini, Ulrich (2001⁹): *Musikinstrumente – erfinden, bauen, spielen.* Stuttgart/Düsseldorf/Leipzig.

Maturana, Humberto R./Verden-Zöller, Gerda (1994²): *Liebe und Spiel: die vergessenen Grundlagen des Menschseins.* Heidelberg.

Milani Comparetti, Adriano (1995): *Von der "Medizin der Krankheit" zu einer "Medizin der Gesundheit".* In: Janssen, Edda/Lüpke, Hans von: *Von der Behandlung der Krankheit zur Sorge um Gesundheit. Konzept einer am Kind orientierten Gesundheitsförderung von Prof. Adriano Milani Comparetti.* Frankfurt/Main.

Milani Comparetti, Adriano (1998): *Fetale und neonatale Ursprünge des Seins und der Zugehörigkeit zur Welt.* In: *Behinderte in Familie, Schule und Gesellschaft*, Vol. I. Graz.

Murray Schafer, Raymond (1972): *When words sing.* London.

Neumann, Katrin (2001): *Hörphysiologie und Hörstörungen – ein Überblick.* In: *Musiktherapeutische Umschau*, Vol. 22. Göttingen.

Orff, Gertrud (1974): *Die Orff-Musiktherapie.* Munich.

Orff, Gertrud (1980): *The Orff Music Therapy.* (English translation: Margaret Murray). London.

Popper, Karl/Lorenz, Konrad (1985): *Die Zukunft ist offen.* Munich.

Prause, Manuela (1995): *Möglichkeiten eines multisensorischen Ansatzes in den USA zur Steigerung der Wahrnehmung von Musik, Klang und Sprache.* In: *Hörgeschädigten Pädagogik*, Vol. 49. Heidelberg.

Prause, Manuela-Carmen (2001): *Musik und Gehörlosigkeit. Therapeutische und pädagogische Aspekte der Verwendung von Musik bei gehörlosen Menschen unter Berücksichtigung des angloamerikanischen Forschungsgebietes.* Cologne/Rheinkassel.

Robbins, Clive/Robbins, Carol (1980): *Music for the Hearing Impaired. A recourse manual and curriculum guide.* Saint-Louis, USA.

Sacks, Oliver (1990): *Seeing voices.* London.

Salmon, Shirley (1992): *Musik und Bewegung mit schwerhörigen Kindern in Kooperationsklassen.* In: *Orff-Schulwerk Informationen*, Nr. 50. Edited by: Hochschule für Musik und Darstellende Kunst "Mozarteum" in Salzburg, "Orff-Institut" and Orff-Schulwerk Forum Salzburg; Frohnburgweg 55, A-5020 Salzburg; *http://bidok.uibk.ac.at/library/salmon-musik.html*, 12/2007.

Salmon, Shirley (2001): Wege zum Dialog – Erfahrungen mit hörgeschädigten Kindern in integrativen Gruppen. In. Salmon, Shirley/Schumacher, Karin (Ed.): *Symposion Musikalische Lebenshilfe.* Hamburg.

Schumacher, Karin (1999): *Die Bedeutung des Orff-Schulwerkes für die musikalische Sozial-und Integrationspädagogik und die Musiktherapie.* In: *Orff-Schulwerk Informationen,* Nr. 62. Edited by: Hochschule für Musik und Darstellende Kunst "Mozarteum" in Salzburg, "Orff-Institut" and Orff-Schulwerk Forum Salzburg; Frohnburgweg 55, A-5020 Salzburg.

Schumacher, Karin (2001): *Ammenscherze und Sprachentwicklung. Entwicklungspsychologische Erkenntnisse für die Arbeit mit noch nicht sprechenden und sprachgestörten Kindern.* In: *Orff-Schulwerk Informationen,* Nr. 66. Edited by: Universität Mozarteum Salzburg, "Orff-Institut" and Orff-Schulwerk Forum Salzburg; Frohnburgweg 55, A-5020 Salzburg.

Sherborne, Veronica (1990): *Developmental Movement for Children. Mainstream, special needs and pre-school.* Cambridge.

Spitz, René A. (1988): *Vom Dialog. Studien über den Ursprung der menschlichen Kommunikation und ihrer Rollen in der Persönlichkeitsbildung.* Munich.

Stöcklin-Meier, Susanne (1980): *Sprechen und Spielen.* Regensburg.

Widmer, Manuela (1997): *Alles was klingt. Elementares Musizieren im Kindergarten.* Freiburg/Breisgau.

A World of Sound and Music –
Music Therapy and Musical Speech Therapy with Deaf, Hearing Impaired and Multi-Handicapped Children

Claus Bang

Music as Therapy

Music therapy is the controlled application of specially organised music activities with the intention of furthering the development and cure during the treatment, education and rehabilitation of children and adults who have motor, sensory or emotional handicaps. The handicaps might be reading retarded, speech retarded, mentally retarded, motor handicapped, emotionally disturbed, blind, sight deficient, deaf, partially-hearing, psychotic, autistic, aphasic, and dysphasic children or adults.

The aim of the music therapist is centred on the client, and is not starting from the music. For example, the music therapist starts from a diagnosis, and the music activities are planned and chosen according to the specific needs of the clients. A client may be involved individually or in a group with other clients, both actively creating music and actively listening to music with the purpose of further development favourable to the client. One of the most important points of music therapy is to concentrate on the individual person and to start from his problems and difficulties. As for all other forms of treatment and education of handicapped persons, it is crucial in musical therapy to motivate and stimulate the client to an achievement and then support and stabilise this new development in any imaginable way.

Man is considered to be a unity and not looked upon as a being that is divided into two parts, body and soul. All doctrines of in-depth psychology and psychotherapy presuppose a therapeutic therapy as a part of this. Music therapy is a supplement and an auxiliary just as are teachers, psychologists, psychiatrists, physicians, physiotherapists, ergo therapists, speech therapists, advisers, parents and others.

Often music therapy has turned out to be the only practicable way to obtain therapeutic and pedagogic results. These results, brought about by music therapy as an improvement of the condition of the handicapped person and his potential in communication, perception, action and behaviour, and social prospects, have all been proved in scientific papers. It is, however, not always possible to objectively measure the improvement of a physical or psychiatric handicap by means of modern statistical scientific methods. It is to a high extent dependent on subjective, individual, emotional forces, which may be liberated through increased contact and exchange with the environment. This is to an increasing degree acknowledged in all treatment, education and rehabilitation teams. In our work with the handicapped, it is above all, important to procure conditions of life acceptable to the handicapped, where they have the possibility of self-expression and of communication. Music therapy satisfies all these efforts in an optimum way.

The Goals of Music Therapy

The most important goals of music therapy, which are working at Aalborg School, are:
1. Establishing contact and communication
2. Sensory training and development
3. Physical and motor training and development
4. Social training and development
5. Liberation of social-communicative processes
6. Activation and liberation of emotional processes
7. Development of speech and language
8. Intellectual training and development
9. Incitement to develop new interests alone or in the company of others
10. Musical training and development
11. Development of self-reliance and self-discipline
12. Relaxation and diversion from problems

The music therapy programme at the Aalborg School, comprised of all the pupils from the pre-school age up to the upper forms, consists of activities, such as instrumental group activities, musical speech therapy, singing therapy, expressive motor training for the multiply handicapped pupils (each receiving individual therapy), group improvisations and orchestra-playing in varying groups, dancing (i. e. folk dancing and dancing games), where all pupils are divided into five or six groups; and organ performance is optional for the oldest pupils. By means of the experience, which we have had since 1961, with the different activities, offered to our hearing impaired and multiply handicapped pupils, we are able to establish that music therapy has had results for the above mentioned goals. However, music therapy is not a goal in itself. Music therapy is one of the most important means of developing an acoustic-visual-motor unity, and an optimal means of communication in a total world – including the handicapped.

Music is Communication

All of our pupils at Aalborg School (like most handicapped persons) might be characterised as having communication impairment in the sense that language limitations of a sensorimotor or emotional character are understood as an obstacle to communication and function in society.

Music can establish contact without language, and through music therapy we find unused potentials in other communicative paths that assist with developing language. Since music produces a means of communication of a predominantly emotional character (non-verbal or pre-verbal communication), it is of importance and has great application exactly where verbal communication is not used because the spoken language is not understood. To the contact impaired persons, who are most often receptive to music, music will become the theme through which communication can take place. Communication may be described as verbal, emotional and is motor interactive. When verbal and motor communication does not function sufficiently, the emotional expression must be tried in order to reach the mind. As an emotional form of communication, as an unambiguous means of communication, music can replace the ambiguous verbal communication.

As a form of communication music is one of the possibilities of human interaction. As is the case in the development of social psychology, music therapy demonstrates unmistakable tendencies to understand music as an emotional way of communication, as a means of contact, the therapeutic application of music there is a possibility of making the treatment include interaction disturbances, or through communication, to tackle communicative disorders.

To all people, but in particular to the communication handicapped, to hear music and to make music means communication. He, who is actively making music, can by means of the music, communicate with himself and thus re-establish his identity with his own body. Passive receptive music therapy, when the client is exclusively listening to music, may also turn out to be effective, as it offers the client a possibility to turn his attention to the music as a theme, and possibly create an object relationship.

Using the traditional terminology of music therapy, music offers the client some of the following therapeutic active resources, namely to listen, to be creative, to participate. Through music the handicapped person will have an opportunity of gathering experiences from the musical structure, experiences of self-organization and experiences of relating to others.

Music is a unique source and intermediary as to order energy, ability establishing contacts, actualizing self-knowledge, and not least, establishing or re-establishing human relationships.

Music appeals to the human being as a whole and influences the total personality in a way different from other forms of speech and language therapy. The integrating and emotional effect of music diminishes the abstract, which often accompanies man in many of the traditional situations of learning language.

The language-retarded person can only learn language through verbal action. But, the language-retarded person can also *learn to learn* through musical action. Music is a language for all people. In the severest cases when it is not possible to learn through the language, music as a special human resource for communication is indispensable. Through music, an interactive development can be initiated for every human being.

Music – a Way to Speech and Language

Music and speech are based on perception and interpretation of sound starting with an auditory experience. In music therapy as well as in speech therapy, we are engaged in the auditory processes and the production and perception of sound. In both kinds of therapy we try to assess the pupils' or patients' reaction to sounds and all the factors involved in the developmental process. The auditory perception comprises the ability to distinguish between different sounds, their pitch, timbre, intensity or duration, all the characteristics, which contribute to the meaning of sound. Music and speech concern ability to remember and to imitate sounds.

Sounds, which have not yet been integrated into musical patterns as melody or rhythm or in verbal patterns as language, already contain elements of intensity, duration, pitch and intonation. The four characteristic elements can be perceived in spite of a severely reduced function of the brain.

Speech therapy can start with sounds that have not yet been structured into meaningful patterns. In treatment we shall then have to analyse the character of the sound produced and perceived, and engage ourselves in gradual process through which man transforms sounds into a meaningful language produced by his own body by means of physical movements which he is able to control, co-ordinate and use consciously. Any deficiency or blocking of the auditory system or of the ability to move is therefore a hindrance for the acquisition of language.

The resemblance between the construction of a music language and of a verbal language makes music a very important aid in speech therapy. Music language is first and foremost referred to as the perceptual and mental processes, such as hearing, memory and imitation of sounds heard, together with motor control of the necessary physical movements. When we speak an amalgamation of the elements attended by symbols of speech and music is taking place. During perception of speech and music the process is leading along the path in common to the sensory fields of projection and to the various centres processing information. Music activity and active listening to music can produce functions supporting the acquisition of language, of attention and perception, the transfer of movement to sound and of sound to movement, such as an experience of the unity of language, music and movement.

Musical Speech Therapy for the Hearing Impaired

The development of man is accompanied by sound, which is such a highly integrated part of the environment that very often we do not consciously perceive these sounds. What we call silence is only a relative conception. Consciously or unconsciously, we learn from our birth the surrounding sounds. Our normal means of communication is with linguistic sounds, which we first perceive and later imitate. To those with normal hearing sound is an auditory perception, but the sound waves, which are produced by a vibrating sound source and are transmitted to us through the air, can reach us in other ways. They can be felt through the skin and the bones in parts of the body, in addition to the ears. This sound perception cannot be compared with what we hear, but it enables the deaf person to be in contact with the surrounding world of sounds.

To the deaf person music is thus primarily a series of vibrations, which are perceived and transported to the brain along other lines than the auditory organ. None the less, these vibrations can carry rhythms, sounds and melodic sequences, and cause reactions in the deaf person leading to activities of great value to him. The rhythms and tones, so to speak, are experienced from within as vibrations connected with the auditory input (kinaesthetic and auditory rather then visually) gives rise to a spontaneous desire of the hearing impaired person to transform the rhythmical-musical influence perceived into his own forms of expression, such as movements, mimicry, speech and singing.

Of the many human activities, speech is presumably the most rhythmical and musical. At the same time, speech and language are the most valuable instruments for communication and memory. Therefore working with hearing impaired children's speech and language is most essential. One of the additional handicaps in the case of hearing impairment is that the control of the voice is lost completely or partially, often resulting in monotonous or forced, strained and squeaking voices.

This is to a high extent hampering these pupils in their communication with those who are able to hear. The rhythm of speech is a rhythmic movement of the speech organs, such as respiration, voice and articulatory movements of the mouth, together with the sounds from the larynx. We hear the speech movements, and thus hearing is a sensorimotor process.

Practising music and movement will train the auditory and vibratory sensorimotor functions and the memory of such sequences and their use. Consequently, musical activities are indirectly training the basic functions of speech and language.

Music and language offer so many points of resemblance that the basic elements of music can be employed as a means of teaching the hearing impaired and other handicapped groups to break the verbal monotony, to speak rhythmically and melodically, thus developing and improving communication with the normal hearing.

The crux of music therapy at the Aalborg School is therefore the speech training and language stimulation through music, the musical speech therapy, which is started when the pupils are two or three years old, and which is then integrated in the daily teaching of articulation and speech by co-operation between parents, advisers, teachers, speech therapists and the music therapist. By this form of therapy we try to improve the voice levels and the voice qualities of the pupils, at the same time systematically teaching the accentuation in intensity, duration, pitch and intonation by utilising the pupil's residual hearing by means of hearing aids, the ability of sound perception in the whole body, and the contact-vibration sense, particularly in the limbs.

Sonor Tone Bars in Practice and in Research

In musical speech therapy a great number of special musical instruments are used, such as the Sonor tone bars, the frequencies of which are from 64 to 380 Hz, a range where the greatest part of the deaf have some residual hearing. This means that the residual hearing to a certain degree can be activated and utilised through work with the tone bars, which possess very specific acoustic-vibratory qualities. Since 1972, we have concentrated the use of tone bars in musical speech therapy because of the remarkably good vocal responses from our hearing impaired and multiply handicapped pupils to these sound stimuli. The Danish Research Council for the Humanities has with grants, during the years of 1973–1976, supported my research project "Physiological Sound Functions, Perception and Reproduction of Sound in Profoundly Deaf and Normal Hearing Children Exploring the Use of Tone Bars in Sound Analysis and Musical Speech Therapy".

The purpose of the project is an examination of the voice material of profoundly deaf and normally hearing children, aged 5–15, and an analysis of the effect of musical speech therapy with Sonor tone bars on the qualities of these pupils' voices and vocal function. The analysis includes tone, intensity, duration, frequencies, intonation, compression, modulation, learning the half glottal stop, reduction of nasality etc. Further, the intention of the project is to determine if the improvement of deaf children's speech and language, as a result of this tone bar therapy, will cause an increased comprehension of those surrounding the deaf and consequently improved possibilities of communication in society.

At the Aalborg School, l have tape-recorded the spontaneous voices of 30 deaf pupils and 30 children with normal hearing, aged 5–15, and their vocal responses, using the BA-sound, applied to 26 different tone bars in a series of different test-positions, each of them showing different paths of perception. At the Institute of Phonetics at the University of Copenhagen, l have transformed the tape-recordings to curve materials on the sonograph and mingograph equipment. The curves have been measured for data processing and examined statistically in co-operation with assistant professor Allan Dresling of the Institute for Electronic Systems, Aalborg University Centre.

On the basis of the analysed materials, two mathematic models of calculation have been developed for a qualitative evaluation of vocal improvement of the responding and the spontaneous voices. The purpose has been to make a comparison between the voice qualities before and after the training with the tone bars, and on this basis to define pedagogic and therapeutic lines and methodical instructions concerning the use of tone bars in the professional treatment of voice disorders and speech training of hearing impaired pupils. Concurrently, with this work, experimental measurements have been carried out in co-operation with assistant professor M. A. Børge Frøkjær Jensen from the Audiologopaedic Research Group at the University of Copenhagen, on the electronic instrument, which he has developed, measuring improvement of voices by a spectral analysis of the voice. Further, Allan Dresling, supported by the Danish Natural Science Research Council, has developed a general model of data analysis for automatic processing of data from the electronic measuring instrument used for voice analysis.

In order to determine the value of the tone bar therapy as part of the speech and language treatment of mentally retarded, motor handicapped, and multiply handicapped (e. g. deaf-blind and psychotic-autistic pupils) the project is also designed to develop training programmes for the use of the tone bars with these handicaps. In the normal school too, there is a marked need for the use of the tone bar method when working with voice improvement. For the pupils with hoarse, noisy or monotonous voices the tone bar therapy has shown considerable improvement of the vocal tone and modulation.

We feel that the use of the tone bar therapy has broadened to even more fields, such as the fact that special education has started new research of the physiological sound functions. Based on the experiences, which have been achieved, the committee for deciding articulation and voice treatment methods for hearing impaired in the Nordic countries have decided to introduce training programmes using the tone bars. Through the close co-operation of the teaching and treatment teams organised concerning musical speech therapy, we can, as a result of intensive training, achieve an improvement of the handicapped person's possibility of perceiving and reproducing the rhythm and melody of speech and of language, the result which will mean better modulation, an increased mastering and understanding of language and thus, development of handicapped pupils' potential communication.

The Results of Tone Bar Therapy

We can after more than forty years of practise determine, that the Sonor tone bars offer a possibility of training and developing the ability of profoundly deaf and severely hearing impaired children to perceive and reproduce tones and rhythms. By this means the pupils are given the opportunity of perceiving and reproducing the melody and rhythm of speech. The tones of the bars are within a relatively low frequency range, 64–380 Hz. Most deaf persons have some residual hearing in this range, and here it is rather easy to perceive the frequencies by means of the tactile sense. This means:

1. That the residual hearing can to a certain degree be activated and utilised
2. That the deaf person when touching the resonance box with his hands receives a strong vibratory contact, which on account of his well-developed sense of vibration enables him to distinguish pitch
3. That the strong vibrations at the moment of striking the tone bar will be perceived directly by the body. The low frequencies will be perceived by the lower part of the body, and the high frequencies by the upper part of the body. Even profoundly deaf children are able to perceive the sound of the tone bars at a distance of several metres.

In the following areas concrete improvement in voice and speech through the therapy with Sonor tone bars have been proved:
- Pitch and frequency span, its regulation in the spontaneous voice
- Intonation, compression, intensity of the spontaneous voice
- Sonority of vowels, motivation for structured articulation
- Voice malfunctions caused by stress, changes at puberty etc.
- Accentuation in intensity, duration and pitch. Elements of Prosody.

Training Arrangement with the Tone Bars

The pupil is placed on a chair in front of the teacher. The tone bar must lie on the pupil's thighs. If only one tone bar is being used it has to be placed across the thighs. When, later on, two tone bars are used for training accent modulation the tone bars must be placed along the thighs. The highest tone, which is used as a stressed, accentuated element, is placed at the side of the dominating hand.

When training the pupil's capability for perceiving sound in the body the tone bars are placed on a chair or a table. The pupil is not supposed to have any direct contact with the bars, the table, nor the chair. At group practising in the classroom the tone bars are placed on the table, and the exercises change between contact and no contact with the tone bars.

Fig. 1: Claus Bang with a deaf boy beating a tone bar (Photo: IGMF)

The Training Procedure

The pupil is asked to babble, e. g. say "bah-bah" with his spontaneous voice. In this way the teacher will find the level of the pupils' spontaneous voice. If necessary he may check the pitch through finding the tone on an instrument.

The tone bar with a tone one octave below the pupil's spontaneous voice is the first one to be used when working with deaf pupils. Thus the child will experience a frequency found in his own voice. Using a tone, which is one octave lower, will intensify the experience of the frequency, as the low frequencies are registered very strongly having consequently the most motivating effect. The response of the pupil will be one octave higher.

The tone bar chosen is struck with a hard mallet with a big head covered with felt. The bar is hid just above the opening to the resonator. It is of importance to make sure that the pupil does not touch the tone bar proper with his hands, but is only grasping the resonance box. The pupil is asked to give a vocal response to the stroke with a bah-sound or another babbling sound. It must be pointed out that the b-explosion is the sound most properly corresponding to the explosive sound produced by a stroke on the tone bars. All vowels can of course be used, when the pupil can pronounce them.

At first the pupil is instructed to say the bah-sounds synchronously with the tone bars being struck. In this way the pupil find the correct frequency most quickly. Later it is of importance to instruct the pupil to postpone his bah-response until the sound of the tone bar has died away. Thereby it is easier for the teacher to hear if the pupil's tone is correct. At a rather early stage the pupil is able to strike the tone bar himself.

When the pupil has had the experience that the tone bar is producing the same tone as the pupil himself, the moment has come when the teacher must estimate whether the pupil's voice is too high, too low, or within an acceptable frequency range. The figure below showing the tone bars will be helpful (Fig. 2) Here the tones A (two octaves below middle c) to e (below middle c) and a (below middle c) to e (above middle c) are marked. The upper group a to e around middle c corresponds to the voices of hearing children, and is therefore suitable for methodical speech and language practice. When the range from A to e below middle c is struck on the tone bars, the children will imitate them one octave higher from a to e above middle c.

If the spontaneous voice of the pupil is on a higher tone than e above middle c, the teacher must try to lower the pitch of the voice by successively using tone bars with gradually lower frequencies until the voice has reached the e. Then this tone may become the upper tone of the pupil's interval, i. e. be the tone used in accented, stressed elements of words and phrases. If the pupil's spontaneous voice is on a lower tone than a below middle c, the teacher will have to train in the opposite direction, until the voice has reached the higher pitch.

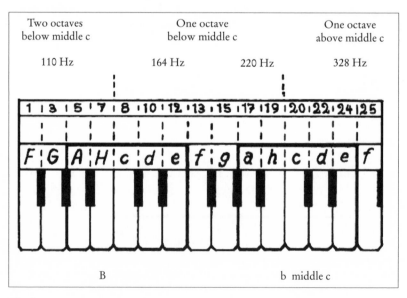

Fig. 2

Sonor tone bars in the range A–e (110 Hz–164 Hz) evoke a response from the pupil in the range a–e (220 Hz–328 Hz), which is the frequency range wanted for the voice of the pupil.

Training the Melodious Accent

My experience from practise and research with approx. 5,000 hearing impaired and deaf pupils is that the major third, the interval of two whole tones, is the interval most easily remembered by hearing impaired pupils and sufficient even for a deaf person to demonstrate that it is possible to make the pitch of the voice higher or lower. Consequently a pupil who has learnt e above middle c, will have to learn the lower tones d#, d, c# above middle c and finally middle c, which is the major third below e above middle c and thus has to be used as the lowest tone of the interval of modulation.

On the other hand a pupil who has learnt a below middle c, must learn the higher tones b flat, b, middle c, and at last c# above middle c, the major third above a and therefore the upper tone of the modulation interval, which has to be used in stressed, accented elements of speech. The eight tones of the range from a below middle c to e above middle c and accordingly also the eight corresponding tones of the octave below from A to e can form four separate major third intervals thus giving four separate modulation intervals (Fig. 3).

a   b flat   b   middle c   c sharp   d   d sharp   e

Fig. 3: The four separate intervals of modulation

It is our experience that hearing impaired and even profoundly deaf pupils are able to learn to combine the loud sound, the long sound, and the high sound from instruments and from the voice producing stressed, accented speech elements as e. g. BAH, mum, up, bee. Reversely they can also learn to combine the soft sound, the short sound and the low sound from instruments and from voice as unaccented elements of speech as e. g. of, and, to, in. In this way the hearing impaired and deaf pupil has got the opportunity to work to a certain degree with all three accents of speech, namely variations in intensity, duration and pitch.

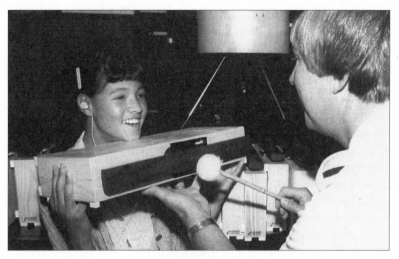

Fig. 4: Voice treatment with Sandra who is deaf (Photo: Ezra Rachlin)

Speaking and Singing

In the music therapy programme, speaking and singing are closely related fields, because both have tonal modulation and stress or accent certain syllables or words in a sentence. When singing, the words use tonal modulation by means of the melody, and the accentuation is expressed through the rhythm. Musical use of words and phrases emphasising the natural modulation and accentuation of speech underlines the sense of the words and increases their use. For hearing and speech handicapped pupils, this is a very effective stimulus motivating them to sing with a greater interest in the verbal content.

Singing helps them in their attempt to learn to speak. When, at the same time, the song contains a meaning and the words have been set to music with the normal accent and modulation of speech, singing will be of pedagogic and therapeutic value. The handicapped person is deeply attached to his singing. In this case, the musical instrument is part of him and he experiences singing as a means of spontaneous self-expression. To sing and to sing with others may in many cases give our handicapped pupils a feeling of freedom in relationship to many of the consequences of their handicap and the related restrictions.

Playing and singing are united in our play-songs, with movement, dramatics, sign language, instrumental performance etc., accompanying the song. In this way the language is, so to speak, carried by the melody and movement, for the linguist this is processing of information. By means of singing, a further development of the musical speech therapy, we have the best possibility of improving the vowel sound, which is crucial for comprehension. When the children are young, they will usually produce vowels before consonants, which are more rhythmical than the melodic vowels. Most infants recognise the melodic element before they catch the rhythmic structure of the song. Deaf children are no exception. Their singing is modulated and very expressive.

Fig. 5: Deaf children singing and playing around the grand piano
(Photo: Viggo Kragmann)

Music is Movement

Particularly during the first years of life, sounds and music are perceived directly by the body. This is also true even to a higher degree with the hearing impaired child who compensates for the reduced hearing, and as a supplement to limited residual hearing, perceived by his whole body. Therefore, music and movement are inseparable. Formerly, the deaf were often designated as "eye-creatures" because of their auditory problems they rely strongly on their visual resources. Music therapy with these children unmistakably confirms that the best way to bring about a visual and an auditory combination is by the use of the motor element. Thereby, we experience the deaf as a total being who through music, receives a multi-sensory impact on all senses. By means of the musical activities, the handicapped child has the possibility of expressing bodily, such as through mimicry, sign language, feelings and ideas which he is not yet able to express in words. The child has a possibility of co-ordinating his voice with music and movements in a relaxed spontaneous way, while the articulation problems, for the time being, are insignificant.

One of our most important therapeutic principles is to build on what already exists in the child and make it appear in the consciousness of the child. Through music therapy the handicapped person discovers and realises his potentials rather than his limitations.

Stimulation, through physical action and motor training, contributes to the initiation of linguistic development. The pupil's awareness of his body and of his motor functions, the kinaesthetic perception and feedback is extremely important for auditory perception and linguistic skills.

We have arranged a special rhythm music programme of movement and language stimulation for the pupils. The rhythm stimulates and activates them to perceive and imitate the accentuation and modulation of music and language. It trains rhythm, different bars, tones etc. At the same time, the programme maintains the attention and concentration of the pupils. This creates the possibility of experiencing the rhythms and the music while concurrently exercising them in movement, drama, play and dance, in co-ordination with speaking and singing. The human body, especially the human voice, is the most superb means of expressing music.

When the pupils are singing, playing, as well as dancing, these various musical activities can give them both passive and active auditory training. The sound effect of the child's physical efforts will be perceived, and in this way, physical efforts and auditory perception or sound perception with the body will form a whole. The interaction of the sensory training and the motor training is crucial and also forms the basis of our auditory training programme in music therapy, "A World of Sound and Music".

Fig. 6: Indian Dance with deaf children in "Pocahontas" (Photo: Jesper Dall)

Improvisation and Response

The music therapy work with our hearing impaired and multiply handicapped pupils is varied and differs highly because of the extensive individual considerations
having been taken into account. We must concentrate on how music can develop
the potential of the individual pupil. Consequently, towards the end of the sixties
we introduced, at the Aalborg School, an individual music therapy treatment for
our multiply handicapped pupils, in particular, to serve as an alternative to, and a
preparation for possible later musical group work.

These severely handicapped pupils' need for activities relating to music is, as a matter of fact, far greater than that of the other pupils. What is essential in these cases
is to find a way of opening up their music experiences and activating them *within
the music* by means of developing various means of expression that are possible for
the pupils, such as breathing, singing, mimicry, body movements, beating a drum
etc. We are able to move ahead in music therapy as far as the potential of the pupil
allows. *The music must be adapted to the pupil, not the pupil to the music.*

It is necessary to be very flexible in regard to instrumental methodology, because of
the problems of co-ordination, hearing loss, field of vision, apprehension of space,
or physical restrictions, which may demand a simplification of the task. As for our
multiply handicapped pupils, very few are able to use a conventional musical instrument. In such cases simple instruments, offering efficient musical possibilities
to the pupils must be used.

With a suitable sound accompanying the instruments which are easy to play, we
try to develop a sort of free improvisation which is neither strict in requiring certain music rules to be followed, nor does it allow wandering off into fortuitous
playing. The pre-requisites of this activity are the creation of psychological – not
musical – preparation by taking various situations and conditions into consideration. Only then will the basis of an optimum readiness for the experience of playing arise. The psychotherapeutic requirements of being experience prepared must
definitely precede the musical achievement. Only then will the activity develop
as desired. With a mostly receptive-listening attitude towards the first impulses
of sound, the aim is a musical activity, as elementary as it may be. This preparation and waiting for the pupil to take over the music material himself ensures the
intended therapeutic results. Participation by a pupil demonstrates liberation and
motivation from within.

Creativity is certainly first and foremost – to create and to produce something
without knowledge of the result. Man cannot be taught creativity. His creative
powers can be furthered and supported. Therefore, attention should be paid not
only to the musical performance, but what is more important, to the path that has

led to the performance. Nevertheless, the performance, however elementary it musically may be, can serve as a diagnostic as well as a therapeutic assistance.

If the therapist knows how to adjust the improvisation of his instrument, or perhaps of his voice, to the pupils own productions or response to the musical stimuli and the pupil, as far as he is concerned, is able to engage himself actively in music and expend on the musical contact he had with his own musical language we have via the music, started an interchange, and this is the basis of Music Therapy. This, obviously, demands a differentiated methodical procedure, which psychologically opens and makes use of the specific possibilities of sound, music and social intercourse, which is part of the spontaneous elementary playing. Hereby a connection is brought about between the musical and the social dimensions supporting that improvisation advantageously can be used with greater effect in the music therapy as a genuine means of expression and communication for the handicapped pupils.

Music and Musicality

Music is one of the best ways of keeping the attention of a human being, because it is a constant mixture of new and already known stimuli. The active and attentive condition, which can be obtained through adapting the music to the handicapped pupil, is an excellent resource for all kinds of learning. Music becomes as much a therapeutic assistance as does pedagogy. An example is that the method of presenting special instruction to the handicapped pupils becomes also a resource for the handicapped to choose at his own discretion as his behaviour.

It has been possible for most of our pupils at the Aalborg School to develop by means of music therapy, so that they spontaneously react to music stimuli, move, talk, sing or play, and create music selecting their own means of expression. Consequently, it must be a free kinaesthetic experience, which does not imitate or echo a musical stimulus, but an expressive creativity emanating from the pupil himself.

We regard music, among other things, as a form of structured sound, just as in language, and musicality as the ability to react to the musical stimulus and to create music. The person who is listening, or with other senses, perceives the numerous variations of those musical sounds, is, himself, creating music.

All children need to have their natural rhythmic and harmonic powers encouraged and stimulated through music if provided the possibility of playing on suitable instruments. It might also be of importance to give some more thought to the kind of music, which the child hears at home and at school. The sounds and the music that surrounds us have a lasting influence on the way we experience life.

Fundamental human features are contained in the various ways of experiencing music, whether one is handicapped or not. All persons, more or less, respond to musical stimuli, and so, they are all musical to some extent or another. In the most severely handicapped person, a musical being can be found, and this being can, by means of music therapy, be granted the opportunity to be included in participation in music and not be isolated because of a handicap. Music therapy should be a right for all children and adults with or without handicaps.

Music therapy appeals, not only to the handicapped, but can also open up new prospects for the so-called "normally developed", perhaps even in particular for the intelligent pupils who in some schools, may be handicapped – hampered by the system. One asks if it is not very relevant to understand music therapy also as an alternative or at least a supplement to the existing teaching of music and singing in the primary school, especially when considering the perspectives of the integration of handicapped pupils in the normal school. Also in the musical field, the handicapped can teach other people. The experience of reversed integration at the Aalborg School demonstrates, undoubtedly, that music therapy is one of the very best means in which endeavours to integrate are successful. It is very essential to give the handicapped individual the optimum potential of experiencing himself as being on the same level as others and of the same value. It is a moral, civil and legal right for handicapped persons to receive a level of services in the arts equal to that of the non-handicapped. When we stop discriminating musically against children who are different, the slogan "Music for every child" can become a reality.

It is my hope that we with our joint efforts and exchange of ways and means can contribute in a significant and concrete way to develop teaching, therapy and treatment methods for children and adolescents for whom music is therapy and for whom music therapy open new possibilities and perspectives in *A World of Sound and Music*[1].

---

1   http://www.clausbang.com

Literature

Bang, Claus (1971): *Ein Weg zum vollen Erlebnis und zur Selbstverwirklichung für gehör-lose Kinder*. In: Wolfgart, Hans (Ed.): *Das Orff Schulwerk im Dienste der Erziehung und Therapie behinderter Kinder*. Berlin.

Bang, Claus, co-author (1972): *Musikterapi*. Gyldendal Copenhagen. (Swedish edition: *Musikterapi*. Natur och Kultur, 1975).

Bang, Claus (1972): Editor and translator of Danish, Norwegian and Swedish *Children's Play Songs* by Paul Nordoff and Clive Robbins.

Bang, Claus (1976): *Musik durchdringt die lautlose Welt*. In: *Hörgeschädigtenpädagogik*, Nr. 13. Hamburg.

Bang, Claus (1978): *Musik – ein Weg zur Sprache*. In: *Musik & Medizin*. Neu Isenburg.

Bang, Claus (1979): *Music in Therapy for Hearing Impaired – Ways & Means*. Oxford.

Bang, Claus (1979): *Verden af lyd og musik*. In: *Education*, No. 3. Ministry of Education, DK.

Bang, Claus (1980): *A World of Sound & Music*. In: *Journal British Association Teachers of the Deaf*, No. 4.

Bang, Claus (1984): *Eine Welt von Klang & Musik*. In: *Hörgeschädigtenpädagogik*, Nr. 2. Heidelberg.

Bang, Claus (1998): Introduction to *A World of Sound & Music*. In: *Nordic Journal of Music Therapy*, No. 7(2).

Bang, Claus (2005): *A World of Sound & Music. Music Therapy for Deaf, Hearing Impaired and Multi-Handicapped Children and Adolescents*. On 3 dual-layer DVD+R with material for treatment, education, training and research.

Bang, Claus (2008): *A World of Sound & Music. Music Therapy for Deaf, Hearing Impaired and Multi-Handicapped Children and Adolescents*. NEW: Online-Web Version in English. See: http://www.clausbang.com for further information.

Birkenshaw-Fleming, Lois (1965): *Teaching Music to Deaf Children*. An application of Carl Orff's "Music for Children". The Volta Review.

Bitcon, Carol Hampton (1976): *Alike and Different*. Santa Anna CA, USA.

Levin, Gail/Levin Herbert (1974): *Learning Through Music*. Boston.

Nordoff, Paul/Robbins, Clive (1977): *Creative Music Therapy*. New York.

Robbins, Carol/Robbins Clive (1980): *Music for the Hearing Impaired*. Saint-Louis MO, USA.

Music Therapy with Deaf Children

Giulia Cremaschi Trovesi

Gently Encountering the Emotional World of the Deaf Child

"Let's try to imagine the possibility of putting a cello inside a double bass; inside the cello a viola; inside the viola a violin. The result, like in a Chinese puzzle, would be one instrument inside another. From the same, externally visible instrument, we could then hear the sound of four. When bowing the chords of the double bass, the strings of the cello, viola and violin would accordingly vibrate. The bodies of resonance, one inside the other, amplify the harmonics according to precisely defined proportions. The harmonics in every fundamental vibrating sound correspond in correct proportion to the length of the strings and the volume of the resonator. The same takes place in our body."[1]

From time being humanity has always sought identity and reproduction in the design of musical instruments. In each detail the human body resounds to the presence of the world. The human voice echoes within the body in order to reproduce the noise and sounds made by nature. In turn the human voice is continually recreated through the construction of musical instruments. Each instrument is an extension of the human being. The resonating bodies of musical instruments are reproductions of our own resonators, the so-called "resonator cavities". The vibrating organ is the essence of ourselves[2], is our "being in the world" representing individual vibrations which describe the realm of contact with those of similar disposition. Music and word have a common origin. Voice is a cry, vocalisation, song, homeopathic play. Voice is the expression of emotion. Over generations human beings have improved their ability to reproduce the sounds of nature by voice and to communicate with others through spoken word.

We are so used to speaking, to take listening for granted, that we have forgotten how each of our own gestures is the result of perception and learning. The verb *perceive* comes from Latin *per capio*, that is "I take through myself". To perceive incorporates physicality in its entirety. To perceive means: to follow the direction of hearing in order to grasp, practise and process sound. To perceive is to relate personally to the material world and to the presence of others.

---

1 Cremaschi Trovesi 2001
2 The philosopher Edmund Husserl speaks about *Körper* (the body as object, inert, not perceiving), about *Leib* (the perceived body, the point of motion), of the "linguistic body" and of body pattern (the ability to assume different postures according to given situations).

When this overlapping of relationships overtly begins to take a sole direction, we are placed in a situation which is fraught with difficulties, pathology, deprivation, exclusion, disability. An excessive egotism separates us from society and surroundings. An excessive relationship to material objects diminishes contact with others. This is a common situation among deaf children and children with relationship problems (psychosis, autism), who enjoy playing alone and refuse the company of others. An excessive centring on others removes us from the material world, which is the case with blind children who are able to relate to others however not to material objects.

The *resonant body* is continually connected to reality. When exaggeration in one of the named directions occurs, the resonant body shows particular behavioural patterns, tension, postures, gestures, movements and facial expression. The interpretation of body language requires particular sensibility and preparation for nonverbal expression. Edith Stein says: "Our body, starting with our face (eyes, forehead etc.) is like a *living score* where very precise musical notes are recorded which can be further described as 'traces' of character."[3]

How is the *living score* 'manifested in a deaf person'? How can hearing people read this score whilst maintaining the prejudice: "Deaf people cannot hear?"

The body of a deaf person vibrates in sequence with the world and in accord with the vibration of musical instruments. Through my experience with deaf persons and children[4], I can verify that the *body* is the protagonist of hearing. The *resonance* of the grand piano results in the sympathetic vibrations of the different substances that form our organism (resonance in bones, muscles, nerves etc.).

Scientific Aspects

Sympathetic vibration is the source of emotion. The sonorous waves, differing in frequency, volume, overtones (harmonics) and length, are perceived by body resonance. Studies in acoustic physics demonstrate that low frequencies correspond to large resonators, and high frequencies to increasingly smaller ones[5]. An example clarifies the concept: the difference between the lowing of the cow (large resonator) and the twittering of a bird (tiny resonator). Life inside the maternal womb (the "first orchestra"[6]) is rooted in the sonorous-emotional, sympathetic vibrations that bind mother and child. This is the original co-vibration which will map future experiences. To perceive the mother totally in oneself is the deep sense of being heard,

3   Cremaschi Trovesi 2002
4   The listening experiences with 485 deaf children are described in the book *Il Corpo Vibrante*.
5   cf. Helmholtz's resonators
6   Cremaschi Trovesi 1996

of learning to hear and to inwardly listen. Deaf babies resonate with their entire body in accordance with their mother's emotional sound waves just like any other person. After birth they are ready to proceed in their own individuality – a process which is ever and always subjective.

When we speak about sounds with reference to the deaf we normally say: "they hear vibrations". Let's ask ourselves: "What are vibrations?" Each sound occurs through vibrating movement. To understand *how* a deaf person can perceive this, it is necessary to consider:

- Sound is a complex phenomenon.
- Perception of sound waves is complex.

When we speak about "vibrations" we refer, without being aware of it, to fundamental sounds without harmony.

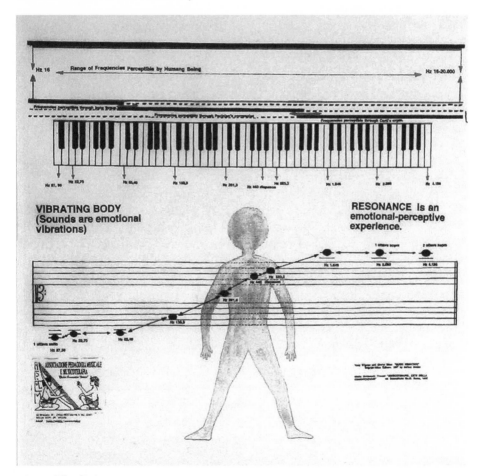

Fig. 1: The living score

This table represents:

- The range of frequencies of a piano from 27.50 Hz to 4,184 Hz[7], corresponding to almost all frequencies heard by mankind (16 Hz–16,000–20,000 Hz)
- The sound waves through corporality, in coherence with the principles of resonance as formulated by Helmholtz: large resonators for low notes, small ones for high notes
- The term "tone pitch" refers to human corporality and corresponding vertical posture. High sounds resonate in the higher cavities (head); progressively they shift down to low sounds, i. e. subject to the force of gravity which we perceive in lower resonant cavities (abdomen, legs, feet).
- The body is a resonator which receives sound waves throughout its entirety. The reception of fundamental sounds and harmonics occurs via a transmitter which includes complete head to foot physicality. Mankind resounds in the reception and production of sound waves (the voice). Many more frequencies as can be produced are received.
- Musical notation arose in order to represent the ascending and descending movements of voice within the body[8]. The first neumes form the original idea which subsequently progresses to square notation and thus to the pentagram.
- The musical notes written on the score indicate fundamental frequencies. The harmonics do *not* appear in written form. Their appreciation is subjective. A piano wire in the low register can produce 120 harmonics. At which level can a deaf person perceive harmonics? This is the problem: persons with particular audiometric curves (generally classified by the connotation "deaf") are able to *hear* but not to *discriminate*. The distinction depends on the higher harmonics that characterize the timbre of each sound. For example with the vowel "I" the harmonics in a masculine voice (the fundamental is about 120 Hz) reach over 2,700 Hz. A person that can't perceive 2,700 Hz doesn't hear "I", but perhaps "A" or "O", vowels whose harmonics are between 1,000 Hz and 2,000 Hz. The guttural voice of many deaf people mirrors the way they hear. The high voice that you can find in deaf people is actually a harmonic of the guttural voice sounding in the head.
- The notation has been transferred from voice to musical instruments.
- With the passing centuries we have forgotten that notation arose to represent the movements of the voice in the body. Consequently we came to give it a conventional value based on instrumental practise.

---

7 With the harmonics 16,000 Hz and more can be reached.
8 Guido d'Arezzo (11th century): *Micrologos*

Fig. 2: The vibrating body is listening – the child depicts "where" sounds are received.

Body Resonance

I spoke about *body resonance* in 1981 in an AS.PE.I publication (Italian Pedagogy Association), under the title: *The deaf child's integration, reality and perspectives.* In 1983 the French Marie Louise Aucher published a book on "Psycho-phone", *Vivre sur sept octaves* where she comments body resonance. In 1997 Tony Wigram and Cheril Dileo also deal with this theme in the book *Music Vibration*, in which they demonstrate that body is the great perceiver, not just the ear.

The answers given by deaf children to the sounds they perceive, if they have been introduced to music in a creative atmosphere with positive acceptance, are unbelievable for hearing persons. These answers must be attentively studied whilst observing the following differences:
- Deaf children without a hearing aid
- Deaf children with a hearing aid[9]

---

9   Today we have to distinguish between external hearing aid, retro-auricular or endo-aural, and internal aid, cochlear implantation. External hearing aids are amplifiers of sonorous waves; the listening is analogue, similar to hearing persons. Cochlear implantation replaces the perception sending electrical impulses to the acoustic nerve.

My first experiences were made in an institute for so-called "deaf-mutes"[10] – children from four to fifteen years old whose hearing aids were in a very poor condition. Their responses to sound were so evidently manifested that the institute rented a grand piano for me in the second year. I worked as a voluntary expert, authorized to practise music therapy with the deaf. At the same time I worked with deaf children and gave courses in speech therapy and psychomotorics at the Institute of Audiology at the University of Milan[11]. Thus I could compare the answers to the perception of sounds given by children without acoustic support in the institute, with those of the children equipped with acoustic support in the Polyclinic. One common factor linked all: deaf children were eager for direct contact with sound. Notable differences were recorded with reference to the correct use of hearing aids.

To understand what was happening in front of my eyes, my hands, my hearing, I had to begin to study over again. The deaf children's answers challenged my knowledge as a music teacher. I realized that playing, studying music and analyzing scores was not enough. Questions, that for many seemed obvious or even superfluous, were clamouring for my attention:
- What does listening mean?
- What is the difference between Hearing and Listening?
- Which emotions develop in a person who re-discovers hearing after years of silence?

These are questions that do not involve ears as sensory organs; they are more concerned with emotions, with attentiveness, with intentionality, with communication and *empathy*. While I was offering these children the world of sounds, encouraging them to lie across the piano, they were opening the world of empathy to me; a form of hearing which penetrates to deep and direct contact. Eventually I realized that the deaf had re-found the very contact which they had experienced whilst inside their mothers' womb.

The feeling of security conceived before words and which, through song, gives mankind the gift of speech. I worked with children in the institute. Society, culture, science had already decided their future for them: they would be "deaf-mute". In direct contact with sounds, they behaved differently. Their expressions, always fraught with questions about what was going on in the outside world[12], used to

---

10 In 1974 the Italian Government passed the law 104 concerning educational integration for children with handicaps. For the deaf, too, access was gained to integration and educational integration. Now, deaf children grow up, study and learn together with hearing children.
11 These references regard the 1970s and the beginning of the 1980s in the Institute for the Deaf and until 2000 at the University Polyclinic.
12 Thirty-years ago a deaf person defined his eyes as "cameras". He explained to me that his eyes recorded everything. He does not forget anything. The "camera" records and chronologically links the events. It is a camera without sound.

freeze just at one point. Through mimic and posture, we understood that they were listening. The children let their bodies co-vibrate with the sonorous waves of the piano. *I used to play, reading these living scores standing in front of me.* There was no music stand on the harmonic piano case; there were these children showing me a new world. I played using low and yet lower sonorities; contrasts between high and low sounds, with vivacious, brilliant, quick rhythms, as quick were the children in answer to the sounds.

Up to then I had never understood why the playing of octaves was so important:
• A low doubled octave involves the whole listening body.
• A doubled octave in high sounds emphasises the brilliance of the timbre.

I was speaking through the piano. Hearing was occurring within the children; hearing is not external; it is the link between "inside" with "outside". The children were rediscovering emotions learnt in the maternal womb, the "first orchestra". Their behaviour was the very negation of the term "deaf-mute". The process leading to deaf-muteness gradually suffocates the perceptive capacities of the deaf.

One of the principle characteristics of deaf children's re-education collapsed like a house of cards in front of me: the predominance of the senses. According to this principle sight replaces hearing. No, this was not the case: Through movement (for example, joint and simultaneous hand clapping with closed eyes) the deaf children succeeded in proving their ability to listen up until the last key of the piano (4,184 Hz). They were swimming against the current. Inside the institute two directions were beginning to crystallise.
• The adult imposes instruction relevant for the education of a non-hearing person; consequently deaf children assume 'deaf and dumb behaviour' (concept of re-education).
• The musician gives children the freedom of self-perception; children are willing to sharpen their attention. The availability of well adjusted acoustic devices enables an almost average listening capability for each child. (Music therapy: the therapy is considered as very gradual and individually designed for each child.)

Deafness is terrible. A person surrounded by hundreds people and not capable of understanding anything they say. Deafness is separation, forced solitude and isolation. The deaf were teaching me that, even without hearing, you can learn to listen. Whilst developing corporeal sensitivity they were learning to profit from acoustic devices. Learning to listen was equally possible for them by concentrating on improvement through the power of music. Listening improvement means learning to concentrate in order to support increased perception of harmonic formants. Thus I was able to learn that sound reception for a deaf person is characterised as follows:

- Body resonance
- Remaining vestiges of hearing
- Amplification of hearing vestiges through correct application of acoustic devices

Nothing mentioned can function without the *will* to listen. *Will* is *subjective*. It emerges from the sensation of acceptance, appreciation, respect and lack of criticism. It is generated by the *we* in *empathy*.

The Method

I realized that there were both grave as well as unconsidered problems: correct diagnosis and an equally correct adjustment of acoustic devices. I think that the following points will always be the basic problem of deafness[13]:
- Correct adjustment of acoustic devices
- Respect for each child's individuality of perception
- Belief in the child demonstrated by all adults, whether parents, tutors, specialists or doctors

"To establish a rapport, a relationship between me and someone else, to communicate something to another etc., a corporeal relationship, a connection created by physical processes must take place. I have to approach this person and start a conversation. Thus space plays an as equally important role as time."[14]

Between the children and me the following was happening: Our bodies were vibrating to the same sonorous waves. The children's space, vibrating in accord with the piano, became the time of their experience. My emotions resulted from theirs. They were the creative source of my improvisation on the piano in order to reflect their joy and their vitality, which was increasing from day to day. The children wanted to learn the relevant words in order to describe what was happening. The nonverbal dialogue triggered the wish to speak. The words crossed from me to them and vice versa as a significant element of our communication, our emotions. In short, we really spoke[15].

---

13 We can understand the dimension of these problems, when we equate the difficulties in the prescription of glasses in short sighted children who refuse to collaborate.
14 Stein, Edith (1985): *The problem of empathy.* Rome
15 I learned this, too: many words are not needed for an utterance. Just one word, only one verb can capture the significance of a situation. I began to wonder about the "inherent" value in each word, even more "inherent" in a vowel or a consonant. I felt the need for further study to be able to understand the import of just one word.

As years go by, and with subsequent experience, I have increasingly understood that my job as music therapist for deaf children (and also for others) was to give them the opportunity to be themselves. The rest followed automatically. It wasn't a problem of the grade of deafness; it was a problem of reciprocal listening[16].

With the terms Matching, Pacing, Leading, NLP (Neuro-linguistic programming) aims to focus on a therapeutic relationship. Matching means reflection, Pacing is accompaniment and support of the child on its way, and Leading describes the guidance of a child towards constructive action. Thus an *"a posteriore"* analysis would be possible. In practise though, it is impossible to differentiate moments of reflection from moments of support or leading. The *dialogue* in music therapy occurs within modalities which are executed and re-created step by step. Trained experts realise that they are in control of the relationship of reflection and support. It is a question of focussed reflection and support accompanying each step of the therapeutic method. Matching involves Leading and Pacing; Leading involves Pacing and Matching; Pacing involves Matching and Leading in the energetic flow evolving between child and therapist who is constantly guiding the situation and, from the nonverbal, subsequently designating the direction of development. Guidance is performed by clinical improvisation on the piano, which in itself includes the infinite variants of sonorous dialogue. Each gesture is nascent. In music therapy the import lies in the emergence, in the transition from present to future that characterizes the temporality of sound, of music, of life. Emergence lies in the Leading because an inner change is "directional", i. e. the experience *"in fieri"* is a therapeutic and vital genesis.

The courses at the University Polyclinic gave me the opportunity of learning the theoretical fundamentals of speech therapy. I worked hard and thought deeply before drawing any conclusions. I saw some deaf children who developed well and others who in time, sometimes a very short time, showed both behavioural disturbance and dysfunctions which could have led to psychosis or autistic withdrawal. Deaf children with behavioural and relationship disturbances (aggressiveness, escape, disinterestedness) were prescribed music therapy. Which were the aspects that favoured success or led to failure? Success or failure did *not* depend on the degree of deafness. A child could possess serious third degree deafness and nevertheless make positive developments in verbal communication. Success or failure depended on the child's environment.

Also in the case of behavioural disturbances the children acted quite differently when in direct contact with sound (body resonance). They went on a "chase"

---

16 I used to, and still do, let the children listen blindfolded as soon as they show capability and pleasure in hearing. For us this is one of several enactments. With blindfolded eyes, the children demonstrate increased sensitivity for sounds that adults, even when present, are hardly able to recognize.

for sounds – rhythms – movement. I had a lot of musical instrumentals available, amongst others the Orff instruments that I brought to the lessons. The theoretical foundations which I was beginning to develop came from a thought, from the perspective of the individual in a world that did not coincide with the technical principles of re-education. I did not wear a white coat, I did not give orders and I did not demand achievement. The children's body, in direct contact with the case of the grand piano, became a resonant, singing organ seeking speech. Their eyes sought mine; their hands suggested my movements on the keyboard. They indicated sonorous registers in their search for contrasts between sonorities. They stretched out along the piano to touch my hands. Word was generated automatically, as an undeniable necessity. The word was an instrument used to inter-communicate, to enjoy the feeling of togetherness, to unite our emotions.

Often the mothers (and fathers) who were present could hardly understand what was happening. It seemed to be a game[17]. Whilst I was interacting with the children, I was endeavouring to answer the parents' questions. Finally there was only one answer: One's own self-confidence had to be found in order to communicate this same confidence to the child.

The older children used to give vent to their emotions by energetically banging the drums. The higher the children lifted their arms in order to hit the drum, the more their bodies were flooded by sonorous waves, the more flexible their diaphragms became leading ultimately to the spontaneous utterance of voice. Each gesture, necessary for playing an instrument, caused physical movement, which in turn gradually led to equilibrium between gesture, breathing co-ordination, vocal expression and spontaneous and natural genesis of the word. Through creative, musical *dialogue*, through *clinical improvisation on the piano* and through *body resonance*, children were able to eradicate previous experiences in order to absorb newer ones[18]. I discovered their spontaneity; I witnessed their abandonment of aggressive and oppositional behavioural patterns. I shared and supported their wish to learn the words in order to be able to describe what they were experiencing. Song arose spontaneously. This process of rebirth led me to better self-discovery, to relive my infantile emotions, my love for music and the joy of sharing the "beauty" of music and art with these children.

---

17 *"Gioco"* (game) derives from *"gioia"* (joy). Our activities were in fact based on emotions of joy. How could the parents of a handicapped child feel joy? Gradually the parents realized that a handicap can equally be a resource.

18 Experiences which were related to diagnostic controls, parents' fear, to family discussions, to counselling with new specialists etc.

Theoretical Fundamentals

Let's try to think of material. We can:
* Analyze and use it to make a dress
* Retrace the past in order to discover "how" our ancestors came across yarn and weaving

It is a case of procedures that arise from differing interests and lead to different goals. Analysis of the material refers to the existing product.

The choice of threads, of yarns, of colours, of designs gives evidence as to how the human being discovered the ability to weave. Was it a memorable event when human hands first twisted a natural fibre? We'll never know. We just know that, without this action, we would not have clothes. The experience implicates the first personal involvement in starting the search for something to link intention to action, to participation and communication. Thus we can interpret verbal language and observe it from different points of views:
* Analysis of adult language and dissection in relevant components
* Correlation of ontogenesis and phylogeny in order to equate the progress of mankind within the development of a child

"Often the power and the practical efficiency of analysis make us blind and oblivious to the holistic moment of comprehension, which, nonetheless, is at the origin of each of our experiences and learning procedures. This, in itself, consequently leads to our belief that elements which emerge from the analysis are fundamental and not the progeny of one's own analytic activity on the vague basis of primordial comprehension. Language suffers from exactly this error of perspective. Starting with the applaudable analysis and transcription of oral speech, supported by the stylized signs of the alphabet, (one of the most perfect and persistent creations of the Greek intellect), we have for example unwittingly convinced ourselves that the "letters" (vowels, consonants, syllables) are the building blocks that constitute language "in itself". That the truth is not as simple nor in fact consistent with reality can be proved by the fact that no child has learned or would learn to speak on the basis of a preventive, separate and analytic education of the sounds of the language which form the words: The child learns in coherent units (e. g. Mummy, Daddy)."[19]

---

19 Carlo Sini, introduction to Cremaschi Trovesi, Giulia (2000) *Dal suono al segno* (*From sound to sign*). Carlo Sini, lecturer of theoretical philosophy, at the University of Milan, member of the Accademia dei Lincei, and of the Istituto Internazionale di Filosofia is the author of *Semiotica e Filosofia*, 1991, *Etica della scrittura* 1992, *Filosofia teoretica* 1994, *Filosofia e scrittura* 1994, *Gli abiti, le pratiche e i saperi* 1996, *Idoli della conoscenza* 2000.

In music therapy as a humanistic model[20], knowledge is enacted. From the depth of experience existence emerges, self-generated action, personal responsibility for self-expression. The processes of transformation follow naturally. The deaf child makes his voice heard when in direct contact with sound. He interweaves "his" story with the sounds, with the voice, with the natural and spontaneous occurrence of verbal language. Nonverbal dialogue provokes the formation of word. Just as the naturally twisted fibres form the threads; the threads subsequently the weft, the wefts then the clothes, thus the child practices his own self in voice, playfully generating articulation noises with his mouth by watching the movements of his mother's lips or those of his music therapist or other persons as is the wont of all children. Reading lip movements is the way we all used in an imitative-creative process with which we learned to speak. Thus games were sung, counting rehearsed and nursery rhymes recounted. The nonsense and dissonance of the nursery rhymes encourage the formation of words in all children, and equally in the deaf child. The sonorous waves are waves of energy which humanity has embodied over the ages with voice and dance. Body resonance, clinical improvisation on the piano, the eurhythmy (organization of sounds – rhythms – movements), the playing of small idiophone musical instruments[21] suitable for children's hands, is the knowledge which the child experiences and shares with the music therapist, with, when present, one or both parents.

Fig. 3: The symbolic game is the origin of mother tongue.
The child, spontaneously, sings its "Am".

---

20 The model was elaborated at A.P.M.M. "Giulia Cremaschi Trovesi" (Association of Musical Pedagogy and Music Therapy).

21 The child plays with the available material. Instruments are varied and the choice is free. Through the child's own choice he identifies himself within the game (symbolically), he tells "his story", he rids himself of the burdens which could become intolerable and he unfolds towards dialogue. Behaviour never occurs by chance. The adult is responsible for the interpretation of the inner significance of childlike behaviour in order to assist progress in future development.

The interpersonal relation in music therapy becomes possible through the vibration and co-vibration of the same experience. Only the acoustical musical instruments have the co-vibration i. e. they are composed of harmonic cases which amplify vibratory waves created by membranes, chords, "arias in movement". I feel it is important to report on a certain episode. Considering our procedures it hardly surprises us if deaf children start to explore the piano keyboard in order to compare differing sounds in various registers. Gradually, almost inadvertently, the child learns to read music through conscious awareness of voice[22]. Reading, exploring the keyboard, learning to play is a process which develops over time. One day I asked a deaf thirteen year old girl, who plays the piano (she plays pieces by Bach, Schumann, Kabalewsky etc.) if it was the same for her to play the grand piano or her electric keyboard at home. She looked at me, deeply astonished. "No! No! It's not the same! All the keys of the piano vibrate under one's fingers. They are *all different*! The keys of the electric keyboard *do not* communicate *anything*."[23]

Music is composed of: *rhythm*, *melody* and *harmony*. *Rhythm* alone is not yet music; rhythm is a framework which supports melody. Each *melody* integrates harmony or further possibilities of harmonic arrangements; *harmony* is the foundation on which music itself is based. The advantage of keyboard instruments (piano, organ) is that they permit simultaneous rhythm, melody and harmony. The grand piano is simultaneously a string and percussion instrument, with a wide range of sounds (from 27.50 Hz from the first left key up to 4,184 Hz for the last right key). A wire in the low register of a good piano produces up to 120 harmonic sounds and the case can equally include an adult's body in its resonance.

During the various stages of development the music therapist becomes increasingly aware of his communicative role whilst playing an instrument. The music therapist can, at any time, find those sonorities, those chords (harmony), rhythms and melodies through which he "speaks", leads, supports, provokes, accompanies, approves, reacts etc. according to what characterizes the "we" of the therapeutic relation. *Empathy* is personified by the clinical improvisation on a piano. The improvisation on the piano gives answer to the melodies, to the sonorities of a harp, of string instruments (violin, viola, cello and contrabass), of wind instruments (trumpet, horn, flute, clarinet etc.), of percussion instruments (membranes, ethnic instruments etc.), of idiophone instruments, whereby rich, fascinating musical combinations can be achieved within fleeting moments of time.

Eurythmy describes the organization of sounds, rhythms and movements. The gesture of each child, capable of holding and voluntarily using tangible materials

---

22 cf. reference to Guido d'Arezzo
23 This is one of the several examples that I could list in order to demonstrate that handicap can be a resource.

(wraps, scarves, ribbons or others) is positively assessed by clinical improvisation on the piano. In musical therapeutic activity, the occurrence itself construes the essence. On the piano, the professional expert follows the child's movements; the sensitivity of his accompaniment encourages the child to feel protected and accepted, thus continuing its movements whilst actively listening. A musical therapist who is not sufficiently trained, can miss moments of significant hearing and thus thwart a constructive process which would have otherwise led to successful results.

What happens to the parents who are present during therapy? The answer is simple. Whoever is present during unforeseeable events can only profit. It is difficult to explain in words what happens during the therapy as it is the sonorous material which characterizes this discipline. Let us proceed according to following points:

- The parents (at least one of both) know the child's history.
- The parents are accustomed to the child's behaviour.
- The parents, knowing the child's characteristics, are aware of the importance and significance of customary gestures, new gestures, and atypical gestures.
- The parents can give information as to unusual activity.
- The parents can take advantage of the professional's therapy in order to relate to the child under different aspects in order to appreciate the child's progress.
- The parents and the expert discuss the reasons for reconsideration and adoption of new procedures.

The presence of parents allows easier processing of family systems, with no long discussions, periods of instruction or critical attitude. Through the presence of the parents, the therapist is able to progress without having to decide alone. The child is the centre of attention and is encouraged to work together with those who are accompanying him. Musical improvisation makes all this possible. A development procedure of a therapeutic kind is initiated, encouraging all those who are taking part to accept a different "register" or new total perspective. Whilst working with deaf children it often happens that one meets deaf parents.

The same attentiveness as with the children is of utmost importance, an increased sensitivity towards those who as adults rediscover the world of sounds. Deaf parents welcome the sounds, which they were unable to perceive, through love for their children. They allow their children a different deafness as they themselves experienced i. e. to be a deaf child who learns to listen, who spontaneously learns to speak, who laughs when it hears music.

Working Instruments

- Idiophone musical instruments[24]
- Percussion musical instruments
- Membrane musical instruments
- Ethnic musical instruments
- Wind musical instruments
- String musical instruments
- Different kinds of bells
- Big posters with illustrations of numbers, refrains or other didactical material
- Eurhythmic materials (ribbons, material, foulards, hoops of different sizes etc.)
- Handcraft materials to encourage the development of speech in mute children
- Papers, marking pens or other materials

How?

Music therapy for deaf children primarily means playing with common daily noises and sounds. In a true and honest communicative relationship the child unfolds towards listening. It realizes the consideration of an adult and behaves accordingly (significance of feedback, by which the child feels the other's authenticity). Before a deaf child is prepared to listen it puts the adult to the test. Through diagnostic control the child has already realized that something is somehow different. The diagnostic results are followed by family crises, and marked reactions from the parents. Adult emotions, especially parent's emotions, do not escape the attention of any child. Thus a deaf child learns to develop awareness, and to absorb others' feedback.

The emotional context in music therapy is also a novelty for the child. It's important to register moments of childlike astonishment; the resulting feedbacks are a constructive basis for the future. It is possible to co-operate with one or two or even three children. The sporadic presence of one or more siblings offers the following possibilities:
- To acquaint the sibling with what the deaf child is doing, what the "enactment" of music therapy involves
- To include the sibling in the activities so that he can suitably profit
- To demonstrate that the sibling, diagnosed with a particular handicap, has "normal" aspects that enable him to play, to be a child

---

24 An idiophone instrument, suitable for children's hands, when rubbed or massaged under the foot sole (let's think of castanets, clappers, small rattles etc.) allows the entire body to co-vibrate. It is important to experiment in this area in order to understand how far our civilisation has neglected the significance of physical transmission from head to sole.

- To allow the sibling to ask questions, express doubts or other feelings
- To remove the mysterious "aura" which can be created by the expression "music therapy"
- To encourage a happy relationship context between siblings who do not play together at home
- To communicate clearly to the sibling that there are no preferences

The musical therapeutic meetings take place once a week and last for one hour.

Rehabilitation and Integration in School

In 1974, in accordance with law 104, the Italian state school system regulated the integration of handicapped children in classes with "normal"[25] children. The music therapist, with a humanistic further educational training according to the A.P.M.M. model, is also a musical teacher. The preparation and further education within the scope of education and special therapy allows him to perform activities in the classroom related to the education, in this case, of handicapped children, the deaf as well as the hearing. The concept of listening, which generally refers to music, is understood here as "listening to the person". Musical activities aim to allow hearing children to experience that their deaf companions require special attention regarding their acoustic environment in daily school routine. As soon as these children become aware of the problem[26], they independently assume responsibility for other pupils and those with hearing aids, they demonstrate both maturity and serious participation. They are grateful to the adult who has given them responsibility and, in time, their commitment increases. The deaf and integrated child feels that he is being listened to and respected. He experiences the opportunity to interact in an equal relationship and, through self-awareness, to respect others.

---

25 Children without a disability (Ed.)

26 To show the function of acoustic aids in relation to the reception of sound waves; to experiment body resonance at the piano, to experiment with the transmission of sounds in the ambience of other musical instruments, to place palms on doors in order to feel the transmission of sound waves etc.

Literature

Cremaschi Trovesi, Giulia (1976): *Musica nella scuola.*

Cremaschi Trovesi, Giulia (1976): *Musica nella scuola*. Operative book.

Cremaschi Trovesi, Giulia (1987): *Musica Ragazzi.*

Cremaschi Trovesi, Giulia (1988): *Dal suono alla parola, dal suono alla musica*. Psychopeda-
    gogy of music.

Cremaschi Trovesi, Giulia (1996): *Musicoterapica, arte della comunicazione.* Rome.

Cremaschi Trovesi, Giulia (2000): *Dal Suono al Segno.* Bari/Bergamo.

Cremaschi Trovesi, Giulia (2000): *L'incanto della parola.*

Cremaschi Trovesi, Giulia (2001): *Il Corpo Vibrante.* Rome.

Cremaschi Trovesi, Giulia (2002): *Metamorfosi e musica.*

Inner Rhythm

Naomi Benari

When I first began to teach dance to profoundly deaf children, I immediately became aware that a new approach was needed. Together with the children, I developed a method which I called "Inner Rhythm". In the following pages I will describe the path I took, the problems I encountered along the road, and examples of the ways I found to overcome them. It was an exciting process from which I learn a lot and from which I am still learning.

Why Teach Dance to the Profoundly Deaf?

For many people, music and dance are inextricably linked. In fact, there are some societies where the word for dance is synonymous with that for music. So, why teach profoundly deaf children to dance when they cannot hear the music? There are of course many reasons. All children benefit from dancing. Above all, it is fun. It also raises awareness of one's own body, of space around it, of shape, and of others, and it enhances social skills, as children learn to dance with each other. Through dance muscular tone, flexibility and strength are acquired, as well as critical ability and self-discipline. Above all, it is a vehicle for self-expression which, for very young profoundly deaf children whose verbal ability, whether signed or spoken, is not yet developed, is particularly important.

The Age at Which to Start Dancing

In spite of the enormous growth of dance in popular culture – pop videos, musicals etc., there is still a prejudice among some children, boys in particular, that dance is not for them. Some adults including those in the teaching profession, also feel that dance is somehow an inferior activity and a waste of time when there is so much to teach the children. However, there is less resistance among teachers of very young children, and less prejudice among the children themselves at an early age. Dance is pleasurable, and by ensuring that every task is set in the form of a game, the perception of dance as fun is reinforced, and there is less resistance to dancing when the children grow older. This is true of all children.

Segregation or Mainstreaming

The argument on whether to mainstream or to segregate profoundly deaf children has been ongoing for decades and in the UK, after increasingly mainstreaming children with disabilities, the pendulum is beginning to swing back in favour of designated schools for some of these children. With regards to dance, I have found that many profoundly deaf children do not initially have sufficient self-confidence to dance alongside their hearing peers, and will often tend to copy them, rather than taking the initiative on their own. For this reason, I prefer to begin by teaching these children by themselves. Only later, when their self-confidence is established, I will agree to teach them together with their hearing peers.

Focussing Attention

It is relatively easy to gain and hold the attention of, and communicate with hearing children, simply by speaking or, in a large dance classroom, by raising the voice. Hearing people hear whether they want to or not, but the hard-of-hearing receive communication through their eyes, whether they are watching signing or are lip-reading, and this is a voluntary activity, which requires concentration and is at first often tiring. In addition, in a dance hall, where the children are running around in all directions, it is even harder to gain their attention, and it is necessary to find ways of focussing the children's attention. As most young people enjoy games, I always start my sessions with a "watch me" game. First, the children run or dance around until I signal "stop". This ensures that all eyes are focussed on me, and the children are ready for further communication. For those who enjoy competition, the last person to stop moving is "out", and so on until there is a winner. The game can be modified to watching a drumstick on a large tambour, and at a later stage, this can be modified further as the drumming becomes slow or fast, and gradually introduces different simple rhythms.

Another game for encouraging focussing and communication is "Follow-the-Leader", where the children initially follow the movements of the teacher, and then those of a peer. Again, these can be developed and modified to become rhythmical, including slow and fast movements, accented and soft ones, phrasing, rests etc.

Pulse

Once channels of communication are open, the class can begin. My first surprise when teaching young, profoundly deaf children was that many had no awareness at all of the pulse, the beat, of music, and they would often stop while dancing to scratch or talk, and then carry on. In my search for a way to inculcate an understanding of dance, I started from the premise that if deaf children could not hear the music and had no knowledge of the regularity of pulse, or of the variations of rhythm possible in dance, I had to help them become aware of the rhythm which is in the body, and from there of the rhythm, dynamics, breath, and phrasing, which is in every dance movement. We all have a heartbeat and pulse and our own Inner Rhythm.

I started by trying to help the children become aware of their own pulse and heartbeat, with the hope that they could then walk in time to it. But it was very difficult for any of them to feel the pulse simply by holding the conventional places where it can be felt, and I realised that I had to find alternative ways. I then asked them to breathe deeply, as speed of breath can control speed of movement, and found that many could not do so. I tried various tasks employed by speech therapists, such as keeping a balloon in the air with their breath, or racing peas by blowing at them through a straw, all with little avail. We finally had a breakthrough when, at the suggestion of one of the children, I asked them to run until they were exhausted, and found that it was now not necessary to try to find the pulse, as they were breathing deeply and evenly. I began to devise movement sequences with large movements which necessitated deep breathing, and which the children executed beautifully and rhythmically.

Conscious breathing is difficult for anyone, and is an integral part of the training of many professional dancers. It is therefore not surprising that the children found it hard to do this consistently, and if excited or nervous would breathe faster or unevenly, but if all movements were wide and executed with full extensions, involving the whole body, the breathing became deep and the movements even and flowing. I also showed the children how breath could help with technical feats, such as jumping or swinging, or actions which require slow sustained movements such as a slow-motion replay or a walk on the moon. Every class or workshop I give now starts with a very energetic warm-up section, in which large movements, particularly of the torso, are used; this necessitates deep breathing, and it is thus easier to create movements with pulse and rhythm.

Rhythm

The next stage was the development of rhythm. By asking for two movements to one breath, or one breath to last for two movements, the idea of working rhythmically was established. The rhythms were gradually made more intricate, and finally the children themselves were able to devise rhythms to which to dance short sequences. Sometimes a class decision would be made on a rhythm; sometimes they would work in pairs, each pair agreeing their own rhythm; at other times they would work in pairs with one child setting a rhythm for the other. After being given time to develop their ideas and to practice their dance sequence, the children would "share" what they had done; that is, they would show their work to the rest of the class. This had the added benefit of increasing self esteem, and also of giving confidence in performing in front of others when, at the end of the year, we would put on a complete performance for the whole school, on a story or theme chosen by the children.

I always start every task with making definite demands, in the expectation that when the children are familiar with the requirement and with the tools with which to fulfil it, they will use their own creativity to take it further and to make it their own. After having worked for some time in this way, I realised that my work had many similarities with that of Emile Jaques-Dalcroze, a music teacher of hearing children at the turn of the 20th century. He found that many of his pupils could not keep time when playing the piano or singing, but that when they marched at the same time, they kept perfect time, and he developed a system of movement training which emphasised understanding of the different time values of notes. His system has been taken up by the dance world rather than by music teachers, but I recommend reading about his method, as it is as relevant for children with hearing impairment as for hearing children, bearing in mind that, while marching may be sufficient for hearing children, larger movements requiring deep breathing are more helpful to the hard-of-hearing.

Vibrations

It is widely accepted that there are very few profoundly deaf people who do not hear anything at all. Many can hear very low sounds, and those who cannot hear anything at all can often feel the vibrations. However, to my surprise, I discovered that the feeling of vibrations often has to be taught, and for this, the use of tone bars which the children can hold close to the body or can place one hand on as they drum with the other, is particularly good. These are heavy and can most easily be played while sitting, but large tambours, which can be heard not only by the player, emit big vibrations and can be danced to by others. Dancing while holding a tambourine is fun and reinforces awareness of beat. As outlined above, a simple pulse can be followed gradually by more intricate rhythms, composed by the teacher and finally by the children for themselves, or for other children to dance to.

As children become more familiar with feeling vibrations, they will also become aware of feeling different pitches in different parts of the body. When this happens they can then begin to understand pitch, even though they may not hear it.

Fig. 1: Experimenting with frame drums

Music Notation

For some profoundly deaf children, it is easier to learn about the concept of music and rhythm by seeing them on a page. At first I was wary about introducing this to young children, but found that most picked it up surprisingly easily, and were soon writing their own simple rhythms to dance to. I started with quarter notes and rests, for example: | | | − , and then introduced eighth notes: | | ⌐| | . With these three symbols, many interesting rhythms were invented and danced to, so easily that I was able also to teach them about dotted rhythms. By accenting some notes: | | | | , the concept of bar lines was introduced, thus broadening the children's understanding of music notation, and more importantly, bringing light and shade to their dancing, as accented, louder, notes led to stronger movements.

Sound Sources

It is always best to work with live music, and if the dance teacher is able, or has a colleague who is able to play the drums or a piano, for example, this is the best way to accompany the dance classes of profoundly deaf children. They can be greatly helped to become acquainted with a rhythm or phrase by putting their hand on the instrument for a moment to feel the vibrations. However, this is not always possible and many teachers use pre-recorded music. Where possible, use a tape recorder with variable speed, as most dance music is played for adults to dance to, whereas children have shorter legs and faster heartbeat, and therefore need the music to be slightly faster.

Fig. 2: Dancing together

It is best to put the speakers on the floor, where the vibrations can best be felt. However, this does not always help, as the dancers will also pick up the vibrations of other feet on the floor, which can be confusing. This brings us back to Inner Rhythm, as the surest way to dance and move in time and rhythmically, is to rely on one's own inner rhythm, established and maintained by conscious breathing.

Inner Rhythm for All

Often, profoundly deaf children will dance more musically than their hearing peers because many hearing children have become accustomed to listening to pop music with its insistent loud beat, whereas the profoundly deaf child who has learnt Inner Rhythm will pay attention to the musical accompaniment, its variations in speed and rhythm, its accents, phrasing, light and shade and will dance accordingly, whether by feeling the vibrations, watching a drum stick, or listening. Above all, they will breathe consciously as they move.

The preceding pages outline my approach to teaching dance to profoundly deaf children. The system described was developed to help profoundly deaf children to learn to dance rhythmically, thereby increasing their understanding of rhythm and music. It is not set in stone, and I hope that teachers in the future will use it as a starting point for their own ideas, or will even disregard it totally and will devise their own methods.

It has been found that by starting with the rhythm of a dance sequence, hearing children and even professional dancers, find it easier to learn complicated movements and dances, and are able not only to dance rhythmically, but to dance musically as they breathe consciously, because music and rhythm are an integral part of dance. Inner Rhythm is for all.

Literature

Benari, Naomi (1995): *Inner Rhythm – Dance Training for the Deaf*. Chur. An accompanying video was also published.

Music and Auditory-Verbal Therapy

Lois Birkenshaw-Fleming

Every child should grow up experiencing the joys of making music. To be most effective the music making must be one that is active and one that joins rhythm and melody with movement, speech and drama. It also must be one that also encourages creativity at every level. Children who are taught this way generally achieve greater success in their academic studies and research shows that they drop out less frequently and have better success in gaining admission to institutes of higher learning. No less a person than Plato insisted on music training as one of the most important components of an education. "I would teach children music, physics, and philosophy: but, most importantly music, for in the patterns of music and all the arts are the keys to learning."

If the description of this active training sounds a great deal like the Carl Orff approach to teaching music, this is no accident. Orff and Gunild Keetman provided a foundation from which many, many active music education programmes have developed. This is true in regular school programmes throughout the world and is also true in approaches to music therapy and music in special education. It is safe to say that the Orff approach has changed the way music is taught everywhere and particularly in the way it is taught to people with special needs. All students can benefit from being taught in this active way but for those who have special problems, music just might become the most important part of their curriculum.

Active music experiences can help release the tensions that occur as these students try so hard to make sense of, and fit in with their world. They can relax in music period and if they are relaxed they are more receptive to learning.

The Orff approach integrates many different learning modalities to help children learn. Children can master musical concepts (and other subjects) by employing their "best" modality. A child who cannot speak can communicate with a drum. A child who cannot sing might be brilliant in movement. A child who is paralyzed from the neck down can play a xylophone with a mallet attached to a headpiece. All things are possible with a little ingenuity. Success in mastering one activity leads to greater self-confidence and the students will then find the courage to achieve success in other learning tasks. Indeed, one of the main tasks for every teacher or leader is to make sure that every child succeeds in at least one activity in every lesson.

Children who have various forms of exceptionalities often have difficulty acquiring clear, understandable speech and acquiring language. This is a vitally important ability for all to achieve, and here again, an active music experience (that includes working with speech, dramatising poetry and singing children's songs and other folk songs of their country) can be an effective and valuable aid.

For children who are hard-of-hearing or profoundly deaf, acquiring the ability to understand and use speech and language is a top priority. It is also a daunting task as anyone who has worked with this population will know only too well. The greater the hearing loss the more difficult the task becomes. For those with a profound loss the main approaches include sign language, lip-reading, the Auditory-Verbal Method and total communication which is a combination of several of these methods.

Almost all deaf and hard-of-hearing people have some residual hearing. It is important to test children as soon after birth as possible and if needed, fit those with hearing loss with hearing aids so they can begin to "learn to listen" as soon as possible.

Although hearing aids have improved greatly over the last decades, they all have limitations in their perception of sound and this is most evident in the perception of speech. The most impressive development in this field is the cochlear implant. Briefly, this is a device that consists of an external microphone (most often worn behind the ear) that picks up sound and changes it into electrical signals that are then sent to a processor. There the electrical signal is changed to a "code" and this goes to a transmitting coil that looks like a small wheel and is placed just over the ear. It attaches to the receiving coil that is implanted in the bone (by means of a magnet). The code is sent across the skin to this receiving coil. Here it is decoded and goes next to the stimulator which sends the electrical signals to specific electrodes that have been implanted within the cochlea. The auditory nerve fibres are stimulated and the signals are then sent to the auditory part of the brain.

Preparing the child for implantation, receiving the device, programming it and working with the child immediately afterwards are steps that have to be done slowly and carefully. It takes a great deal of adjustment on the part of the child who might become fearful when hearing sound for the first time. The result of successful implementation however, can be a greatly enhanced ability to perceive all sounds and most importantly to perceive those used in speech.

Whatever the means of accessing residual hearing, an unbelievable amount of training and drill has to take place to teach these students to listen and then to speak. Auditory-Verbal Therapy is the most common approach used and great success has been achieved by combining music activities with this approach. For the parents working in this way, this becomes a 24 hour task and everyone in the family circle will be drawn in to assist the child's learning.

Auditory-Verbal Therapy:

- Teaches the child to maximise the use of residual hearing, regardless of the degree of hearing loss
- Is parent/child-centred therapy in which parents observe and participate in therapy sessions to learn techniques and methods for carrying on at home on a daily basis
- Regards the whole child with specific emphasis on developing skills in hearing, speech, language and cognition[1]

The therapists guide the early programme starting with introducing vowel and consonant sounds that would come first in the speech of hearing children (a, oo, ah, b, d and so on). These speech sounds are called the "Learning to Listen Sounds" and are the easiest sounds to hear for children who have a profound hearing loss. They are commonly used in most Auditory-Verbal therapies. Practice can be given in learning these sounds by including them in little chants e. g.

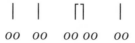

$$| \quad | \quad \sqcap \quad |$$

oo   oo   oo oo   oo

Words containing these sounds can also be made into little chants e. g.

$$\sqcap \quad |$$

hear the train.

These activities combined with singing songs such as the one that follows, also reinforce learning to listen in a lesson (in this case) about a train.

---

1 Estabrooks/Birkenshaw-Fleming 2006

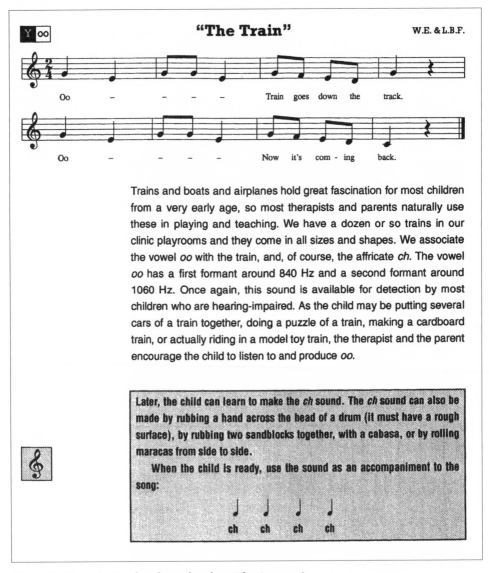

Fig. 1: The Train, *in: Estabrooks/Birkenshaw-Fleming 2006[2]*

It is important to sing with the children at every opportunity throughout the day and parents should sing with their children during the training sessions and at other times at home. Singing helps communication, it brings joy to the singer and listener (who inevitably joins in) and it reinforces speech awareness. Both singing and speech require breath control to produce a long, steady flow; both require pitch discrimination and both require rhythm to have the words make sense. Sing songs chosen for content that will foster specific learning. Sing songs for fun from the children's cultural background – songs that have stood the test of time and have survived for hundreds of years. In English as in other languages, the choice is vast. Some examples (again in English) are *Baa Baa Black Sheep, London Bridge is Falling Down, You Are My Sunshine, Ha Ha, This A-Way*, or *Twinkle Twinkle Little Star*. Many of these songs have a movement or game component that again gives practice in developing movement skills and leads to whole body learning.

Older students love to sing popular songs and these are often useful for speech training as there is much repetition in the lyrics. With the easy availability of CDs, music can be accessed by almost everyone. Teens will also need no urging to dance to this music. A caution. One must watch that the very loud amplification so beloved of today's teenagers does not push the resultant sound over the pain threshold for students who are wearing hearing aids. Instruments such as drums or cymbals can also cross the pain threshold for these children when played too loudly.

In the classroom many of the songs can be accompanied by percussion instruments and/or with simple, repetitive motives (ostinati and borduns) created by the students and played on Orff melodic instruments. Songs using the pentatonic scale will lend themselves brilliantly to accompaniments such as these. The bass xylophone is the most useful instrument as the lower pitch of the notes can be easily felt as vibrations and more easily heard. Many students can also hear and perceive vibrations of the higher instruments such as the soprano xylophone or glockenspiel.

The two greatest roadblocks to achieving understandable speech are a lack of (or faulty) rhythm and lack of pitch and inflection. Often one can figure out what a speech impaired person is saying if the rhythm and/or the intonation are correct even though the speech is faulty. As we have seen, singing helps in both areas, and other music activities can also give more direct assistance.

Rhythm in Speech

As with all children who have a hearing impairment, we begin with developing an awareness of the presence and absence of sound.
- The students feel the vibrations of a large bass drum or bass xylophone directly as it is played and when the sound stops, they lift their hands away and say "stop". The next step is to repeat the exercise with the children's backs turned, gradually moving farther and farther away as they learn to perceive the vibrations through the air.
- Walking, running and skipping to rhythms played on a large drum, stopping when the sound stops are valuable exercises in perceiving sound and at the same time it encourages relaxed movement and gets rid of excess energy.

- Students then experience walking, running and skipping rhythms by using body percussion – clapping, patting the knees, and snapping fingers as these rhythms are played on a drum or xylophone.
- Next, they echo short rhythmic phrases, again using body percussion. Then this activity is transferred to hand-held instruments such as small drums, woodblocks or rhythm sticks. The vibrations from these instruments can be felt through the hands, furthering the perception of the sound. When ready, the students create their own rhythms for the teacher and the group to imitate.
- Relate the sound of these activities to simple, one-syllable words such as dog, walk, cat and have the students clap or play the beat as they say the words. Move on to two and more syllables when the students are ready, and clap these rhythms, while always saying the words.
- Later, relate the sounds to music notation, simple rhythmic notation or drawn symbols | | | | as in *dog, dog, dog, dog* or *walk, walk, walk, walk*, and make charts for the children to clap and say. "Running" notes can be shown by ⌐⌐ ⌐⌐ ⌐⌐ ⌐⌐ and combinations of these symbols can express the rhythms of simple speech. An example would be ⌐⌐ | ⌐⌐ | *bread and jam, bread and jam*. Make these more difficult as skill is developed.

Inflection (Pitch) in Speech

This is another area in which music can be a great help in learning. The strongest syllable is most often spoken in a higher tone while the other parts of the word are said in a lower pitch. This can be clearly demonstrated by using pitched instruments along with the voice.

- Have the children show the concept of high and low in movement, listening, then moving appropriately to high and low notes played on instruments. Light scarves and/or streamers can add fun to this exercise and encourage experimentation in movement. Animals and other objects that move high and low can be imitated in movement and voice – birds, cars going up and down hills, airplanes taking off and landing. Always use the voice to accompany the movement in these exercises.
- Work with instruments that have easily perceived vibrations. These could include a bass xylophone, two large drums tuned to two different pitches, two low notes on a piano or, if it is possible to acquire these, tone bars. Tone bars are individual wooden notes set on wooden boxes that resonate to the frequency of the particular note. They come in a full range of pitches, the most useful being those in the low register. If held to the upper body while being played the vibrations can clearly resonate in the child's chest[2].
- Begin with echo activities using just one bar at first. When the child feels confident with this, use two tone bars with different pitches to create different

---

2   Studio 49 and Sonor are two reliable makers of these instruments.

"melodies" for echoing e. g. *high-low-low / low-high-low / high-high-high-low*. (The children always "sing" the words "*high, low, low*" as the notes are played.)

- Combine this activity with two-syllable words, working out the patterns of inflection on the blocks as the word is said i. e. "*apple*" would be high-low, "*tomato*" would be low-high-low. At first use notes that are fairly far apart e. g. low C and the G above. As listening becomes more developed choose notes that are closer together such as low C and the E above.
- As the children mature, differences in pitch can be detected in words of three or more syllables and even in whole sentences. It can be interesting to explore how the meaning of a sentence can be changed with a change in inflection e. g. *I want to go out. / I want to go **out**. / I **want** to go out.*
- Another instrument that can be used effectively for demonstrating pitch and inflection is the rather unlikely kazoo. To make a sound the player has to produce a steady stream of breath and hum across a paper membrane. As this membrane vibrates the vibrations can be felt in the nose and around the mouth. Playing games of high and low, and humming the melodies of songs on the kazoo encourages the ability to produce a steady breath, requires a voiced sound and with its weird sound is fun to play. It is a great choice if the teacher or parents can stand the sound!

These are just a few of the many, many games and activities that can be used in a program of music for deaf and hard-of-hearing children. This approach is based on the premise that learning is most effective when it is enjoyable and when movement, rhythm, melody, speech, drama, singing, playing instruments are all included in the learning process. It is indeed full spectrum learning and one that delights the students while at the same time helps them to learn. If the aim of education for those with hearing loss is to have them be fully functioning, happy and useful members of society, an active music education can be a tremendous help in promoting this. It is worth all the thousand times you have said and heard, "*Do you hear that?*" – "*Yes I hear that.*"

Literature

Birkenshaw-Fleming, Lois (2007²): *Music for All*. Van Nuys CA.

Birkenshaw-Fleming, Lois (2006⁴) *Music for Fun, Music for Learning*. Gilsum NH.

Estabrooks,Warren/Birkenshaw-Fleming, Lois (2006²): *Hear and Listen! Talk and Sing!* Alexander Graham Bell Association for the Deaf and the Hard of Hearing. Washington DC.

Estabrooks,Warren/Birkenshaw-Fleming, Lois (2003): *Songs for Listening! Songs for Life!* Alexander Graham Bell Association for the Deaf and the Hard of Hearing. Washington DC.

Estabrooks, Warren (Ed.) (1998): *Cochlear Implants for Kids*. Alexander Graham Bell Association for the Deaf and the Hard of Hearing. Washington DC.

Orff, Gertrud (1980): *The Orff Music Therapy*. Translation: Margaret Murray. London.

Contact and Development through Improvisation in Music Therapy

Kent Lykke Jensen

In music therapy sessions with children who are hard-of-hearing we have to think of music in a different way than we usually do. We can't use the conventional terms in music, because musical perception normally relies on the sense of hearing. We use music as therapy in a way, so the music is the primary factor in the experience in these sessions. Music is essential to the therapy, since it helps to provide the therapeutic goals and add meaning as well as a general direction to the therapy.

In the music-therapeutic work with hard-of-hearing children, the combination of music as therapy and music in therapy is very important on account of the extended perception that has to become effective. People with various degrees of hearing loss use the whole body as the "ear", and all the vibrations and music are perceived by different areas in the body. There is an area in music therapy known as "Vibro Acoustics", which is doing a lot of research work in this field, examining where we as humans perceive music and the vibrations originating from it.

With this fact in mind and broadening the scope of music, the context of music goes beyond that of merely notes and sounds. If we see music as the product of sound only, we can't work with hard-of-hearing children in a musical way. If we see music as a factor in a process, we have opened the door to the world of music and sound for the children with hearing problems. We give them the possibility to experience musical exhilaration, to feel music, to hear music on the terms of the individual child, and let them be a part of the world of music.

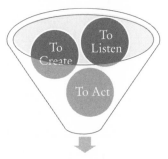

Music Therapy Process

Fig. 1: The 3 elements in music therapy; shows how we work by combining the possibilities to listen, to create and to act in music therapy (Kent Lykke Jensen 2007)

Why use music therapy?

The goal of using music therapy with children who have special needs is very clear. It's all about creating contact between the child and the therapist. Through music I try to create musical contact with the child. In music we create a space where the child and myself are present. We respond to the sounds we make, and we reach a level of communication in music. This communication creates and develops a calm and "safe" space for the child, where we have the possibilities to express what we feel. This happens in the areas of language, body, music and voice.

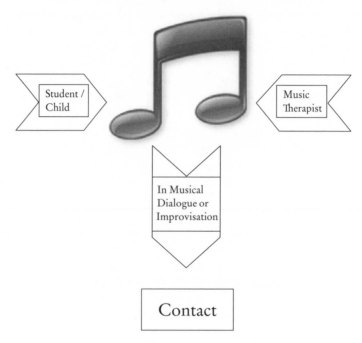

Fig. 2: Through music the child and therapist join a musical dialogue and establish contact (Kent Lykke Jensen 2007).

Improvisational music is a diffuse and complex topic to explain, if we don't clarify the borders of the topic. We can use music as an active part, and as a receptive part of the music therapy. In the active part, the child and the therapist participate in the improvisation. This means that we sing and make music together. We are active and expressive musicians. In the receptive part it is the music, which attempts to reach its goal, which in turn is the child. The media employed can be either a tape or a compact disc, or the music played by the therapist to and for the child. The specific direction of using improvisational music directly for the child is called receptive music therapy. These two examples of a music therapy approach in the work with children will be described in two short case studies.

The goals of music therapy differ according to the needs of the child, and are centred around the problem and type of disability we are working with. Depending on the specific situation of each child, we work with other groups of professional therapists to assess the child's needs and to decide what the work should concentrate on. Doing this we can prepare for the music therapy.

The main goal is to get the chance to "express yourself" in music. The rhythm, timbre, sound, timing, volume and intonation are the foundational elements for communication[1]. All human beings have these elements and have the possibility of using them. Our language uses these elements when we speak and speaking is a kind of musicality.

As music therapists we intend to use this knowledge in music therapy. Language is a big problem for many children; this is the case in the area of hearing loss but also in the area of children with autism. For children with autism, speech is a problem which makes it very hard to express needs and feelings. Therefore it is very important that the children are given the opportunity to develop these skills, so that later on in life they can use these skills in a given situation.

In the area of autism and deafness, there are many benefits of using music therapy. I have listed some of the areas which are used as primary goals and also as secondary goals for music therapy.
• Social training through musical activities (turn-taking and simple musical rules)
• Concentration exercises
• Musical Remembering (exercises that train the memory)
• Physical co-ordination, e. g. the physical co-ordination needed to play a drum set
• Training of language and stimulation of the speech, e. g. songs
• Higher levels of activity
• Training imagination and fantasy
• Training in the use of speech, e. g. learning how to speak in a proper way

For many of the children there is a kind of confidence in the knowledge of what is going to happen and when it is all going to end. In music therapy we use these methods, as I will describe in case study no. 1, but we also use the more unstructured and improvisational methods as I will describe in case study no. 2.

Both cases show the approach and the methods ensuring safe and secure parameters for the music therapy sessions from the beginning to the end of each session and throughout the whole therapy. There can be "structure" in the meeting, from the beginning to the end, or it can be "a free session", depending on the needs of

---

1   cf. Bonde et al. 2001

the child, the object of the therapy and the specific problem. The child *will never* be pushed towards the line where there is no safety and no response.

Music is very effective and, when dealing with autism, music is generally used in three domains. We use it as a means of improvisation as well as a method of dialogue and communication. Even if music is not presented or performed, we can all sing and play when we use music as a means of expression whether we have a disabilty or not. When we communicate with and through music, it is not necessary to make a verbal agreement about what we would like to express. We play it out freely. We improvise according to the specific feeling we are feeling right now and give it a specific sound. In music it is very "easy" to express exactly what our experience is. There is no need to put it into words. Words will turn the feeling and experience into an analytic object and therefore we isolate some of the musical elements and the musical expression is a new input.

Music goes beyond words and it leads to new developmental and empirical processes with the children, resulting in greater awareness and recognition. This process will be integrated and used later on in life in other similar situations. Music creates the frame of the therapy, where safeness and awareness is important, and where the qualitative contact between the therapist and the child is the aim.

Case Study No. 1: A nine year old boy who is hard-of-hearing. Among other disabilities, he was also diagnosed with autism.

I have worked with Robert in music therapy for 3 years. The first years it was as a group therapy, with four other students. Robert was very shy and sensitive to being touched or verbally addressed. Physical contact was impossible, and even sitting opposite one another was not possible. Not even the social workers and I as a music therapist were allowed to come close to him. Robert would only participate in the activities he could control. He was not open for new ideas or suggestions regarding his activities. Robert did not have a verbal language that was understandable, except for a few words. He knew a few lines from some traditional children's songs, and he sang them when he wanted to. It was impossible to squeeze anything out of him.

Since August 2004 we have focussed on the music therapy work with Robert in a concentrated form. This means that we have made a structured frame for Robert, containing a few elements that we know he likes. We have taken the few lines of the songs he hums, and put them together, so we can sing the songs he knows in the music therapy sessions. We repeat the sessions to produce a recognisable process for him. Every morning, for 15 minutes four times a week, Robert comes smiling to music therapy, climbing up onto the grand piano and sitting calmly and waiting to begin.

The frame for the music therapy session is very simple:
1. "Hello" song where we sing *hello* to Robert.

2. "Tickle me" song, where we sing about 2 people (*tickle me* and *tackle me*) who are riding on a bike. Suddenly *tackle me* falls off, and when I ask Robert who is left, he has to respond "*tickle me*".
3. *Row, row, row your boat*
4. Roberts's choice of a song
5. "Goodbye" song

This simple programme is the frame of the individual music therapy sessions with Robert. During the whole session Robert sits or lies on the top of the piano. The vibrations of my playing spread from the piano to the parts of Robert's body that are touching the piano. Just the fact that he accepts the vibrations is a good sign, considering that a year and a half ago he didn't want anything or anyone to touch him.

Robert joins in with the "Hello" song. He sings "we shall have music again". He knows this line is coming, and he knows that he can sing it, and therefore we end the singing when he has sung the line.

In the song of "tickle me" Robert knows he can decide when we have to tickle him. He builds up an expectation of the tickling and knows that he can make it happen. He can control the activity and the song, and he knows that we will respond to him, and there is contact and awareness focussed on him. We reach Robert with this amusing and playful song to get into physical contact with him, but remember he is in control of "when" the tickling happens. This creates a new situation to hold on to; he can wait up to one minute before he answers. Robert shows that he is confident with us and that he is responding to the musical activity. When working with Robert, the autonomy that he is granted is as important for the therapy as it is for himself. Robert is allowed to say "stop", and we stop. There would be no benefit in pushing Robert in any specific direction at this point of his therapy and on his current developmental level.

In the song *Row, row, row your boat*, once again we are allowed to establish physical contact with Robert. He shows us that he is rowing the boat and how high the waves of the sea are. He holds our hands while we sing.

Robert chooses to sing a song, and this is typically a children's song. Robert joins the singing at varying stages from session to session.

At the end we sing the "Goodbye" song to indicate that the therapy session is coming to an end.

The progress which Robert has made in the last year and a half is close to indescribable within the understanding of Robert's overall development. In the music therapy sessions we can communicate with Robert, we can hear that his language has improved, and that he is now using more and more verbal rhythm in his language. In the part "Robert's choice" he shows us that he is now able to pick one specific song when he is offered a choice of three. Robert is not as physically shy as at the beginning and he jumps onto the piano all by himself.

It is also important to say that the team working with Robert is very competent and professional, and that I, as a music therapist, am working together very closely with the different groups of professionals. Everybody involved benefits from the well-functioning interdisciplinary work. This also means that we have the chance to work in a more concentrated and focussed way with Robert, on the process and his overall development.

This case is an example of a highly structured music therapy, and a structure that Robert knows. He has confidence in the programme because he knows what we are going to do. The only part that varies is "Roberts Choice", where we encourage Robert to make a choice from different possibilities.

Case Study No. 2: Michael is a nine-year-old boy with mild hearing loss. Among other disabilities he has also been diagnosed with autism.

Michael is retarded and does not use language as a form of communication. Michael knows a few words, which he uses as his "mantra" and which give him confidence. He is directed by his impulses, with no consideration of the situation he is in, and he is very much in his "own world". Michael responds to music and it is possible to create "turn taking contact" with Michael in music.

A year and a half ago Michael avoided all types of contact. No eye contact, no physical contact, not even when we played clapping hands. No social contact at all. He always used his tongue to feel all the instruments which was not appropriate behaviour. Michael would run away if he had the chance. Not because he did not like the music therapy sessions, but because this was his typical behaviour.

In the first year of music therapy I tried to be very structured in the music therapy programme with Michael, proceeding similarly as described in case study no. 1. This structured form of music therapy, however, didn't help at all. Michael became more unconcentrated, and his facial expression and voice communicated absent-mindedness. At the end of this year I thought to myself: "Let go of all structure and behavioural analysis, and do whatever you are thinking of right now", and somehow I started to think of *Bananas in Pajamas*, the television series with B1 and B2[2]. I started to play the theme on the piano – and Michael at once stopped his movements and

---

2   B1 and B2 are the names of the banana characters in the BBC children's television series *Bananas in Pajamas*.

stood still. He looked at me sitting by the grand piano, and said "nanas in jamas". –
Yes! This was the way to reach Michael in music therapy. I had found my approach
to creating musical contact with Michael. In this case it was my intuition, when I
started to think of those two dancing bananas, and afterwards started to play the
theme. In the music therapy sessions we now use themes from *Teletubbies*, *Postman
Pat*, and a Danish television series called *The Bear Time of Sigurd*. Michael recognises all the themes, and when I stop playing the theme, he hums on until he reaches
a word in the lyrics he knows and he can articulate, which he sings out loudly. If I
don't start to play again he comes over to the piano and puts my hands on the piano
and says "more music – more music – come on – more music".

I have started to play classical music on the piano to Michael. Michael responds
very well to this. He lies down on the floor and looks straight up at the sky. It
seems to me that Michael feels safe in the situation, and he knows there is space and
room for him, and that his reaction to the music is respected. Michael also looks
inside the piano when I play. He likes to tease me by holding the dampers and
touching the strings on the piano. He laughs and says "air" – referring to the *Aire*
by Bach. I start to play the *Aire* and he responds by lying on the top of the piano
very calmly and looking at me and smiling. This is a response to a musical effect
that I find very important. Michael's high level of activity is directly related to the
music played to him.

I think that Michel is benefiting from the music therapy. In the music therapy sessions with Michael there is no structure, but I see Michael listening more intently and
with a greater awareness to what is going to happen. The only framework is provided
by the "Hello" and the "Goodbye" songs, which Michael knows by now and of
which he sings a few words, when he is ready to start and to end the session.

What we will work on in between these two songs, we only find out when we have
heard Michael's response to the musical material from the piano and the singing
and the sounds I make. The responses that Michael gives are verbal sounds, but also
some rhythms of his own played on the window, which I then respond to.

I have illustrated the general framework of the music therapy sessions in figure 3.

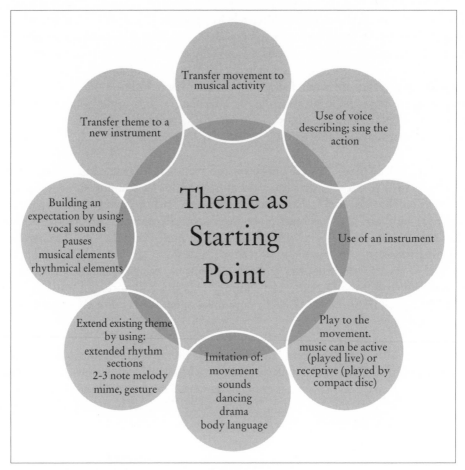

Fig. 3: The development of the theme in a musical improvisation (Kent Lykke Jensen 2007)

We seek a theme which we come across spontaneously depending on the situation. This can be a phrase from a song or a casual movement. From rhythm, timbre and sounds I start to work with Michael, within the musical frame (Fig. 4). Either together or separately we can move from the starting point to examine new possibilities in the musical interaction and in this way reach a common movement in the dialogue. When we have finished we can return to the starting point and our initial theme.

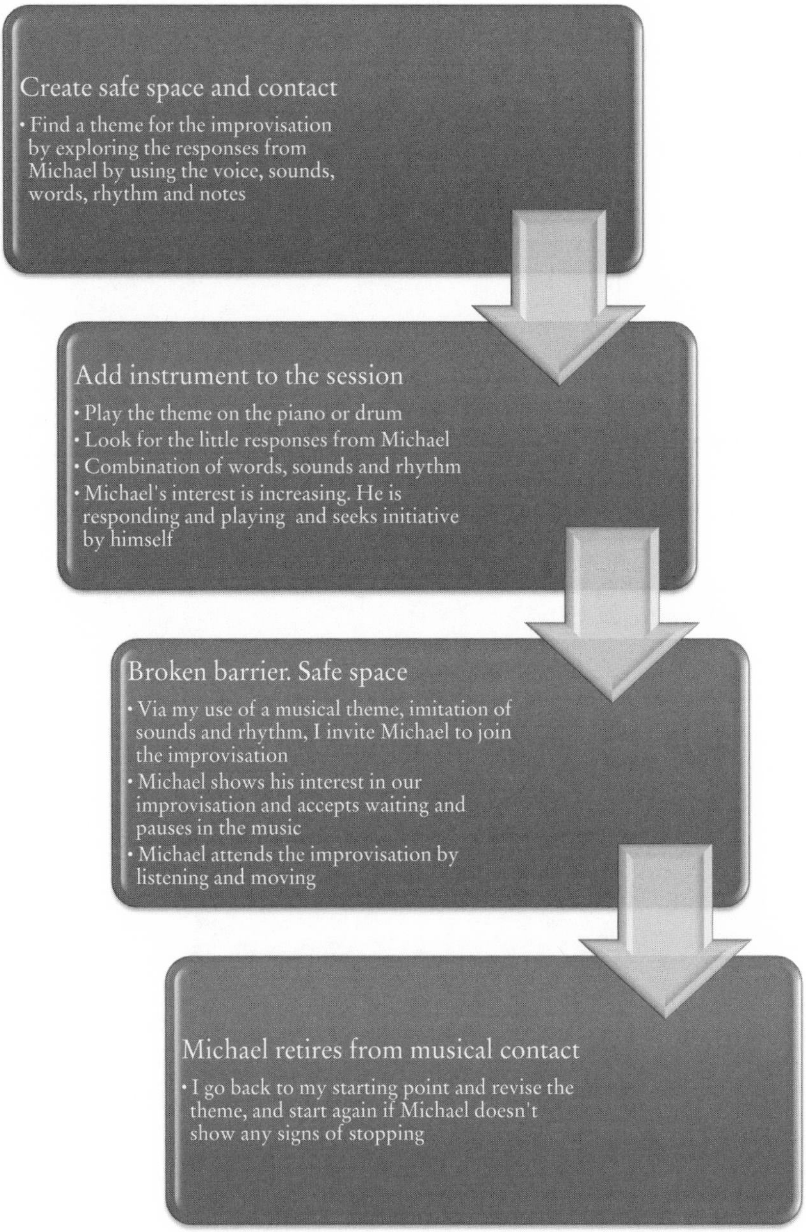

Create safe space and contact
- Find a theme for the improvisation by exploring the responses from Michael by using the voice, sounds, words, rhythm and notes

Add instrument to the session
- Play the theme on the piano or drum
- Look for the little responses from Michael
- Combination of words, sounds and rhythm
- Michael's interest is increasing. He is responding and playing and seeks initiative by himself

Broken barrier. Safe space
- Via my use of a musical theme, imitation of sounds and rhythm, I invite Michael to join the improvisation
- Michael shows his interest in our improvisation and accepts waiting and pauses in the music
- Michael attends the improvisation by listening and moving

Michael retires from musical contact
- I go back to my starting point and revise the theme, and start again if Michael doesn't show any signs of stopping

Fig. 4: (Kent Lykke Jensen 2007)

Finally, I can say from my experience that the children who come to music therapy, benefit from the activities. The development of all the children has taken a positive direction. It is not only the music therapy, but music therapy definitely contributes to the child's personal development. It is possible to establish contact, initiate personal development and begin to look at the process instead of the musical product. The children will later in their lives benefit from the experience they have gained in music therapy. In music therapy, we "feel" the music, we "hear" the music and we "play" the music.

So let's meet around the piano.

Literature

Bonde, Lars O./Nygaard, Inge/Wigram, Tony (2001): *Når Ord ikke Slår Til. En håndbog i Musikterapiens teori og praksis i Danmark.* [*When words are not enough. A handbook of Music Therapy Theory and Practice in Denmark.*]

Holck, Ulla/Nygaard, Inge/Hannibal, Niels (Ed.) (2003): *Musikterapi I Psykiatrien.* Aalborg Psykiatriske Sygehus – musikterapiklinikken. [*Music Therapy in the psychiatry Aalborg Psychiatric Hospital.*]

Dafolo, Nielsen (1998): *Det skrøbelige barnesind – en basis bog i børnepsykiatri.* [*The fragile children's mind – basic book in psychiatry of children.*]

Jensen, Kent Lykke (1998): *Musikalske aspekter.* In: *Døvblinde nyt.* [*Musical aspects.* In: *News for the Deafblind.*]

SiLaSo – Sign Language and Songs

Wolfgang Friedrich, Marion Honka

Students in Europe we work all alike,
We're signing and singing –
Sign Language and Song[1]

An idea and its transnational application within the framework of the European Union's Comenius Programme[2]

1. Development of the Project

Forerunner

"Opening Doors across Europe", our first Comenius project[3] from 2002 to 2005, introduced us to the practical experience of "looking beyond our noses". Co-oper-ation with the Uffington Primary School in England and the preparatory school El Real in Spain demonstrated the importance of allowing pupils and teachers to seek contact with other nations, as well as making it possible, as a school for hard-of-hearing children and youths, to experience an exchange with hearing pupils speak-ing different languages. With the use of various communication media such as pic-ture, script, art, video, language and signing, typical national events, daily routine as also traditions and customs became clear and descriptive. However, music and songs were, without doubt, the most attractive feature of each school visit in the respective partner country. In this moment rhythm, dance and movement lifted language barriers for even our hard-of-hearing pupils and content was imparted of its own accord.

New Structures at the Centre

"Hearing" and learning from our partner schools has introduced new structures to the Centre for the Hearing Impaired in Würzburg: On the basis of the "Assem-bly" in English schools, where the entire school community meets in an organised

---

1   from: *SiLaSong* 2006/07
2   *http://europa.eu/scadplus/leg/en/cha/c11082.htm*, 12/2007
3   *http://www.bezirk-unterfranken.de/aufgaben/schulen/kks/leistungen/schulen/gs/in-dex.html*, 12/2007

structure to exchange information, to sing together and celebrate, we have introduced a Monday morning meeting. All preparatory school pupils meet every Monday morning in order to exchange information, to announce forthcoming weekly events, to introduce projects and special happenings and to celebrate in case of birthdays or awards, using the English pattern as described above. The meeting is held within a framework of music with vocal support and appropriate sign language. The songs and the signs are self initiated by the pupils in joint co-operation.

Experiences from a Project in the Neighbourhood

The annual inter-school project known as "putting up the maypole" together with the neighbouring state primary school demonstrates the significance of the joint experience made by hearing and hard-of-hearing children with music, dance, movement and signing as unifying elements. The May song in simple language (cf. Friedrich, p. 239) with catchy melody, accompanied instrumentally and with sign language, is a musical act for every pupil, notwithstanding individual hearing potential, where each can directly and actively take part according to individual capacity.

Laying the Cornerstone for SiLaSo

Previous experiences gained from the first Comenius project, as described, the active conversion and implementation of a new community form at school as well as successful experiments with the annual "neighbourhood project" were the mosaic tiles from which the total picture began to emerge, thus engendering the requirement for its subsequent completion through "action".

Questions we asked ourselves:
- Would it not be possible, in spite of the national nature of each sign language, for a common, independently developed sign treasure trove to exist?
- Could a repertoire of songs be constructed from those already existent plus the newly composed?
- Is it possible to develop versatile, physically independent ways of expression?
- Would the production and subsequent application of digital audiovisual media for the immediate, uncomplicated and unlimited exchange of procedure results be successful?

The desire to acquire ideas, suggestions and concepts as to if and how songs and signs for hard-of-hearing children and youths in various other schools in different countries were applied, led, besides the already mentioned points of origin, to the conclusion that these questions should be answered by working on a new Comenius project.

Acquisition of Participating Partners

Acquiring suitable European partner schools in the field of education for deaf and hard-of-hearing children was at first more difficult than had been imagined. A tender, fed to the distributor engine in the search for any planned Comenius project, showed no results. An announcement on the web only produced an enquiry from a regular school in Turkey, but unfortunately from no other specific establishments for the hard-of-hearing. Again we were confronted with the usual questions:

• Are the aims of the project too high?
• Are the teachers and the pupils thus too challenged?
• Does the problem lie in the feasibility of linking song and manual expression?
• Is the obstruction to be found in the heterogeneous nature of the hard-of-hearing pupils and the consequential differences in communication?

Finally, through our later associated partners, we were able to make direct and personal contact with single educational centres for the hard-of-hearing in Europe. We were able to communicate directly and, as these exchanges progressed, it was possible to describe our plans which, in turn, aroused increasing interest.

At the first project planning meeting in Würzburg in January 2005, an according proposal was composed and submitted. Unfortunately this proposal received only 51 of the necessary 53 points and was refused, meaning we were unable to start. After a further meeting in Salzburg in the spring of 2006 "SiLaSo" was successfully authorised for the school year 2006/07 with the following partner schools and associated partners:

• Aalborgskolen, Specialskole (Aalborg, Denmark)[4]
• Dr.-Karl-Kroiss-School, Training Centre with emphasis on hearing (Würzburg, Germany)[5]
• County Institute for the Hearing Impaired, Josef-Rehrl-School for Deaf and Hard-of-Hearing Pupils (Salzburg, Austria)[6]

Representatives from the field of special needs education as well as from music education have presented themselves as associated partners for academic guidance and for the accomplishment of projects with students:

• Department for Music and Dance Education at the Orff Institute, Mozarteum University (Salzburg, Austria)[7]

---

4   http://www.aalborgskolen.dk, head of project: Kent Lykke Jensen
5   http://www.dr-karl-kroiss-schule.de, head of project: Wolfgang Friedrich, graduate Music Therapist, senior teacher for children with special needs
6   http://www.josef-rehrl-schule.salzburg.at, head of project: Katharina Ferner, graduate in Educational Science, teacher for children with special needs
7   http://www.moz.ac.at/department.php?nr=14010&lang=1, Mag. phil. Shirley Salmon B.A., P.G.C.E.

- Chair in Deaf and Hearing Impaired Pedagogy, Ludwig Maximilians University (Munich, Germany)[8]
- Chair in Musical Pedagogy, Julius Maximilians University (Würzburg, Germany)[9]

2. Basic Ideas and Targets of the Project

Schools participating in the project, work with hard-of-hearing children and, in the sense of reversed integration, also with hearing children. The development of every child's personality can be supported by a range of musical subjects offered at school. Music, movement and sign language are important means of communication and expression for our children.

The targets of this project are:
- Elaboration of a treasure trove of songs, repertoire of songs with signing
- Discovering the treasure trove of songs from the other schools
- Development of culture and care of shared songs for all participant countries

SiLaSo is to be understood as an experimental field. Not the necessity of scientific argumentation is at the centre but, rather the extensive range of collectable variety and the possibilities offered by musical activity within the context of school.

The desired consequences:
- Support in the development of the children's personality: motor skills, communication and expression
- Qualitative improvement of work at school: content and composition
- Influence on the school's cultural position
- Influence on the public's attitude towards the competence of sign language (sign language as a form of expression not as auxiliary support)
- Possibility for deaf and hearing persons to play music together
- Integrative co-operation between pupils (children with different abilities, needs and language)

The project as a whole is relevant to all grades as well as being interdisciplinary e. g. Monday Morning Circle or Project Weeks. The detailed elaboration of single project assignments, as well as the practise of treasure trove songs, mostly occurs within the individual class associations and the appertaining educational framework, mainly Rhythmic Musical Education (RME).

---

8   http://www.paed.uni-muenchen.de/~gsp/index, Prof. Dr. Annette Leonhardt
9   http://www.musikpaedagogik.uni-wuerzburg.de, Prof. Dr. Friedhelm Brusniak

Si-La-Song

SiLaSo-Team 2006/2007

2. Dansker' spiser fisk, Tysker' spiser pølse, Østrigere spiser Knödeln. Hvad spiser du?
   Dänen essen Fisch, Deutsche Weißwurst, Österreicher Knödel. Was isst du?

3. I Danmark har vi havet, Tyskland har en flod, Østrig har sø'er. Hvad kender du?
   In Dänemark gibt's ein Meer, in Deutschland einen Fluss, in Österreich Seen. Was kennst du?

4. I Danmark har vi slotte, Tyskland har en fæstning, Østrig har en borg. Hvad kender du?
   In Dänemark gibt's das Schloss, in Deutschland die Festung, in Österreich die Burg. Was kennst du?

5. I Danmark har vi måger, Tyskland har får, Østrig har kø'er. Hvad kender du?
   In Dänemark gibt es Möwen, in Deutschland Schafe, in Österreich Kühe. Was kennst du?

6. Danskere sir' „Farvel", Tyskere „Tschüss", Østrigere „baba". Hvad sir' du?
   Dänen sag'n „Farvel", Deutsche „Tschüss", Öst'rreicher „baba". Was sagst du?

Fig. 1: Si-La-Song

Students in Europe we work all alike, we're signing and singing, Sign Language and Song. (2x)

1. *(In) Denmark we say "Hej", in Germany "Hallo", in Austria "Servus".*
   What about you? – Students ...
2. *Danes like to eat fish, Germans like wurst, Austrians like dumplings.*
   What about you? – Students ...
3. *Denmark has sea, Germany has rivers, Austria has lakes. What about you?*
   – Students ...
4. *Denmark has castles, Germany too, Austria as well. What about you?*
   – Students ...
5. *Denmark has gulls, Germany has sheep, Austria has cows. What about you?*
   – Students ...
6. *Danes say "Favel", Germans say "Tschüss", Austrians say "Baba".*
   What about you? – Students ...

3. Pertinence to the Curriculum

In the curricula of German-speaking countries musical education for the children with hearing loss is often described as Rhythmic Musical Education. It should always be an integral part in the development of a child's entire personality. The basic requirements are movement and music, as well as voice and materials, later including instruments.

The Austrian curriculum stipulates that experience should be gained in the following fields:
- Sensitisation of perception
- Development of physical expression as well as increased physical experience
- Indoor and outdoor orientation
- Expression, flexibility, communication and interaction, fantasy and creativity

The targets are:
- Sensitisation of the senses
- Social learning and development of creative abilities
- Self-competence
- Stress equalisation regarding both individuals and groups
- Increase of awareness and memory potential through multi-functional processes

The Bavarian curriculum describes the following targets and will be discussed in the excerpts given below:
Educational emphasis is focussed on the encouragement of perception and active participation in music and movement. This includes independent composition, singing and playing music together, listening to music and movement to music,

drawing and drama. Rhythmic Musical Education includes education through music and education in music.

In the specialised curriculum for all grades and language study groups in primary and secondary schools five overall areas are stated: These areas are especially suited to the appropriate combination of different rhythmic musical interactive forms, as well as the experiences and interests of hard-of-hearing children.

Perceiving and Experiencing

Rhythmic Musical Education encourages the perception of both the personal as well as the objective environment, as well as self-awareness. This is performed through conscious awareness of self and others, by being part of contemporary events in time and space, through self-experience as an individual part of a whole and awareness of the group. Together with the support of visual, auditory and tactile perception, training of the sense of vibration is of utmost importance for hard-of-hearing children.

Rhythmic Musical Education supports the development of personality. The pupil experiences himself in an area of conflict between independence and assimilation. Within the rules and structures which he must conform to, he learns the possibilities of movement, action, discovery and decision. He must find an equation between existing prerequisites and own opportunities. The pupil takes on the responsibility for the success of a task and thus gains self-confidence, self-assuredness, decision-making as well as social competence.

Movement

In this area movement, as an elementary physical form of expression, is considered. The pupils discover and extend their own possibilities of movement, use their own creative imagination and experience enjoyment in movement and dance. Here the important task is to encourage a positive body relationship.

Hearing loss is often combined with dysfunction of the sense of balance as well as impairment of motor skills, with time and space orientation as well as body awareness. Movement experiences, modified both in quantity and quality, influence self-awareness and self-esteem and a sense of achievement dependent on physical movement. Movement and dance can reduce inhibitions, encourage differentiated perception and motor skills and strengthen physical awareness and self-esteem. The development of own body awareness permits the pupils to find new possibilities of making contact and communicating in the social area.

Speaking, Singing and Signing

Pupils explore manifold possibilities in playful contact with rhythmic elements, the ability to express themselves and communicate with voice, language, their entire body and by signing. The target is the promotion of individual ability through song, mimic, gesture, pantomime, body language and signing, as well as the appropriate speech and song training. Limitations occur due to the differing hearing and speaking capabilities of the pupils. Thus, for example, it is advisable to choose songs with a low pitch range and regular intervals, as well as short explicit texts which coincide with the pupils' range of words.

The pupils recognise the basic function of speech whilst listening, speaking and singing and whilst attempting own creations with mime, gesture, pantomime, body and sign language. These varied creative possibilities serve to ensure communication as they appeal to feelings, convey moods and needs as well as providing additional information on intended messages.

Playing Games and Making Music

When pupils play instruments the focal point is sound experience and active enjoyment of music. The pupils are first playfully introduced to instruments before they are taught how to use them and the relevant instrumental technique. Instrumental playing encourages more manifold and diverging perception; promotes body awareness and trains self-co-ordination as well as co-ordination when playing together with others. The pupils test and expand their sense of vibration and their individual acoustic impressions. The limited musical development of hard-of-hearing children often causes rhythmical hindrance; it means certain limitations when introducing them to melody and harmony can only be gently approached. Thus the choice of instruments is of utmost significance. Pupils must be addressed correctly according to their relevant development grade. Instruments have an own methodical-didactic place. They can be used as rhythm instruments, melody instruments and as harmony instruments. Playing instruments encourages and expands acoustic training.

Hearing, Exploring and Notating

Hard-of-hearing children should receive basic and continuing contact with multifarious sound material in order to construct and expand sound experience. Explorative sessions with instruments then help to familiarise these experiences which, in turn, leads to sound compositions. It is important to ensure a balance between impression and expression, which is an essential elemental of rhythmic musical education. Graphic notation records first attempts at composing and enables them to be repeated. Learning traditional notation is deepened when learning an instrument.

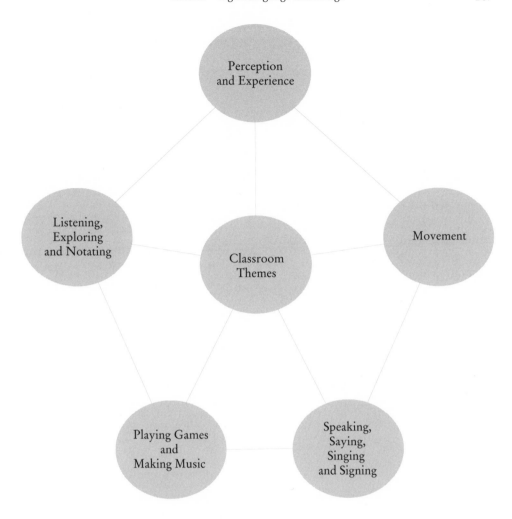

Fig. 2: Linking the areas of RME for all annual grade themes, in: Bavarian Curriculum for RME[10]

From the above depiction it can consequently be deduced that the incorporation of currently developing content and the targets of SiLaSo projects must be an integral part of school curricula.

_____

10 Excerpt from the special curriculum Rhythmic Musical Education for the primary and secondary schools of the Remedial Centre for Hearing Impairments, Munich 2007

Schule sind wir

Melodie: SiLaSo

Fig. 3: Schule sind wir (We are a school)

We are a school, we are a school, we are altogether here.
Children, teachers and assistants, parents, cleaners, everyone.

4. The Connection between Song and Sign

Accessing Various Musical and Communicative Approaches

Today the heterogeneity of school pupils, with reference to hearing capability, speech level and communicative participation, is basically a collective issue for the hard-of-hearing. This differing community of pupils (including those with Asperger autism) must be offered a common denominator where exchange, according to varying levels of expression, is permitted.

Experience from daily instruction shows that rhythm, music and song permit an enormously important access to verbal and non-verbal exchange as well as to empathetic commitment and relationship.

It was commonly agreed, at the beginning of the project, that the resulting (language) range was not to be seen as completed expertise offering individual pupils a detailed language and musical "special programme" but as an access and practical experience of the diverse contributions from pupils, revealing who, when, how and with which resources they could contend. Thus a procedure for all kinds of musical production was introduced with simultaneous verbal and manual accompaniment from a variety of possibilities: mimic, gesture, body language, verbal communication with accompanying sign language, pure signing, newly developed signing (drawing), up to and including sign poetry. An additional cornucopia exists when one considers what each individual country's language as well as its sign language can offer.

Development of Transnational Signing

In retrospect, and given the results of the first project year, the initial difficulties and misgivings accompanying the thought of combining German, Austrian and Danish song texts and signs were completely unfounded. A tentative approach using already existent songs and (most) simple welcoming songs (see Practical Intentions and Actions) was able to put pay to any reservations and motivated both pupils and teachers alike to adopt presentations common to the specific country, to integrate these in their daily school life or even to make further developments and perform this revised version to the partner country.

Whereby, there are no restrictions concerning the sole use of contemporary signs. On the contrary; the search for suitable signs which can either be in the context of the signs of each respective country or, on the other hand, individual artistic creations can be seen as the design of an "individual sign treasure trove". In this respect it was clearly seen that it was primarily due to school exchanges, where in situ songs, texts, signs and many new ideas were compiled, revised, practised and occasionally even rejected, that the ultimate version of a song was finally produced.

Finally it must be emphasised that the connection between song and sign can occur along different paths of access. The more usual way is the development of signs to songs; vice versa songs to signs is also possible.

5. Practical Intentions and Actions

An overview of former projects, as well as those planned for the future, depicted on charts (Project Calendar)

In 2006

- *A Welcoming song* with signs was composed. Signs for all the children's names were found and classes introduced to each other (pictures, photos etc.) Development of a new in songs in sign language e. g. *We are a school*.
- Participating teachers met in Aalborg to plan the project. A *SiLaSong* was developed and the criteria for evaluating the project were discussed.
- At the partner school meeting in Würzburg the new project submittal was compiled, project work exchanged and presented.
- The project week in Salzburg saw the exchange of teachers and the results were performed in public.
- The first video conference took place and there was a school visit in Aalborg. Here songs from other countries were presented and studied, the integration of songs in school events was discussed as well as the design of web site and the questionnaire to be used for the evaluation.

Further Actvities for 2008 Include

- The development of further sign songs in partner schools; elaboration and recording in digital form; exchange between partner classes
- Designing a file system on the SiLaSo homepage and elaboration of "welcoming songs"
- Teachers from the partner schools will meet in order to conduct a project week in Würzburg with workshops in musical theatre, sign poetry, rhythm and percussion, and songs.
- A project meeting in Aalborg for the children's congress and preparation of material – development of further sign songs in the partner schools, digital video recordings, and exchange between partner classes
- Developing children's songs and pop songs for the SiLaSo homepage
- Further education course "Music and the Hard-of-Hearing" in Salzburg
- Children's congress with workshops and presentation in Salzburg
- Evaluation and project meeting in Würzburg
- Development of further sign songs in partner schools, digital video recordings, exchange between partner classes

- Elaboration of the category Movement and Dance Songs and Poetry on the SiLaSo home page
- Start of the project "One World – One Sign" (model: "One World – One Voice")

In 2009 the Following Activities are Planned

- Development of further seasonal sign songs in partner schools, digital video recordings, exchange of partner classes
- Elaboration of category Seasonal Songs and songs in simple language
- Concert trip Salzburg to Würzburg
- Teacher exchange Würzburg-Aalborg to conduct musical workshops
- Joint final meeting for evaluation and reporting purposes

Together with current on site project work, two larger undertakings have been planned: The children's congress in June 2008 has scheduled meetings with groups of pupils from respective partner schools in Salzburg. There, in diverse workshops, SiLaSo songs and signs will be construed and practised, so that they may be used as an introduction for a subsequent concert trip (Spring 2009). This concert trip will exhibit SiLaSo repertoires performed by pupils and teachers for pupils, teachers, parents and further public.

Alluding to "One World – One Voice" a current project of a "special kind" has been targeted: "One World – One Sign". The idea is to interest musicians and artists to contribute work which then flows together to form a sign and music performance.

Building Blocks of Project Action

Actively involved in the project are currently the participating pupils and teachers of each partner school. Up to now parents have taken part in relevant project presentations and the first questionnaire submission. The associated partners of the universities and institutes lend scientific accompaniment and help to extend contacts. Experts (e. g. deaf native speakers) offer workshops during the project weeks and can lend support with signing queries.

All work results are exchanged between the participating partner schools via DVD, video conference and mail. As further significant contact medium for the results please see the respective homepage (http://www.silaso.eu). For improvement, expansion or alteration of the previous modus operandi a questionnaire was presented for the first time in the summer of 2007. Pupils, teachers and parents had the opportunity to submit reports on the previous development of the project.

The total project results will be outlined and in a final report with relevant analysis with the assistance of the accompanying project evaluation.

6. Prospects

As can be understood from the general outline for planned activities, the implementation of the accordingly planned project task is of primary importance. Both pupils and teachers are equally interested in the processing and implementation of the new content and in the work results of the relevant partner countries.

Moreover the initiation of the project represents an important factor for all participants. In spite of established partners from Denmark, Austria and Germany, an expansion in form of access for all those interested, from any branch of expertise or country, is targeted. By means of request for active participation and expansion of the existing repertoire, the reciprocal enrichment should bear fruit through the project. Not the insistence on previous own results rather the exchange over school and country borders should be the focus, as at the start of the project. The use of modern communication technology, i. e. internet, offers a realistic and practical basis for these schemes. Exchange via the (still under construction) internet portal with reciprocal networking, should invite interested persons and simplify contact establishment. Especially with regard to participating pupils, this communication platform can and should be used. In the long run, i. e. after the end of the official duration of the project, the existing interests and contacts should be pursued when possible in network form and thus on a more comprehensive and extended (country) level.

The SiLaSo team wishes you fun and enjoyment.

Part IV: Fields of Practice

The Significance of Music in Early Learning Programmes

Christine Kiffmann-Duller

Today, the application of music in audio pedagogical early learning is indisputable. Even though musical access may differ from family to family, either vocal or instrumental rendering, the use of sound appliances or the compilation of song texts, all have become an integral part of my work which aims to develop, consolidate and improve the communicative competence of partially hearing children. In my report, I intend to deliberate on the following points and thus connect theoretical basics with practical examples.

- Significance of music for children and their parent persons
- Development of hearing, discovery of language
- Development of "speech rhythm" as an important parameter for understandable language
- Influence of music on socio-emotional maturity
- Practical examples

Music has a different meaning for each individual. The simplest definition, as found in text books, describes music as a combination of tones[1]. However it is certainly very different whether in a musical work of art form and content merge to a harmonious total, be it a case of lullabies or nursery rhymes, military songs or marches, folk music or dance melodies. Hearing children experience a multitude of musical impressions and imbibe "moods" – different situations, accompanied by background music or musical presentations given in a special atmosphere. Let us not forget to make the world of music also accessible to children with partial hearing, so that it is right from the start a natural part of their daily routine.

It seems paradoxical: although we know that we do not actually hear with our ears, it is our ears that perform the first steps in the hearing procedure. Hearing is not the assimilation of sound occurrences performed by the inner ear, but rather the mental processing and evaluation of this sound information. Thus it is important to give partially hearing children 'musical brain food' in order to facilitate the accommodation and processing of 'musical qualities'. Joachim Ernst Berendt writes: "Hearing energises our brain. This happens because though our eye projects the picture it has absorbed onto the retina, i. e. only transfers the information relevant to this picture to the brain, the acoustic organ cannot produce a picture of what it

---

1   cf. Pahlen 1973, p. 8

has heard, it is forced to relay the entire information received to the brain. Here finally a sort of 'audio picture' materialises – an equivalent to what the eye in its visual field can already design on the retina. Thus hearing – the use of music in early learning – encourages thought processes."[2] Within the scope of early acoustic learning it is important to address the mechanisms of central speech analysis and infantile mental maturity[3] in order to understand the creation and maturation of brain structures – "primary growth orientation of nerve fibres, the development of myelin sheaths (myelinisation) around nerve tracts and the creation of synaptic connections and their stabilisation"[4]. The resulting recognition of speech is an achievement of the mature brain. This detail maturity needs external stimuli which, in their turn depend on intact processing performances. The neural networks necessary for this task must first be formed and then mature in their functioning. For this maturation of the human hearing system there are critical periods, so-called "time-frames", which can be effectively exploited by early audio pedagogical learning.

Rhythmical-musical work is concerned, amongst other, with the significance of prosody in speech[5]. In the discovery of language, prosody plays a paramount role. First children absorb the sound characteristics of a sentence, a word, and reproduce with mainly indistinct articulation. For this reason the melodious, rhythmically structured speech proposition for partially hearing children is of great importance. It gives them – with the support of efficient hearing aids, respectively after a cochlear implantation – the opportunity to assimilate speech, to discover speech structures. Antonius van Uden, the great Dutch educational scientist for the hard-of-hearing and the deaf had already established that "[...] A lack of rhythmical arrangement is an equally serious mistake (today I personally would say obstacle) as falsely articulated pronunciation. And not just because of the lack of comprehensibility, but rather more because of the memory for speech and the structure of language. A school for the deaf which ignores the rhythmical structuring of speech cannot be called a school using spoken language methods, even if they do teach the children to speak, because they disregard the most important aspect of spoken language."[6] Even though this statement was made some years ago, in my experience it has not lost its validity.

Feeling music and *hearing music* are differentiated on account of the way the way hard-of-hearing and deaf people perceive music. For those who have profound hearing loss tactile perception plays an important role. For the deaf "feeling music" is contact (e. g. physical contact with the floor, loudspeakers, balloons or dif-

---

2 Berendt 1996, p. 86
3 cf. Pearce 1994, p. 101ff.
4 Klinke, in: Leonhardt (Ed.) 1998, p. 83
5 cf. Uden 1980, p. 35
6 Uden 1980, p. 86

ferent types of drums) and resonance where body cavities (e. g. chest or stomach) oscillate and are thus able to perceive vibrations[7]. Children who are deaf or hard-of-hearing also like to sing – I have often witnessed this during my long years of work with them; they have the right to experience music. However the contents which we select and develop for these children must be carefully chosen and suited to individual needs. In recognising a potential in elemental music making and, by using rhythmical-musical tasks, we give deaf and hard-of-hearing children further opportunities to express themselves creatively.

Music effectively encourages character formation. Playing music together positively influences the development of a sense of community, of social behaviour and of psychomotor accomplishments, it builds dialogical performance, develops sensitivity towards others and increases concentration and endurance. In the development of young deaf or hard-of-hearing children music plays an important role in many regards: in the perception of the mother's melodious voice or the voice of other parent persons, in the evolvement of the feed-back cycle 'Production of Sound – Hearing – Reproduction', in the discovery of speech via prosody, in the development of listening carefully and intently, as well as in the socio-emotional development with the use of music, to name only a few aspects.

How do I incorporate music into audio-pedagogical learning? I would like to illustrate this topic with some examples from my practical experience.

Paul (1 year, 2 months) moderate deafness, equipped with two BTE (behind the ear) hearing aids since his fifth month, loves music. His mother comes from Bulgaria and equally has "music in her blood". Paul loves to be cradled by his mother and carried through the flat; an uncle from the mother's homeland began this ritual. Together with a (Bulgarian) lullaby this has become an integral part of Paul's advancement. With temporal (slower and faster) and dynamic (at once loud and then again very quiet) accentuation this game offers many possibilities of variation. As I myself cannot speak Bulgarian, I record the melody and then hum in accompaniment or sing "la, la, la". With this interaction the mother finds her own initiative and activity positively confirmed; whereby it is very important in early learning with babies to support parents in their natural interaction, to give them reassurance so that they learn to speak to their babies in a rhythmical sing-song even though reactions, at times, may take a while to become evident. A further focal point in the work with Paul's family is "stillness", in the stillness after waking Paul tries out his voice, in this stillness he can make new perceptions and (re)discover familiar experiences.

Victor (2 years, 6 months), profound deafness, lives with his deaf parents and hearing grandmother. Regular wearing of hearing aids was not a matter of course

---

7   cf. Salmon 2001, p. 65

at the beginning of our sessions. His musical experiences were few when we began his audio pedagogical early learning programme. In addition Victor was not used to obeying rules; the beginning and end of a game were unknown to him. Two examples of musical promotion brought special success: the use of a recorder for performing new songs to Victor as a means of demonstration and a sung question and answer game. The alto recorder made of bamboo – kept in a crocheted bag – soon became an integral part of the session with Victor. Always at different times I drew it from the bag or reached for it: "Victor, listen I am going to play something for you", was my usual introduction to the ritual. Victor sat beside me, sometimes in front of me on the table and showed little interest and even less patience to begin with, thus, at the beginning, my tunes were short: "Oh, the recorder is tired, it's going back to sleep. Bye, Bye!" I then said. It was my aim to make the beginning and the end of our game an event, to listen to and "practise" the progress of a game and each time to re-awaken Victor's interest. Soon the recorder became a concept; naturally Victor wanted to blow into it too. For this purpose I have small children's recorders, I am the only one who plays on my own recorder, again for some (partially hearing) children a new experience: I cannot have everything I want. Gradually with time my tunes became longer and Victor's patience in listening improved. For some time he had been able to say "…ired. Bye, Bye!" or he demanded, "… corder come". We were overjoyed when having devotedly listened Victor began to "sing" as my tune ended. Deaf parents, too, are interested in the musical advancement of their (hard-of-hearing) children, and are willing to cooperate as far as they can. I feel it is important to mention that I of course use sign language, if it is the main way to communicate in the family or the parents' wish. Very often sign language "opens the door" in a dialogue with the partially hearing children of deaf parents, the basis for the development of the spoken language as a second language.

Now to sung question-answer-games. Before I sing the first songs with the children, I use a singing voice in simple dialogue games. Speech gets a better accentuation and it is fun. Victor's grandmother helped me with this game: in a chest there are a multitude of toys which Victor can name. Each player packs three items into his bag whilst the others are not looking. Now the game starts: sung question, "Do you have a car?" Sung answer, "Yes (I have a car)!" or, "No, no, no!" When the answer is "yes" the player must return his play thing to the chest. Together with toys and everyday activities, the "audio training sounds" form the basis for hearing-orientated language acquirement in auditory-verbal development[8]. They offer the child the possibility to discover first sounds and sound combinations, to assimilate them and then to progress to active use. Also important here is the special observance of prosodic characteristics such as high/low, short/long, rhythm and intonation, so that not just sound but rather a tone pattern is offered.

---

8   cf. Winkelkötter 2005

Tanya (5 years, 4 months), deaf, both ears with cochlear implants (left ear when she was about 1 year old, right ear at the age of 3 years, 7 months) attends nursery school in her village. I am repeatedly surprised at the repertoire of songs that Tanya brings home from the nursery school. I can still remember the first pages of her song folder: "My boat, it rocks backwards and forwards, when the wind blows it rocks all the more ..." or "Sunshine in the garden, sunshine in the house. Sunshine I'll catch you and never let you go." At some point Tanya began to join in and then to sing alone. She liked to go to sleep listening to songs from a nursery school CD. As Tanya always aims at "top performance" I offer songs which bring tranquillity with texts to encourage thought. An example from the book *Mit Liedern in die Stille* (*With Songs towards Stillness*) by Dorothée Kreusch-Jacob[9]: "Fetch yellow from the sun and turquoise from the sea, fetch brown from the earth and fetch white from the snow. Close your eyes in order to see more. Come, regard it inwardly, and know you can really trust yourself." I find precisely the refrain of this song wonderful for (partially hearing) children in our time and age. I accompany this song on the guitar for Tanya and her brothers before we listen to it on the CD. The meditative songs together with the exercises promoting tranquillity which are suggested by Dorothée Kreusch-Jacob have proved very successful in my work with older children. It is certainly important for (partially hearing) children to understand the texts, respectively for them to understand the idea of the singing games.

Alfred (5 years, 6 months), severe deafness, first received hearing aids when he was 3 years, 6 months. After about six months I brought a small book of well-known children's songs with me when I visited the family. My first concern was to find out, which songs the mother was familiar with. Then every evening there was a good night song with the relevant pictures. After some weeks Alfred had already learned five different children's songs; he turned to the right page as I sung the popular Austrian songs with both small animal and human characters. The next step was to find instruments for the individual actors: a clapper for the ducks, the small drum for the rabbits, the triangle for the birds, a howl tube for the forest etc. and thus devised new sound stories. The songs from nursery school exceed Alfred's learning ability: so together with the nursery school teacher and the teacher for special needs we adapt one to two songs per theme. In this way it is possible to take advantage of the challenge within the group using simple singing games.

Work in audio pedagogical early learning and family care is done within the context of the family, this means if I take up the theme "music" in my work with the children, this happens only after an appropriate information transfer with the parents. Here, as has already been mentioned, individual access naturally differs greatly. There are parents for whom music plays an important role in everyday life,

---

9   Kreusch-Jacob 2000, p. 50

who themselves make music and play an instrument. There are also flats where, to begin with, the radio or television is always on. Based on the co-operation with the parents and our practical work together, I want to create an understanding and joy for the use of music. One of the most important targets in auditory verbal work with deaf and hard-of-hearing children is to make it possible for the child "to integrate hearing in his personality"[10]. The use of music supports this target in a variety of ways – as described in the practical examples.

Finally an aspect which, together with the employment of music in remedial education, still finds little regard. Joachim Ernst Berendt writes: "Could it be that the aim of all hearing is to listen to the inner voice? Let us listen to the German word *Gehorsam* (obedience). In the middle there is *Horchen* (listen). All the many interpretations which we give to the word *Gehorsam* in everyday language – to obey a head of the household, a church or a superior – are a misuse of what the word itself can mean: to obey yourself, to be obedient to your own self."[11]

By hearing and listening to music children develop an ability which is beneficial to obeying and listening – also within. A quality which is significant in the personal orientation of each individual and which I should like to summarise with the following words: "Pause for a moment and listen to your heart and then do – with joy – what is to be done."

Literature

Berendt, Joachim E. (1996): *Ich höre also bin ich*. In: Vogel, Thomas (Ed.): *Über das Hören*. Tübingen.

Klinke, Rainer (1998): *Hören lernen: Die Notwendigkeit frühkindlicher Hörerfahrungen*. In: Leonhardt, Annette (Ed.): *Ausbildung des Hörens – Erlernens des Sprechens*. Berlin.

Kreusch-Jacob, Dorothée (1996/2000): *Mit Liedern in die Stille*. Düsseldorf.

Löwe, Armin/Schmid-Giovannini, Susanna (1999): *Sprachfördernde Spiele für hörgeschädigte und für sprachentwicklungsgestörte Kinder*. Internationales Beratungszentrum Meggen. Lucerne.

Pahlen, Kurt (1973): *Mensch und Musik*. Munich.

Pearce, Joseph C. (1994): *Der nächste Schritt der Menschheit*. Freiburg.

---

10 Winkelkötter 2005
11 Berendt 1996, p. 85

Salmon, Shirley (2001): *Wege zum Dialog: Erfahrungen mit hörgeschädigten Kindern in integrativen Gruppen.* In: Salmon, Shirley/Schumacher, Karin (Ed.): *Symposion Musikalische Lebenshilfe. Die Bedeutung des Orff-Schulwerks für Musiktherapie, Sozial- und Integrationspädagogik.* Hamburg.

Uden, Antonius van (1980): *Das gehörlose Kind – Fragen seiner Entwicklung und Förderung.* In: *Hörgeschädigtenpädagogik*, Supplement Nr. 5. Heidelberg.

Wagner, Elisabeth (1992): *Quacki, der kleine freche Frosch.* Munich.

Winkelkötter, Elke M. (2005): *Auditiv-Verbale Therapie.* Workshop notes.

"Now I Can Hear the Grass Grow" – Orff Music Therapy with Children following Cochlear Implant

Regina Neuhäusel, Ursula Sutter, Insa Tjarks

Anna and Manuela[1] are two children who were born deaf. Their parents have decided to have an electronic hearing aid implanted. They want their children to grow up within the hearing world.
The children have different developmental conditions. Whereas Manuela shows no developmental problems, Anna has additional handicapping conditions. From the time of her birth, she had to have several operations due to organic malformations. Today, she shows clear signs of both motor and mental delays.
Both children were treated at the Kinderzentrum München during the two year period of rehabilitation following the operation.

The Kinderzentrum München, Germany's first centre for Social Paediatrics, was founded by Professor Theodor Hellbrügge and has been in operation for over 30 years. It consists of a specialised clinic (inpatient) and an outpatient department for Social Paediatrics and Developmental Rehabilitation. It provides social paediatric, multidisciplinary diagnostics, guidance, counselling and therapy for children with motor, mental and social-emotional developmental differences.

Children should be diagnosed and treated as soon as an imminent or manifest developmental difference is suspected. At the Kinderzentrum München, an interdisciplinary team of paediatricians, psychologists, therapists, nurses and teachers as well as counsellors and caregivers work together effectively in order to enable the child to reach the most autonomy and independence possible within his family and society.

CI-Rehabilitation at the Kinderzentrum München

An important area of emphasis in treatment at the Kinderzentrum München is the rehabilitation of children who have received a cochlear implant (CI). A special concept for the rehabilitation of these children was developed as early as 1990.

The Kinderzentrum München co-operates with different hospitals that are responsible for the implantation of the CI. The Kinderzentrum is included in the process of establishing the indication for the operation. Each child is examined by a paediatrician, a child audiologist and a developmental psychologist.

---

1   names changed (Ed.)

The operation in which the CI is implanted is performed only after the child has been examined, the parents counselled and the indication established. The rehabilitation process at the Kinderzentrum begins eight weeks after the operation has been performed. Relatively stable groups of four children come six times a year for a four-day inpatient treatment. All impressions and results are brought together within the interdisciplinary team in order to define the points of emphasis for therapy for each child.

In addition to adapting the programming of the speech processor, guidance and counselling by a speech therapist and a developmental psychologist as well as intensive speech therapy are included in the rehabilitation program. Furthermore, all children receive two sessions of group music therapy, carried out by two music therapists.

Music therapy was included as a therapeutic measure within this concept because it has proved to be useful for the following reasons:
1. Not only the adjustment of the processor is important after the children have been provided with a CI. Auditory stimulation should be initiated as soon as possible[2]. Instruments and materials for play are especially interesting and inviting and increase the child's willingness to use his newly gained ability to hear.
2. In addition to the auditory stimulation, the development of the children's communicative and social competencies should be prepared and built up. In music therapy, the child has the possibility to express himself at first through musical activity without the use of language. Since these activities always take place within a social situation, the children's communicative and social competencies can be stimulated and supported. The effectiveness of Orff Music Therapy in supporting preverbal communicative abilities has been demonstrated in a study by Plahl (2000).

Music therapy within a group has proved its worth. Social communication is dependent upon language to a large extent. Children with hearing problems often experience misunderstandings when interacting with others[3]. They therefore often feel isolated and exhibit problems in social behaviour which is frequently perceived as aggressive and aversive[4].

One area of emphasis in Orff Music Therapy is the area of social behaviour. Music therapy treatment can promote improvement in this field. The group setting enables the children to acquire competencies in social behaviour by observing each

---

2   Haus 2005, p. 224
3   Sarimski 1986, p. 60
4   Fengler 1990, p. 73

other, learning from each other and recognising and respecting one's own limitations and the limitations of others. These social competencies can form the basis on which further communicative abilities are developed.

In order to explain why Orff Music Therapy is especially suitable for children with hearing disabilities, we will describe the procedures used and illustrate these with case studies.

Principles of Orff Music Therapy

The music therapy approach that was developed by Gertrud Orff at the Kinderzentrum München is an active, multi-sensory approach. The child is viewed as a whole. This means that his physical, mental and emotional development as well as his family situation are taken into consideration. The characteristics of his development serve as a point of orientation for the establishment of indications and the formulation of goals for therapy. In turn, the indications and goals for therapy are adapted to the course of the child's development. Because of these factors, Orff Music Therapy is classified as developmental music therapy[5].

Orff Music Therapy shares its concept of music, the idea of spontaneous, creative music-making and the instrumentarium with Orff-Schulwerk. In both, music is described as *"musiké"*, a Greek term referring to the "total representation of humans in word, sound and movement"[6] which includes the idea of the unity of rhythm, melody, movement and language.

Creative, spontaneous music-making in Orff-Schulwerk creates a dimension of music for children, enabling them to express themselves, experience themselves as a person and to make music with others within a pedagogical situation. In Orff Music Therapy, the activities used should be so motivating that the child can act musically in the sense of *musiké* and take part in the activities. This enables communication to be established and development to be stimulated[7].

Orff Music Therapy is also a *multi-sensory* approach to therapy. The use of musical means – language, movement, melody and the handling of instruments – is organised in a way that engages all the senses. Play activities can combine sound with other sensory experiences (visual, tactile, kinaesthetic), enabling the children to process these simultaneously[8].

---

5   Voigt 2001, p. 242
6   Orff 1980, p. 9
7   Orff 1980
8   ibid.

An important characteristic of Orff Music Therapy is also the *interactive orientation* within its application. In developmental psychology this type of procedure is termed "responsive interaction". The therapist accepts the interests of the child and is willing to interact at his developmental level. She takes up on ideas that the child offers and helps him to develop these further. She observes the child sensitively and adapts her therapy procedures to the child's development. Gertrud Orff used the term *ISO* (Greek, meaning *like* or *similar*) to describe the behaviour of the therapist when she adapts her activity to the developmental situation of the child, thus encountering him at that level[9].

At the same time, the therapist challenges the child's developmental potential when she brings new stimuli or impulses to the therapy situation. These impulses are intended to recapture the child's attention and to give him possibilities to broaden his competencies. Orff used the word *provocation* (in the sense of the Latin word *provocare*, to call forth) to describe this behaviour of the therapist[10]. Because of this type of responsive procedure, the stimulation of communication and interaction form the central point of emphasis in therapy.

Indications, Goals and Procedures in Music Therapy within CI-Rehabilitation

Every decision regarding therapy is based on the results of thorough paediatric, neurological and developmental psychological diagnostics. The results of these diagnostics enable us to establish the child's developmental profile which shows us his individual strengths and weaknesses. For this reason, the developmental level of the child is continually assessed. Observations regarding auditory and language development play a central role in formulating goals for therapy. Additional developmental problems, for example in the areas of motor or cognitive development, have a strong influence on progress in the acquisition of language. Therefore the early diagnosis and assessment of additional developmental differences is very important.

One of the specialties of the Kinderzentrum München is the treatment of multiply handicapped children with hearing differences. Because of this, about one third of the children in CI-Rehabilitation have multiple handicaps or developmental differences.

Formerly, mostly older children between the ages of four and seven years received cochlear implants. Today most of the children we see are between the ages of one

---

9 Orff 1980/1989; Voigt 2001
10 ibid.

and four years. The emphasis for therapy with these young children is developing social interaction as a basis for developing communication through language. The list below is a compilation of important goals for therapy and examples of procedures in therapy.

Some goals for *improving social behaviour* are:
- Promoting attention behaviour
- Improving concentration and perseverance
- Development of co-operation and interaction/communication
- Development of group skills

Goals in the area of *stimulating the social aspects of language* are:
- Development of motivation to vocalise or to speak
- Development of dialogue behaviour, i. e. turn-taking
- Development of an understanding for signals, e. g. recognizing, understanding and carrying out the course of a game
- Development of imitation as an important prerequisite for learning language

The following practical strategies are necessary in order to pursue the goals listed above:
- Arousal of the child's initiative through active participation in play
- Development of mutual play sequences
- Development of turn-taking within play sequences
- Development of communicative activity within musical play

As we mentioned above in our description of Orff Music Therapy, our *method is interaction oriented*. The point of orientation is the social and communicative competencies that the child has. Our suggestions for musical activity are variable. They are always adapted with regard to the developmental level of the children and the specific possibilities for the group. We can divide these suggestions for musical activity into seven different areas:

1. Situation Songs and Traditional Songs

The course of a session is structured by a predetermined greeting song and a song used to close the session. These songs give the children two important points of orientation in the session, the beginning and the end.

Rondo form makes it possible to take up on ideas that the children have and integrate these in the musical activity along with repeated musical passages. Here an example: A song, such as *Komm wir wollen tanzen* (*Come, we want to dance*) by Gerda Bächli, can be varied in the B-section to include sound gestures that the children suggest. These gestures, even if they are expressed by chance, can be imitated and a song text can be added ("we're clapping, stamping, plashing" etc.). This type of activity can strengthen the motivation of the child to take part in what is going on. At the same time, the development of language comprehension can be supported by the simultaneous use of language, gestures and sound.

Situation songs can complete the auditory impression that results when instruments are played spontaneously and creatively by summarizing the activity being carried out using language.

Example from clinical practice: A child plays the lyre which is tuned to G-pentatonic. This can be accompanied by a sort of lullaby in 6/8-time with a text, e. g. "Anna is playing the lyre for me, eia, eia, eia".

2. Use of Spoken Verse

A verse which is spoken rhythmically, either a traditional verse (for example *Da hast ein' Taler*) or an improvised verse referring to the activity being carried out, catches the attention and rouses the motivation to experiment with the voice. At the same time, the structure of the verse makes it easy to repeat and challenges to speak along. Body instruments and sound gestures as well as accentuated performance on percussion instruments enable the speech rhythm of the verse to be experienced directly. This can reinforce the experience of sound.

3. Rhythmic Musical Movement

The unity of music, language and movement as Gertrud Orff wishes the term *musiké* to be understood is inherent in children. This can serve to support the development of sound perception when working with children with hearing differences. For example, the contrast between sound and silence can be mirrored through movement vs. no movement. On the other hand, a change in movement can lead to a change in sound or sound characteristics, such as tempo. Pitch can be expressed through the height of the body. The following example from clinical practice illustrates the use of rhythmic musical movement in this sense:

The children move freely in the room to a drum rhythm. A signal (the cymbal) interrupts the movement. In this activity, the rhythm that is heard must be transposed into walking or running, depending on the tempo of the rhythm played on the drum. At the same time, the signal to stand still (cymbal) must be heeded.

4. The Use of Instruments and Materials of Play in Free Improvisation

A unit in which the children interact with each other without the therapist's playing along is part of each session. This enables us to observe the children without being involved in play. At the same time, the children are able to interact with each other in a spontaneous way. For example, when two children play the piano together, they gradually begin to relate to one another, then to play together, to imitate and to enter into dialogue with each other.

We can also make interesting observations when the children play using additional materials in multi-sensory activities such as a tall tower holding glass marbles. At first, each child places marbles in the tower for himself. After a while, they begin to play together and a lively interaction takes place.

The children can experience their own competencies through their contact with others in these activities. They use the ability to bring their own ideas into the play situation and to assert themselves, but also the ability to accept and respect the ideas and the impetus of others. We can observe which strengths and weaknesses become apparent within these situations that challenge the social competencies of the children. On the basis of these observations we can develop strategies for further promotion of competence.

5. The Experience of Playing Solos

The inclusion of solo sequences within the play situation is important for the development of self-confidence as well as for the support of co-operation and the perception of the other members of the group. These activities present a challenge for the child. He is placed at the centre of attention during the solo section, which requires a certain amount of self-confidence. However, he must also give up this role and allow another child to have it, which requires that he perceive himself as a part of the group.

Example from clinical practice: A signal (the cymbal) is determined after playing together in a drum circle. When a child causes the signal to sound, he is allowed to play alone. When he plays the cymbal again, everyone plays together until another child takes on the role of the soloist by playing the cymbal.

6. Recognising Signals

An understanding of signals, verbal and nonverbal, is absolutely necessary for communication with others. Simple signal games are designed to achieve first conformities with the basic forms of communication.

Example from clinical practice: All children sit in a circle, each with a xylophone in front of him. One of the children sits on a stool behind the bass instrument. This child determines how the others are to play and signals the end of the improvisation by raising his mallets. Following this, places are changed so that each child has the possibility to set the signals as well as being required to recognise and follow these.

The form of a circle enables the children to observe and imitate each other. Through nonverbal interaction, the structure and rules for play can be understood and transposed into action quickly. In addition to building up an understanding for signals, these activities provide a possibility for supporting the children's social competencies.

7. Auditory Discrimination and Differentiation of Sounds

We often observe that children with hearing disorders experience difficulties in accepting offers, and that multiple stimuli are more than they can cope with. Since children with a CI must learn to hear, they must develop the ability to recognise the meanings of sounds and the differences between sounds.

We offer the children possibilities to take in noises and sounds in structured situations and to integrate these as a new experience. At first it is helpful to experience the stimuli through more than one sensory channel as described under the heading "rhythmic musical movement". The children are able to see what they hear in the actions of the other children and to express what they hear through movement.

It is more difficult to recognise sound stimuli without additional clues. The visual channel is "cut off" by closing the eyes, enhancing the stimulus and enabling the child to concentrate better on the new sound.

Two examples of games for auditory perception can illustrate this principle. In the game "cymbal over the head", all children sit in a circle and have their eyes closed. One child walks around the circle and stops behind one of the children, playing the cymbal above the second child's head. As soon as the second child hears the sound and recognises that the cymbal was played above his head, he opens his eyes. In the second game, two or three instruments are selected and played while the children have their eyes closed. Each child is to recognise the instrument that is played for him by naming it or pointing to it.

These activities must be adapted to the developmental characteristics of each child. The following case examples show how different the developmental levels of the children can be.

Case Example: Anna in CI-Rehabilitation October 2003–March 2005

Anna was provided with a CI in 2003. Two months later she took part in group music therapy for the first time in the course of her rehabilitation week. Anna was 2 years and 8 months old at this time and had a very complex case history. A multiple handicapping condition in the areas of motor, language and mental development was diagnosed in addition to a sensory hearing difference.

Anna vocalised constantly and in a stereotyped way during the first music therapy sessions. This behaviour could be observed whenever the CI was activated. She paused only when she heard strong, loud sound stimuli. For example, when the therapist played on the Big Bom® (the largest log drum), located at one side of the room, Anna was instantly alert and crawled to the instrument. She laid her hands on the corpus of the instrument in order to feel the vibration and tactile stimuli and was attentive at first but lost interest rather quickly.

Structured games in the group which included social signals (e. g. raising the arms to signal the end of the game) or that needed an understanding of the principle of cause and effect in order to be performed (e. g. removing balls from a drum by playing it thus making them bounce off) were too complex for her. She did not seem to understand the play sequences and principles. She showed little interest and was not motivated to become active herself. These games required too much of her.

She retreated from situations in which the children were playing together. She became fussy and either sought closeness to her mother or crawled to another instrument. Anna's mother supported her in such situations. She brought her back, sat her on her lap and sometimes guided her arms so that Anna could produce sound by playing with mallets. This way it was possible to briefly catch her attention time and time again.

Anna also showed little interest for contact with the other children in the group or for their activities. She seemed to be in "her own world".

Because of the problems described above, the following goals were formulated for music therapy with Anna:
- Support of auditory perception
- Support/development of interactive and communicative behaviours
- Development of group perception
- Preparation of language development

Since Anna could not cope with the group situation, additional individual music therapy sessions were provided. These were designed to foster her development through suggestions for play which were adapted to her developmental level. Here

Anna was distinctly more active from the beginning. While she showed little initiative in the group situation, in individual music therapy she chose instruments at times by pointing to the instrument she wanted.

She was very interested in the cymbal and explored it with great concentration during our play together. She played it from above and below with her hand, wanted to hold it herself and grasped the loop. She also used a mallet several times to produce sound.

Anna followed the course of very simple games. She observed me as I moved the cymbal upward, grasped the cymbal and showed signs of joy as I moved the cymbal downward. She smiled at me, made eye contact and was very communicative during this game. She experienced that she could influence what I did during this game.

During the course of rehabilitation, additional developmental progress could be observed within the group situation. A positive sequence of play on the bass drum occurred during the second year of her rehabilitation. The children and the therapist sat around the drum as Anna moved her hands slightly, laid them on the drum head and then pulled them away. The others picked up on this movement and used it as a signal for "stop". When Anna touched the drum head, the others played the drum. When she removed her hands, they paused. She followed the course of the activity, the opposites of sound and silence, and seemed to understand to a certain extent that she could influence the activity of the others.

During the last half year of her two year rehabilitation she seemed to be more open and alert in the group setting. She observed more and directed her gaze toward the group at times. She made eye contact with other children every so often and smiled at them. Sometimes she played the instruments herself. She was explorative when playing the piano and the guitar. For example, she played clusters on the piano and then pressed the keys with one finger. She strummed the guitar, stroked the strings lengthwise and knocked on the corpus of the instrument. She used a mallet several times to produce sound on the Big Bom® or the metallophone.

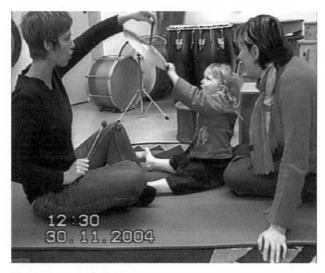

Fig. 1: Anna exploring

We could observe progress in the area of auditory perception as well. Anna reacted noticeably to the sound of the cymbal, raising her head as soon as the instrument was played.

The continuous vocalization hardly occurred at all. Anna's vocalizations accompanied her actions and began to be used communicatively as well.

Her motor skills also showed improvement. She walked when someone held her hand and enjoyed movement games. She imitated arm movements upward and downward during the dance *Komm wir wollen tanzen*. She seemed to take part happily and ran in place.

In summary, we could observe that Anna clearly profited from the CI. At the beginning of rehabilitation she was absorbed in herself, and the group situation was too much for her to cope with. At the end of therapy she showed interest in her environment and noticeably more readiness to interact and communicate. Music therapy certainly played a special part in these developments. Anna showed interest in sound and in tactile stimuli from the beginning. This made it possible to focus her attention and to win her interest for interactive play. At first she showed a short attention span which then became continually longer over time.

The emphasis of the work in the individual music therapy sessions was placed on the basis for social competencies. The goal here was to motivate her to act, to begin to develop simple interactive play sequences, to expand on these sequences and to lengthen her attention span. These single sessions were important for developing skills that made participation in the group possible. At the end of the period of re-habilitation, Anna was much more open in the group setting. She did not withdraw from the situation but seemed to be more independent. She seemed to perceive the group and showed interest for the suggestions for play as well as for the other children.

At the beginning of therapy she almost always vocalised monotonously as soon as the CI was turned on. Whereas her family was pleased at first when she began to vocalise, after a while these vocalisations became strenuous for them. At the end of therapy the vocalisations had changed and become more specific in the sense of communication. The work in the area of social competence affected her language competency positively.

Case Example: Manuela in CI-Rehabilitation March 1996–December 1997

Manuela received her cochlear implant at the age of two years and following sur-gery was at the Kinderzentrum München for seven inpatient stays between March of 1996 and December of 1997.

It soon became clear that Manuela needed a longer phase in which she observed be-fore participating actively and showing willingness to express herself nonverbally and verbally. She followed the first sessions while sitting on her mother's lap. We were not able to recognise any attempts to vocalise or experiment with her voice at the time. Neither could basic principles necessary for gaining language (show-ing behaviours pertaining to dialogue, understanding of signals, and imitation) be observed within the play situation.

After a short time it was apparent that Manuela was an intelligent child who quick-ly grasped situations visually. During the second stay at the clinic, three months after the first, she actively took part in the group session with three other children, followed the course of games and seemed to understand the rules of play. At this time she also began to produce vocal sounds when she felt she was not being ob-served.

The following goals for music therapy were established:
• Promotion of interaction between the child and objects
• Promotion of interaction between the child, adults and other children
• Development of the willingness to use auditory skills
• Support of the social aspects of language

At the age of not even three Manuela effortlessly remained alone in the group situ-ation, unaccompanied by her mother. She still needed slight support for certain ac-tivities (e. g. to show the way to play a barred instrument) at this time. She sought body contact to adults, which gave her the feeling of security. After six weeks of therapy Manuela showed a distinctly more lively temperament along with increasing independence and more activity.

Her first attempts to speak could be observed in music therapy, something that cannot be taken for granted. The use of instruments and structured games allow a great amount of nonverbal communication to take place. Since the necessity to speak is not emphasised in music therapy, we often observe that the children speak more in other therapies such as speech therapy. At the same time, it is interesting to observe that children with CI often let themselves be motivated to language communication in the relaxed situation provided in music therapy.

During one of her stays at the Kinderzentrum, Manuela's older sister attended the music therapy session with her. Anke[11] took up for Manuela, making the very correct and supportive family structure visible. At times she did many things for Manuela, but she also gave her much security.

Manuela skipped one therapy phase, which made her progress in language and independence even more obvious during her next stay. She remembered the structures of the games over a period of half a year and could recall these in the correct situation.

Her self-confidence grew during the last two inpatient stays. She was well integrated in the group even when its constellation was changed, and she was able to express her wishes distinctly. She showed the ability to assert herself – for example, she showed initiative and demanded that she be the first to play the cymbal held over the head of another. Other children in the group were more hesitant to do this. At this point in time she spoke single words and answered in three-word sentences such as "I have blue!", referring to the colour of her mallets. She also determined the colour of her own mallets more often than the others when she was allowed to announce a colour.

Manuela later received a second CI device in the other ear in order to improve sound localization and language perception. The speech therapy following this operation was not performed at the Kinderzentrum München. We saw Manuela again at the age of ten. She had learned to speak so well that her speech hardly differed from that of children with regular hearing. Naturally she oriented herself to the movement of the speaker's mouth. This gave her more security.

Manuela is now in the fifth year of grammar school and has been playing the piano for three years. Music therapy was initiated again at this age in order to improve her singing voice. At first she found it difficult to grasp the melodic contour, but

---

11 name changed (Ed.)

by accompanying the melody, by singing for the therapist and through the weekly exercises she showed progress in singing alone. During the last therapy sessions, part singing was practiced (e. g. by singing in canon). Manuela has shown progress in her ability to stay on pitch, to differentiate between small intervals and to use her singing voice during this period of therapy. She has learned to remember the melody by playing it on the piano before she reproduces it with her voice. Additionally, she has begun to rely more upon her hearing and to experiment with her voice.

In summary we can observe that Manuela is a child who has profited greatly from the CI. On the one hand, she is well integrated in the world of the hearing. She can participate in conversations in everyday life, including using the telephone, and she is very self-confident in her use of language. The fact that Manuela showed no additional developmental disorders coupled with the support she received from her family were important factors influencing her positive development.

On the other hand she has developed the ability to sing melodies. Hearing with a CI has limitations because the small number of electrodes in the implant cannot correspond to the natural ability of the inner ear to make the perception of sound possible. It is very difficult for someone who uses a CI to perceive, differentiate and reproduce the fine nuances of vocal intonation.

Summary

The effects of an early implantation and subsequent support and stimulation on the development of the children and their social environment are illustrated through the courses of therapy with Anna and Manuela. The children began their rehabilitation following the implantation of the CI with very different starting conditions. The development of their communicative abilities corresponded to their individual developmental levels. Anna developed basic competencies such as focussing attention and the development of interest in communicating with others. Manuela's language development proceeded almost like that of a child her age without a hearing difference.

Gertrud Orff wrote, "Orff Music Therapy can fortify other forms of therapy when it is intelligently co-ordinated with them"[12]. Along with the technical care and intensive speech therapy, music therapy contributes to stimulating auditory perception while simultaneously supporting the development of social and communicative competencies in the children. It offers the children with CI possibilities to develop relationships through musical interaction. In order to achieve these goals, it is absolutely necessary to adapt procedures to the course of development of each

---

12 Orff 1980, p. 9

child. Only in this way can the most social awareness possible be developed, enabling an increase in communicative behaviours which form an important foundation of early language development. These experiences show that music therapy is an essential component in the rehabilitation concept for children with CI at the Kinderzentrum München.

Literature

Alvin, Juliette (1998): *Musik und Musiktherapie für behinderte und autistische Kinder*. Stuttgart.

Bächli, Gerda (1985): *Zirkus Zottelbär*. In: *Schwingungen*, Nr. 3. Zurich.

Fengler, Jörg (1990): *Hörgeschädigte Menschen. Beratung, Therapie und Selbsthilfe*. Stuttgart.

Haus, Reiner (2005): *Hört mal wie die Carmen spielt ... – Musiktherapie für hörgeschädigte Kinder*. In: Plahl, Christine/Koch-Temming, Hedwig (Ed.): *Musiktherapie mit* Kindern. *Grundlagen – Methoden – Praxisfelder*. Bern, 222–232.

Orff, Gertrud (1980): *The Orff Music Therapy*. Translation: Margaret Murray. London.

Orff, Gertrud (1989): *Key Concepts in the Orff Music Therapy*. Translation: Jeremy Day and Shirley Salmon. London.

Plahl, Christine (2000): *Entwicklung fördern durch Musik, Evaluation musiktherapeutischer Behandlung*. Münster.

Sarimski, Klaus (1986): *Interaktion mit Kleinkindern. Entwicklung und Störung früher Interaktionsprozesse*. Munich.

Voigt, Melanie (2001): *Musiktherapie nach Gertrud Orff. Eine entwicklungsorientierte Musiktherapie*. In: Decker-Voigt, Hans-Helmut (Ed.): *Schulen der Musiktherapie*. Munich, 242–262.

Music and Language – an Impulse Project for Families with Deaf and Hard-of-Hearing Children

Katharina Ferner, Ulrike Stelzhammer-Reichhardt

"Music is a language beyond words, it is universal. It is the most beautiful form of art that exists, it has the power to virtually set the human body vibrating ... This happens inside the body. It is sounds that begin to dance. Like the flames of an open fire. They rhythmically grow big and small, faster and slower. (...) vibrations, emotions, colours in a magical rhythm." [1]

"The human being is incomplete without music ... " [2]

Completeness, wholeness and development of the total personality – the project "Music and Language" was organized several times in Salzburg based on these fundamental concepts. Over the course of many years approximately ten families with hard-of-hearing children spent a week each summer at Salzburg's Regional Institute for the Hearing Impaired. The objective of these weeks was to provide new motivation for these families in a generally speaking stressful period of their lives. Incentives to relax, to focus on the quality of the relationships within their families and to learn to communicate with the hard-of-hearing child were provided for. Music served as the medium of communication.

This project was developed as a consequence of a certain helplessness: therapeutic and medical concepts can represent an unnecessary burden when the concepts become more important than the personal relationship. This experience has been made at least by most parents and children affected by a diagnosis of hearing impairment. A few common examples: "If your child uses sign language it won't learn to speak." "The child must articulate clearly." "One must practise with the child." "If the child receives an implant, it will be able to hear normally." "Don't let the child read your lips to ensure that it has to concentrate on listening."

It had become more than apparent that an urgent need existed to develop a holistic methodology for the education of the hard-of-hearing. Thus, this project came into existence, the theoretical background of which will be treated in the following discussion. The pictures should provide an impression of the practical work involved.

---

1 Laborit, Emmanuelle 1995, pp. 24–25; French actress who was born deaf (Ed.)
2 Kodály, Zoltan cited in Kreusch-Jacob 1999, p. 8

This Incentive Week served as a chance to retreat, an opportunity for rest and rejuvenation, in which experimentation and communication with other families dealing with hearing impairment could take place. Early intervention teachers also attended the event and from the observations they made during this time developed long-term goals for their continued work with these families. The programme was multifaceted in keeping with the holistic objective. An interdisciplinary team offered a diverse selection of activities, ranging from those focussing on physiotherapy, occupational therapy, logopaedics and sign language to circus-workshops or the making of instruments. No ready-made therapeutic concepts were promoted, but much rather individual approaches based on the specific needs of the family and the child were drawn into consideration. The primary and unifying aspect throughout the entire event remained the use of music.

Music appeals to all of the senses. It should not be considered irreconcilable with deafness, since there are diverse approaches to music and it cannot only be heard, but also felt. One can communicate through music. Every year child-oriented themes were incorporated into the programme, such as the circus, tortoises, horses or the elements, each of which were presented both verbally and musically in every possible way.

Fig. 1: Moving like a horse

The central aspects were listening to music, feeling it and transforming it into movement, thus expressing oneself. To meet these requirements we developed rituals and recurring musical elements that were expanded upon daily and provided space for individual presentation. We decided the approach to music should be as multifaceted as possible, including the use of text, rhythm, melody or dance.

The Family Situation as the Departure Point for Further Considerations

When working with hard-of-hearing children and their parents, the same themes recur again and again. The parents experience an entire scale of emotions during the diagnostic phase including feelings such as anger, sadness, helplessness and/or the loss of orientation in everyday life. Suddenly there is a child in the family with whom the other family members cannot communicate as easily as before. The parents often have a wearisome trial ahead of them in terms of medical and technical care for their child. They have to decide on various therapeutic concepts e. g. verbal auditory training, the use of sign language or surgical intervention. There are a lot of questions and fears that need to be addressed:

- How does my child hear (with and without a hearing aid)?
- It can't be true./It can't be that bad.
- Will my child be able to speak? How?
- How can I be fair to all members of the family? Won't others feel neglected?
- How can I communicate with my child?
- Can we develop a healthy relationship?[3]

The parents of hard-of-hearing children (especially parents with intact hearing) suffer under very high expectations. They are made responsible or make themselves responsible for the success of their child and its ability to speak. There is the danger that the development of the child will be judged based on measurable success exclusively. Manfred Hintermair describes this as "rolling up one's sleeves against the handicap (and often unknowingly thereby against the child)"[4].

Deafness is an exceptional circumstance for the development of the first relationship, especially for the development of language – and the development of language, in turn, from the very beginning corresponds with the development of relationships.

In his book *Mit der Hörschädigung leben* (*Living with Hearing Impairment*), Herbert Ding addresses the most common questions posed by parents. He recommends that parents rely on their own competencies: "But you must be aware that you are not helpless. You will learn to adjust to the new situation. You will more clearly understand what the effects of a hearing impairment are, and will learn to evaluate the difficulties correctly. You will get better at coming to terms with it, and will come to understand that you can overcome the challenges that it presents."[5]

---

3   cf. Ding 1995
4   Hintermair 1997, p. 27
5   Ding 1995, p. 11

Herbert Ding and Manfred Hintermair reconfirm the conclusions we have come to in the course of our own practical experience:

- Working with hard-of-hearing child is at the same time working with their entire family.
- The basis of all work is a child that is accepted.
- Language is communication.

Communication within the family is a decisive factor for the healthy development of the child's personality. The child is never responsible for "how" the family members communicate, but much rather the parents are. Expressing emotions is important for the development of the child's self-esteem. This does not always have to entail words, but the assurance from the parents' side that they love their child as it is. If an uncomplicated method of communication with the child is not granted from the outset, parents need to be educated and to learn from the experience of others who have been affected. At this point the responsibility of the therapist in charge ultimately begins to engage with the child's communicative environment: Which forms of communication are available? Which concepts are the parents pursuing? Do the parents even want to follow the advice offered by the doctors and therapists? Which questions remain unanswered? Which contacts could prove helpful? Who can support the family in its social network?

The main idea underlying this project is to offer the parents relaxation and new insights during this period, as well as the chance to consult other parents of hard-of-hearing children. With this in mind, it is important to remember that our work can only be beneficial when the challenge of successful communication is met.

About Project Work as a Method – or: Why We Decided on Project Work

Projects promote autonomous learning and action. The participants must accept individual responsibility. There is no ready-made programme that guarantees improvement, but rather a broad pallet of opportunities to select from and make use of. It is very likely that such work entails the development of creative and individual problem-solving strategies. What each individual puts in and gets out of this method, is their own responsibility. (Every year, for instance, a sign language course is offered. For many families this provides the first contact with the language of the deaf. For the first time they can observe how their hard-of-hearing children react to it. With some families this experience is decisive in helping them to tread new paths.) Project leaders assist in organising and providing relief. The exchange (e. g. of parents among each other) is an important element which, while needing coordination, often takes place in a very free environment. General communication competence skills are also trained.

Fig. 2: Table drum

The role of the teachers and therapists changes from group leader to co-ordinator and supervisor. The co-operating partners' fields of competence must be transparent and clearly defined.

From an organisational and developmental point of view working on a project provides for the further development of content and organisation: identifying ideas, reflecting on them, testing them, abandoning or realising them. Due to the fact that the project "Music and Language" was repeated several times, it experienced a number of changes and adaptations. The parents' feedback, for example, led to an extension of the programme in the field of physical coordination (riding, occupational therapy etc.).

About the Objectives and the Interdisciplinary Range of Possibilities

The definition of objectives for the project was developed partially from our own practical teaching experience in logopaedics and from the music and movement therapy instruction for small children with hearing impairments. In addition the conceptual decisions were influenced by various approaches discussed in renowned works of research literature, whose authors – teachers and therapists – can all look back on years of experience in working with hard-of-hearing children. From these various sources and concepts (as will be described below), as well as from the considerations concerning the individual family situation of the hard-of-hearing child, we developed the following objectives:

For one week in summer, families should make use of the opportunity in the framework of an impulse-project to

- Exchange experiences with the parents of other hard-of-hearing children
- Be "relieved" of stress (children are supervised so that parents can talk to others in peace or simply have a few hours to themselves)
- Take part in a musical form of language instruction (for hard-of-hearing children) and to receive new suggestions for everyday life at home
- Provide siblings of hard-of-hearing children with their own event in the programme, in which they are at the centre of attention and have time to recognise their own wants and needs
- Learn sign language in the framework of a sign language workshop and be able to observe how deaf people can communicate freely among themselves
- Work creatively with the entire family
- Openly discuss with the parents of older hard-of-hearing children who have technological hearing assistance (conventional hearing aid or cochlear implant)
- Discuss with deaf adults
- Undergo a physiotherapeutic monitoring with the objective of complete relaxation and/or the identification of physical blockades (for parents only)
- Receive a logopaedic assessment in which the pattern of communication and the level of language development are focussed on
- Receive an occupational therapeutic diagnosis for hard-of-hearing children
- Receive psychotherapeutic supervision for parents in both group and individual discussions. This is done to encourage the identification of problems as well as the search for possible solutions.

Therapists and teachers from various disciplines work together to achieve our goals. In the mutual planning phase, the specialised objectives of the individual disciplines are designed to work together synergetically.

- Language therapist: stimulating language through music for hard-of-hearing children
- Music and movement teacher: musical instruction of children as well as the entire family
- Speech therapist: video analysis of interaction between the parents and their hard-of-hearing child as well as counselling
- Early learning specialist: link between the individual discipline and the families
- Occupational therapist: diagnosis and counselling
- Physiotherapist: relaxation for the parents, identification of tensions, counselling
- Psychotherapist: individual and group discussions about "new situations of living"
- Sign language teacher: first contact with Deaf culture and introduction of the basic terms in sign language

- Special education teacher (if demanded): individual care of severely and multiply handicapped children
- Interns from the Institute for Pre-School Pedagogy: support of the parents in their child-care duties, taking strain off them, helping them to relax
- Depending on the current programme – a drama teacher, play therapist, riding teacher, instrument maker: working with the entire family
- Guests in the evening for round table discussions: deaf adults, experienced parents (with intact hearing) of hard-of-hearing children, lecturers from various disciplines (e. g. occupational therapy, psychology etc.)

Music and Language – Backgrounds

Music is language. Speech is communication. Communication leads to and supports relationships. This is a realm of challenges for the work of speech therapists as well as music and movement teachers. The backgrounds and theoretical approaches of our work will be highlighted and discussed in the following section. After a few fundamental considerations on the development of hearing and its meaning in the context of hearing impairment, we would like to introduce the teachers and therapists who have most significantly influenced our work.

Hearing development, for both the hearing as well as the hard-of-hearing, begins in the mother's womb. According to Tomatis (ear, nose and throat specialist, professor for audio-psycho-phonology in Paris) hearing in the womb is a holistic experience: the spinal vertebrae serves as a vibrating tendon between the larynx and the pelvis. The pelvis serves as the resonance chamber. Hearing takes place through the bones in a huge sounding chamber[6].

During the evolutionary process the hearing organ developed from the organ of equilibrium. Robert Jourdain describes the development of the first hearing creatures, namely fish, which first were able to sense the movement of the water only, and in the course of their development came to be able to perceive sound through hair follicle motion[7]. The perception of sound is actually nothing else than a refined form of experiencing pressure change. We have all made the experience of feeling a sound in such a way that we are incapable of distinguishing between hearing and feeling the sound.

This fact encourages us to contemplate the usefulness of the tactile senses for people with hearing impairments. It also motivates us time and time again to transform music into movement.

---

6   Kreusch-Jacob 1999, p. 13
7   cf. Jourdain 1998, p. 35

Experiences gained in free chamber audiometric sessions reflect what children already learn in the wombs of their mothers: they can recognise their mothers' voices better! When the mother sits behind the child and produces sounds, this often results in a better audiogram than when other sources of sound are involved – a phenomenon repeatedly observed over many years by an audiologist in Salzburg during the course of his practice. When working with young children, this effect is particularly striking.

The unimpaired hearing and musical development of the human being develops in various stages: newborn babies can differentiate between tones of different frequencies a mere month after their birth. At the age of six months, babies react to a change in the melody (meaning it has learned to analyse the intervals). The vocal production of the infant child indicates musicality. The child creates notes. Children reproduce the melodies they hear from their mother as early as two months after birth! Between the twelfth and eighteenth month, the child lengthens vowels in a musical manner. It also begins with the first recognisable words, and clearly begins to sing. Initially, the child lacks the feeling for maintaining the harmonic unity within the melody. Already at the age of three years children first begin to reproduce the music of their culture: they develop a sense for tonal intervals and timing[8].

The sing-song, which adults automatically adapt when talking to babies, lyrical melodies, short children's rhymes etc. are the unconsciously produced equivalent to our musical development. Even the observation of what children enjoy, of what appeals to them, gives an indication of their stage of development at any given time. If we withhold this sphere of influence from hard-of-hearing child, we deny them an important and healthy constituent in the development of their personality.

---

8   Jourdain 1998, p. 90ff.

Deaf musicians confirm that deaf and hard-of-hearing individuals also experience a development of their musical sensibility. The well-known percussionist Evelyn Glennie describes numerous multifaceted approaches to music: she has spent considerable time learning to feel sounds. She feels deep sounds in her legs and high sounds in her chest and face. She also describes her approach to imagery: "We can also see items move and vibrate. If Evelyn sees […] the leaves of a tree moving in the wind then subconsciously her brain creates a corresponding sound."[9]

To evoke and express what is in us (images, rhythms, melodies, movements) is the task of musical and linguistic advancement. This applies to deaf and hard-of-hearing children alike.

Fig. 3: Feeling the music

Theoretical Approach

Stefan Koelsch

is a musician and psychologist who studies the processing of music and language in the brain. Recent brain research has done away with the theory that language is processed primarily in the left hemisphere of the brain and music in the right hemisphere. This research justifies every practical application that has been intuitively recognised and utilised: finger games, rhymes, children's songs, lyric melodies etc.[10]

There is a very close connection between music and language. The brain uses the same area, mirrored in both hemispheres, and the same processing rules are at work. "It is not to be underestimated that the melodic nature of singing or speaking is […] the prerequisite for language acquisition: long before a child understands the meaning of a sentence, it recognises the cohesiveness of syntactical units – based on the melody of the sentence and pauses."[11]

A hearing baby learns over 90 % of the words from of a tapestry of sounds, uttered in a lengthy act of cohesive speech. Only about 10 % of words are learned in an isolated form without any context. The brain works constantly by comparing the new with the already familiar[12]. The same developmental steps are also valid for music.

---

9 Glennie 2007
10 cf. Koelsch 2000
11 Broschart/Tentrup 2003, p. 79
12 cf. Goebel 2003, p. 39

Claus Bang

looks back on a long career as a music therapist for hard-of-hearing children at the Aalborgskolen in Denmark. The similarities of music and language are used to improve and develop the typically underdeveloped speech of hard-of-hearing children. Claus Bang also works with chime bars that he places either before or on the child and then causes to resonate. (Contact vibration or good resonance is created also without contact.) The remaining hearing capacity that still exists is activated by sounds in combination with their corresponding vibrations. The following improvements can be achieved with the chime bars:

- Tone of voice and frequency can be modulated in spontaneous speech production
- Acoustic improvement of the vowels and support of articulation processes
- Increased intensity in the production of the plosive B
- Elimination of nasal articulation
- Improved accentuation
- Improved language melody and speech rhythm
- Greater comprehensibility and therefore improved communication[13]

Sentences and dialogues are rhythmically accompanied on two chime bars with the interval of a major third, with the effect that certain language elements are accentuated and thus can be recognised by deaf children. The melodic range of speech should be produced largely in the range of a major third. The pitch of the lower chime bar should match the spontaneous voice of the child, as this will correspond with the vibrations in the child resonating on the same tone. Bang's speech and language development programme at pre-school level includes:

- Paying attention to vibration and sound
- Awareness of the differentiation in terms of strength, i. e. dynamic accentuation
- Awareness of the difference between time and speed, i. e. the quantitative accentuation
- Awareness of the difference in tones, i. e. the melodic accentuation
- Awareness of speech and musical rhythm[14]

These are precisely the elements of language that every baby must learn to recognise and to isolate. They are not only to be found in language, but also in music. Bang's practical approaches find support in the research results of Koelsch[15].

---

13 Bang 1975, p. 2
14 ibid., p. 3
15 cf. Bang 1975, Koelsch 2000

Veronica Sherborne

has developed a form of movement education in which relationships and dialogues play an important role. Although she did not develop her approach especially for children with hearing impairments, her contribution – the development of quality relationships – is an important supplement to our work. She has observed three different types of relationships that affect the quality of motor development:
1. Caring- or mutual relationships (*caring*)
2. Together-relationships (*shared*)
3. Conflicting relationships (*against*)[16]

In *caring* relationships movements such as swaying, rolling, holding, carrying and hugging prevail. These are forms of physical contact that support the child. At the advanced stage, for example, children balance on their parents' knees – a position where eye contact is automatically established and held. These playful forms of a non-verbal dialogue are always observable between parents and children when they can grow and develop in an undisturbed atmosphere.

In the framework of our project, the parents were also present during the musical sessions. In this way we were able to combine *caring* with music. The memories of these hours spent together are still vividly present and as the parents' response confirmed these sessions had a long-lasting effect, also in the home environment.

Sherborne also uses this movement education for children who have learning difficulties and establishes groups in which older children can protect and care for younger children. In the subsequent stages of development the emphasis continues to be placed on body contact and empathy[17].

Naomi Benari

has dedicated herself to assisting deaf children dance. In her book *Inner Rhythm*, she describes the methods and structure of her work. She starts off with the inner rhythm of the children. This, for example, can be defined by their pulse or their breathing. Especially deep breathing (which always precedes movement) can assist a group in finding a common rhythm[18].

Finding a beat shared by all involved is comparable to Sherborne's *caring*. It is something supportive – a common swaying rhythm or a common pace. It is certainly something that can be changed by one person, and thus can be formed and developed into a dialogue. It is a foundation that is strong and supportive and, like breathing, simply exists.

---

16 cf. Sherborne 1998
17 ibid., p. 24
18 cf. Benari's chapter in this book

The target group of the project were pre-school children. According to Benari they are in the phase of "enactment", meaning that the children are totally immersed in the role they are playing in the game or performance. They are what they are pretending to be.

From the age of seven, children enter the "iconic" phase. They perform in order to "be like something". Not before the age of eleven children are first capable of transforming the symbolic content of various qualities. Benari points out that such a development is often delayed with hard-of-hearing children[19].

Benari describes the form of communication between teacher and child as "body language". Many exercises and activities can be explained by simply demonstrating them. Accompanying movement with speech, poetry and imagery is not taken for granted in the work with hard-of-hearing children. Very simple cues such as "stop", "repeat" and "now", assist in co-operative learning. Focussing the children's attention, however, is a pre-condition of working together co-operatively.

Benari's fundamentals influenced our preparations. To us the most important aspect of her contribution appeared to be the work with the "inner" rhythm; the liberation of the child from external pressures and guidelines. The child is truly allowed to express its inner self.

Gertrud Orff,

in her books *Orff Music Therapy* and *Key Concepts in the Orff Music Therapy*, has shown how the Orff approach can be used when working with handicapped children. Her results have become an integral part of our work[20].

The Orff approach[21] provides a stable foundation for musical work with hard-of-hearing children. "By taking up elemental human attributes like language, movement, play, music, rhythm, dialogue and order, it becomes an anthropologically meaningful assistant, because these constituting aspects of humanity are constantly endangered with handicapped children. [...] The exemplary is of equal value as the perfect and the valid."[22] Wolfgart explains very distinctly that the Orff Pedagogy focusses on the children themselves. Music is an approach to realising one's poten-

---

19 cf. Benari 1995
20 cf. Orff 1971
21 This refers to the "Orff-Schulwerk" conceived and developed by Carl Orff und Gunild Keetmann in the 1930s. The most well-known publications are the *Music for Children* (English adaptation: Margaret Murray) published 1957–1966. Since then, there have been numerous international adaptations of the "Orff-Schulwerk", supplementary volumes and developments in its use with different age groups, in social work and with children, teenagers and adults with disabilites (Ed.).
22 Wolfgart 1971, preface

tial. It is not about the matter as an end in itself, but much rather about the human being. This is also reported by Wilhelm Keller, who emphasises the joyous aspects of such work: "Music, which provides no pleasure, is quickly rejected and forgotten, even if it was studiously practiced."[23]

The success of such work is particularly found in certain moments. When working with children it is important to devote attention to these situations. Gertrud Orff[24] lists a whole row of successes in musical work that resulted from such situations. These successes are more likely to pertain to personal qualities, such as extending patience, taking the initiative and being happy about achievements, rather than musical skills[25].

Shirley Salmon

demonstrates the benefit of integrative principles in her work with hard-of-hearing children, but it was her multi-sensory approach that influenced our work the most. Music is a form of dialogue for children with hearing impairments. The ability to participate in a dialogue, which is essential in the development of one's personality, is often accompanied by significant difficulties for the hard-of-hearing child. Due to the hearing impairment, perception, language development, communication, social learning and the development of identity may be affected. Salmon does not presume there are "deficits" in the first place, but rather adapts her work involving music and dance to the individual child's level of development.

Salmon notes that a multi-sensory approach supports development: "My multi-sensory approach is oriented on development, is integrative and dialogue-based."[26] The relationship between teacher and child can no longer be seen as simply a chain reaction of stimuli and response. The (musical) answer should have an open dimension, which means it should provide an incitement to achieve a higher level. The child's answer is what provides the next advancement.

In practice, this could be a song on the drums that contains an open interpretative section in which the child can express itself or listen to others.

It could also be a movement session to piano music. If the tempo changes, does the child react accordingly? Can it perceive the change? Close observation and thorough preparation are prerequisites for this form of work. Concrete suggestions as to how the child can be approached are:

---

23 Wolfgart 1971, preface
24 married to Carl Orff 1939-1953 and collaborated on the Schulwerk
25 cf. Orff 1971
26 Salmon 2001

- Choose instruments that are easy to perceive (ability to feel the vibrations, characteristic sound, challenging, self-made etc.)
- Use of various materials (to identify the characteristics of the material, improve sensory perception, sensibility to forms, order and the ability to establish contact through the material, to promote imagination and creativity)
- Choose topics that are independent of spoken language (e. g. with material, with signs and songs with movement or sign language)
- Movement and Dance (the point of departure is the inner rhythm, reinforcement of the congruence between movement and self-awareness)[27]

Openness is the common ground the musicians and teachers share. The musical work based on these approaches in not restricted. It allows mutual co-operation in spite of impaired perception. The environment is prepared in such a way that independent activity based on one's own needs is possible for everyone.

On the Practical Implementation of Our Ideas

Each of the project weeks – five so far – were based on a specific theme: there was a considerable scope of activities, ranging from physical therapy to reading topics. In each case a creative emphasis was incorporated:
- Fire, Water, Air and Earth
- Bookworms
- Circus, Circus
- Tranquilla Trampeltreu – the Determined Tortoise
- The Joy of the World is on the Back of a Horse

Each day began with music. The morning sessions took place outside in the fresh morning air. This brought all members of the families together and set the tone for the theme of the day. There was a musical part in which sign language was always incorporated. The day's schedule was explained. Symbolic objects helped the hard-of-hearing children to understand. An example from the project week "Tranquilla Trampeltreu – the Determined Turtle"[28]:
- Tranquilla Dance: Circle dance with A and B sections. The A section is comprised of the basic motif (both music and dance) that accompanies us throughout the week. The B section is a free element that changes daily (e. g. movement with chiffon scarves, games with various musical instruments etc.).
- Clarifying the daily routine: For each day a box is opened when sitting in the morning circle. The box contains symbols representing the daily activities (e. g. tortoises for music and language, a spoon for lunch, a pillow for the after-lunch

---

27 cf. Salmon 2001, p. 83ff.
28 cf. Ende 1982

nap time etc.). The children belonging to one group are greeted by their symbol. It becomes clear who is to do what after the morning meeting. The closed boxes are interesting for the children and they are eager to learn about the course of events. By taking part in this ritual, all participants accept responsibility for a smooth operation of the schedule. The hours are always the same, everything happens on time and nothing is forgotten.

- Shared song with sign language accompaniment: e. g. international greetings *Hey, hallo, bonjour, guten Tag.*

The choice of activities was selected for individual family members (hard-of-hearing children, siblings, children in general, the parents) or the entire family. During lunchtime and whenever it had been previously arranged there was the chance to hand over the supervision of the children to interns. This enabled the parents to relax, to attend sessions together as a couple or to simply enjoy a coffee break.

The families were to be provided with something to take home and cherish, while the hard-of-hearing children were to be supported when retelling their experiences to others. This made us devise two forms of written and illustrated documentation:

- The Daily Journal or Diary: Every evening the hard-of-hearing children and their siblings created one page of their daily journal together with their intern responsible. Photos of the most important contact persons were pasted into the journal and the most impressive events of the day were recorded. This was supplemented by drawings and short texts about the day's activities.
- The Project File: The parents collected all materials in a folder, including the songs, sign language materials, summaries of lectures etc., which they could take home for further reference.

The reactions at the parents' sessions were always characterised by positive constructive criticism. The choice of opportunities was particularly praised. The diversity of working and relaxing, listening to experts and exchanging experiences, problems etc. with other parents were considered to be extremely beneficial. The option of having the children supervised by the interns was especially appreciated by all the mothers involved. The parents wished that the impulses provided by music and language could be incorporated into early intervention and always expressed their wish for a continuation of the project in the following year.

The most important aspect of our work was the positive role model that we wanted to convey to the parents: To develop an individual relationship with every child and find methods of communicating depending on the child's level of perception. Accepting the way it is. Not only were the parents satisfied with the project, but the intense exchange between the experts involved was universally appreciated, and some regretted that this form of co-operation could not be implemented in everyday practice. What remained were many fond memories, the feeling of having created strength, and established new goals – or, as one mother put it: "It was so good for us!"

Literature

Bang, Claus: *Musik durchdringt die lautlose Welt*. In: *Musik + Medizin* 1975, Nr. 10, 44-50.

Benari, Naomi (1995): *Inner Rhythm – Dance Training for the Deaf*. Chur. An accompanying video was also published.

Broschart, Jürgen/Tentrup, Isabelle: *Der Klang der Sinne*. In: *GEO* 2003, Nr. 11. Hamburg.

Ding, Herbert (1995): *Mit der Hörschädigung leben. Hilfen für Eltern hörgeschädigter Kinder*. Heidelberg.

Ende, Michael/Schlüter, Manfred/Hiller, Wilfried (1982): *Tranquilla Trampeltreu, die beharrliche Schildkröte*. Stuttgart/Vienna/Bern.

Glennie, Evelyn (2005): *Hearing Essay*. In: *http://www.evelyn.co.uk/live/hearing_essay.htm*, 11/2007.

Goebel, Anne: *Das falsche Lexikon im Kopf*. In: *Max Planck Forschung* 2003, Nr. 2.

Hintermair, Manfred: *Aspekte der Eltern-Kind-Beziehung im Kontext von Hörschädigung*. In: *Hörgeschädigte Kinder* 1997, Nr. 1.

Jourdain, Robert (1998): *Das wohltemperierte Gehirn: Wie Musik im Kopf entsteht und wirkt*. Berlin.

Kreusch-Jacob, Dorothée (1999): *Musik macht klug*. Munich.

Koelsch, Stefan: *Musikalität – Hast Du Töne?* In: *Bild der Wissenschaft* 2000, Nr. 11.

Laborit, Emmanuelle (1995): *Der Schrei der Möwe*. Bergisch Gladbach, 24-25.

Laborit, Emmanuelle (1999): *The Cry of the Gull*. Washington DC, USA.

Orff, Gertrud (1971): *Orff-Schulwerks spezifische Heilkomponente*. In: Wolfgart, Hans (Ed.): *Das Orff-Schulwerk im Dienste der Erziehung und Therapie behinderter Kinder. Festschrift zum 75. Geburtstag von Carl Orff*. Berlin.

Salmon, Shirley (2001): *Wege zum Dialog: Erfahrungen mit hörgeschädigten Kindern in integrativen Gruppen*. In: Salmon, Shirley/Schumacher, Karin (Ed.): *Symposion Musikalische Lebenshilfe. Die Bedeutung des Orff-Schulwerks für Musiktherapie, Sozial- und Integrationspädagogik*. Hamburg.

Sherborne, Veronica (1998): *Beziehungsorientierte Bewegungspädagogik*. Munich/Basle.

Sherborne, Veronica (1990): *Developmental Movement for Children: Mainstream, Special Needs and Pre-School*. Cambridge.

Wolfgart, Hans (Ed.) (1971): *Das Orff-Schulwerk im Dienste der Erziehung und Therapie behinderter Kinder. Festschrift zum 75. Geburtstag von Carl Orff*. Berlin.

Songs in Simple Language

Wolfgang Friedrich

"Spring goeth all in white
Crowned with milk-white may
In fleecy flocks of light
O'er heaven the white clouds stray."[1]

Starting Point and Origin of the Songs in Simple Language

The Centre for the Hearing Impaired in Würzburg wanted to arrange and show a traditional setting-up of a maypole on their grounds together with their neighbouring elementary school. The aim was to have all children singing, dancing and signing together. A May song which is traditionally sung in Frankonia, a region in Germany, would seem strange and incomprehensible to children even when using signs[2].

Songs provide a good framework for numerous arrangements, presentations and modes of play. In combination with signs, movement and instruments many forms of human expression can be found and practised. Setting out from this consideration the range of possibilities for children with hearing loss can be explored and didactical questions answered and solved easily providing suitable song material is available.

Would it not seem obvious to write a new song which meets these requirements? The text and melody should be as simple as possible to suit hard-of-hearing children. This was, roughly speaking, the point of departure in the development of songs written in simple language for hard-of-hearing children. Beside other songs the new May song *Der Winter ist vorbei* (*Now winter is all gone*) was developed (see musical example).

Other songs were composed under the following aspects:
- Children should pick up the text and melody very easily.
- Melody, rhythm and language must be clear and comprehensible.
- The use of a few elemental features should provide for a musically expressive result.

---

1   Robert Seymour Bridges, Poet Laureate, 1844-1930
2   The poem above is an English equivalent, demonstrating how difficult it would be to use this text and make it understandable for the children (Ed.).

- Accompanying the text with signs should be possible in order to support an understanding of its meaning.
- Aspects of the children's everyday lives should be reflected and their linguistic development should be taken into consideration.
- The strong character of challenge should motivate the children to move, speak, sing and sign.
- Short, repetitive phrases help in the learning and practising phase.

13 songs written in simple language were published by Auer Verlag in 2001. Momel, a little boy resembling the goblin Pumuckl[3], leads us through the book and encourages the activities in many ways. The songs, which are not only used in everyday school-life but also in training courses and in-service training presentations, enjoy growing popularity.

Written in simple language, these songs were created for children with hearing loss whose linguistic development (as a result of their impairment) is not on the same level as that of children with intact hearing. There are great differences among the various groups of children or classes, which is why the texts of the songs vary accordingly on an intellectual level. These 13 songs, when sung and signed, follow the grammar of the spoken, respectively sung, language (e. g. signed English) rather than the sign language (e. g. British sign language). However it was a matter of great concern to us that the signs should transport the linguistic contents clearly and in the correct context. (There is also a CD in German to accompany the book.)

The connection between elements of rhythm and music, simple, child-oriented texts and special principles and arrangements for children with hearing loss can be seen in examples from *Momel singt Lieder in einfacher Sprache*[4] (*Momel sings songs in simple language*).

Relation to Basics of Rhythm

Starting off from the 4 basic elements of rhythm, namely *space, time, dynamics and form* , the behaviour observed can be put into relation to other information on children's perception and learning as well as diagnosis. From this perspective adults can develop an understanding for children and be empathic with them.

---

3   A character well-known to children in Germany and Austria who has many adventures (Ed.).
4   Friedrich, Wolfgang/Schmid, Bärbel (2001): *Momel singt Lieder in einfacher Sprache.* Donauwörth

Some children find it difficult to orient themselves in *space*. Already at a very early stage of their development babies with intact hearing turn their heads to the direction of the sound, searching for its source with their eyes whenever they hear acoustic signals, a noise or a call. Non-impaired hearing calls our attention to things which are beyond the scope of our vision. Many stimuli that encourage the exploring and grasping of the concept of space can be considerably reduced due to a hearing difference and irregular auditory concentration.

There are children who find it hard to deal with the concept of *time*, they find it difficult to develop a sense for given time units as well as rhythm in their movements. Their own inner clock lacks a steady beat and they are rarely in time with their environment. These children often react very angrily because they feel disturbed and controlled by others in their on-going activity.

Many children with hearing loss have only few rhythmical auditory experiences to rely on because they have, for example, a hearing radius of no more than a few metres in spite of their hearing aids. For others it is difficult because their brain cannot process rhythmical patterns. Some children are over-sensitive to noise; an audible rhythm cannot compete with loud noises. The development and stabilisation of a sense of rhythm can be impaired by difficulties with the sense of balance, a frequent phenomenon with hard-of-hearing children.

Because of these and other related reasons, some children have poor control over the *dynamics* of their bodies. Their movements are quicker and more erratic than planned. These "insufficiently controlled" children start to run and often overshoot the mark (literally and figuratively). Close observation shows us how much concentration and energy such children need in order to adapt their movements to the task given to the group.

On the other hand slow, less motivated children often have difficulties in maintaining the dynamic tension and attention needed to complete an activity or a sequence of movements.

Sometimes no *form* can be developed because the children lose sight of the goal during the activity. Children cannot see the structure or its principles. In our fast moving day and age there is rarely the chance to repeat anything. Too many new auditory impressions prevent the automation and identification of forms.

Emile Jaques-Dalcroze emphasised the necessity of practice and automation of newly acquired knowledge and accomplishments so that these abilities could be called upon reliably.

Aspects of Structuring the Texts

Important characteristics of the song texts are:
- Simple language. In working on the texts constant specifications or definitions of "simple language" are not so much the basis but rather the experience of on-going communication with the particular group. It is important that the children in a group or class understand "their" song.
- Gentle language. Simple language can also be gentle, even poetic. The rhythm of the words and rhyming verses are important structural elements.
- Vocabulary taken directly from the children's world of experience
- Avoiding pretentious linguistic metaphors, e. g. "Spring goeth all in white"
- Short sentences, if possible without subordinate clauses
- No intricate sentences and inversions. They complicate the texts of many folksongs for children with hearing loss.
- Congruency between the logic of the content and the language
- Greatest conformity between the lyrics and the accompanying signs

It is an absolute necessity for children with hearing loss to accompany the sung language with signs. Gestures and the movement of hands in general belong to the natural means of expression in many children's songs since they are an important element in certain phases of childhood development. Therefore it seems obvious to pick up gestures the children themselves use when working with hearing impaired children.

Experience shows that gestures usually help children to grasp the meaning of the text. Signs can open up the doorway to the rhythmical structure for some children. For other children they are a helpful mnemonic support to learn and remember texts. This applies to deaf and hard-of-hearing children as well as to children with Central Auditory Processing Disorder (CAPD).

Musical Structures

Songs written in simple language should show a simple and clear musical structure. The melodies are characterized by scales and triads as well as series of notes without large intervals or jumps. The songs and their verses are short and often certain phrases are repeated.

The rhythmical structure of the songs should only contain one task for the children. Therefore one musical item could be the consideration of intervals or a change in rhythm. How fast or slow you sing a song depends on the rhythmical and linguistic capacities of the children.

The use of tapes and CDs can be an additional option to the actual work with songs, but should not replace the music made by the children themselves. Live music can adapt to the metre, respectively the changes in tempo of the children.

Aspects in Planning a Lesson

The structure of a rhythmic-musical session can follow a four-phase pattern corresponding with the principles listed above.

1. Warming-up and "Socialisation"

Entering the room and joining the group:
- Children from different classes and groups arrive in the music room.
- They welcome each other with a group ritual.
- Familiar relaxation exercises and a phase of free movement can follow.
- In an exercise known by the children, all senses are awakened: They listen, move, speak and sing and also use their body instruments.

2. Working on the Lesson's Theme

A new element is presented. The children perceive it with concentration, imitate and practise it. This element is integrated into previously known elements. Further elements can be treated in the same way.

3. Absorption, Consolidation and Conclusion

Structures that have been worked on should be repeated until all the children are sure of them. Support can be reduced step by step. Suitably chosen variations, which increase the difficulty of the task, call for further repetitions. The result achieved is observed and appreciated together with the pupils.

4. Farewell

A ritual well-known to all participants is just as essential at the end as at the beginning of the lesson. Each group can have its own specially established farewell song (e. g. with singing, signs and movements).

Children and adults will have fun when playing music with "songs written in simple language" if:
- the children with their abilities remain the most important aspect at the starting-point throughout the entire orientation-phase of the pedagogical process,
- everything that is worked on is divided into small elements,
- complex structures are simplified,
- single elements are worked on individually,
- each step is introduced specifically,

- sufficient time and repetitions are allowed for each step,
- a newly introduced element is incorporated into previously known material and a systematic structure, ranging from simple to difficult, is followed,
- active music-making takes place,
- forms and patterns are introduced and remembered.

These principles are the result of many years of teaching experience. They compile the conditions which should be fulfilled so that children feel secure. Emotional confidence allows concentrated, joyful and successful co-operation.

Two Examples

„Der Winter ist vorbei"

Text: Bärbel Schmid
Melodie: Wolfgang Friedrich

2. Blumen leuchten, Bienen summen,
Bäume blühen, Käfer brummen. – Ja! –
Der Winter...

3. Kinder wollen draußen spielen,
Sonne auf den Haaren fühlen. – Ja! –
Der Winter...

4. Kater wollen abends bummeln
und sich mit den Katzen tummeln. – Ja! –
Der Winter...

5. Vogelmann und Vogelfrau
sind fertig mit dem Nesterbau. – Ja! –
Der Winter...

Fig. 1: May song Der Winter ist vorbei (*by permission of Auer Verlag*)

"Now winter is all gone"

Now winter is all gone, and spring has really won.
1. Children long for open air, want to be in sunshine fair. – Yeah! – Now winter ...
2. Flowers shine and bees are humming, trees in blossom, beetles drumming.
– Yeah! – Now winter ...
3. Children want to play outside, feel the sunbeams as they ride. – Yeah! – Now
winter ...
4. Evening walk for cat and kitten, both with mellow air are smitten. – Yeah!
– Now winter ...
5. Mr. Sparrow and his wife in their new nest hope for life. – Yeah! – Now winter ...

ZfH – Würzburg

Fig. 2: Zfh – Würzburg. *Spoken chorus with signs and instrumental accompaniment composed for the presentation of the new homepage of the Zentrum für Hörgeschädigte (ZfH) Würzburg – the Centre for the Hearing Impaired in Würzburg (http://www.hoer-sprachfoerderung.de).*

Soprano: *Z F H Würzburg, Z F H Würzburg*
Alto: *Come and have a look oh la la.*
Bass: *Who we are, what we do, where we are.*

Outlook

Songs written in simple language are used in the everyday lives of the children and pupils of the Centre for the Hearing Impaired in Würzburg. They are an essential component with many departments of the centre and are recurring according to the seasons. The songs now have a greater range beyond the limits of the centre. Thanks to the new forms of media, they are currently even being integrated into the networks of other cultures.

Inspired by the children's creativity and supported by (more) open systems, international centres for the hard-of-hearing will certainly one day succeed in publishing and exchanging such songs in simple language on the internet.

For inspired they surely are, these songs – inspired by the joy and fun the singing and playing children experience, which in turn sets us all in motion.

The Importance of Play-Songs in Inclusive Teaching

Shirley Salmon

Play-songs offer children at pre-school and primary school age (especially those with hearing loss) a great creative potential which can be extremely beneficial to them. In a multi-sensory approach the play-song serves as an initiating as well as an encouraging factor for a diversity of activities involving music, movement, language and a selection of materials, which in turn lead to various experiences in learning. Different objectives can be aimed at here – those concerning music directly, as well as other fields of development. Linguistic accomplishments are not necessarily the primary goal in this case, the children should much rather be offered the possibility to gain different experiences, playing, moving, speaking, singing and creating in a variety of forms. In a multi-sensory approach using music and movement several senses – not only the auditory – are addressed. Play-songs can offer a broad spectrum of experience and expression which supports the children's general development[1].

Play-Songs – a General Survey

In the play-song, the song itself, movement and certain elements of drama are combined and integrated[2]. Music, movement, language and play(ing) are closely related and can influence and support each other positively. Play-songs are nothing new and have been sung and played by children for centuries. The play-song has a long tradition in musical education – as early as 1919 *Action Songs* (songs with movement) were published by Emile Jaques-Dalcroze, who developed the method of eurhythmics in the teaching of music. Carl Orff, on the other hand, considered the traditional repertoire of children's songs as the basis for Orff-Schulwerk and also emphasized the importance of 'play': "The urge to play develops into a patient activity leading to practice and from there to achievement."[3] It is important that the child be allowed to play, "undisturbed, expressing the internal externally. Word and sound must arise simultaneously from improvisatory, rhythmic play."[4]

Not only in music education, but also in rhythmic musical education as well as in integrative pedagogy and special education, songs that inspire movement, dance,

---

1   cf. Salmon 2003
2   cf. Keller 1970, Haselbach 1971, Plahl/Koch-Temming 2005
3   Carl Orff: *Gedanken über Musik mit Kindern und Laien*. In: *Die Musik* 1932. Berlin, p. 669 (Translation: Margaret Murray)
4   ibid., p. 671

Shirley Salmon

role-play, language and emotional expression represent an important part of the curriculum. In music therapy for children the systematic use of songs is one of the essential tools that therapists have at their disposal. In almost all types of music therapy for children songs are employed to encourage the establishment of contact, to support relationships or to help difficult or disturbing experiences[5]. Songs are not only sung but can be created. *Songwriting* is also an applied method in music therapy[6].

Wilhelm Keller regards the play-song as "the combination of elements from singing with those of movement, ranging from the simple pantomime to dance and the dramatic representation of text scenes; it furthermore comprises the use of musical instruments (including the human body), the transformation of the song into an instrumental piece as well as the purely rhythmical presentation of spoken texts."[7] The story of a play-song can also be of focal interest, for "play- (or dramatic) songs have a scenic core which can be stylised or enacted pantomimically."[8] Integrating songs into a dramatic plot opens up diverse possibilities of activity beyond that of singing itself. This may include dance, movement or forms of drama, vocal and rhythmical inventions, musical effects, making music, accompanying, instrumental improvisation or musical role-playing. Play-songs can be songs based on dialogue, in the form of sung communication, as well as narrative and cyclic songs. With many "new children's songs" the act of singing, as an enjoyable activity, is in itself of central interest. The object here is not only to sing the melody, but also to enact, to play and to experience the story-content, thus involving the whole body, interacting in the group, creating an atmosphere and sometimes stepping onto the stage etc.

A stimulating, *multi-sensory environment* during childhood is of great importance for the development of the abilities and competences an adult needs later in life[9]. "Experiences and sensations *are* learning. Sensations form the base understanding from which concepts and thinking develop. Sensory enriched environments are imperative to learning."[10] The inter-play between physical activity, emotional

---

5 cf. Plahl/Koch-Temming 2005, p. 181. Further goals when using songs in music therapy with children are: structuring, making contact, regulating the relationship, focussing attention, activating, relaxing, possibility of regressing, furthering individual developmental areas (in particular movement, perception, speech and social behaviour), expressing emotions and needs, dealing with experiences and circumstances that are emotionally stressful.

6 cf. Baker/Wigram 2005

7 Keller 1970, Introduction

8 Haselbach 1978, p. 147

9 cf. Hannaford 1995. The main factors are a rich sensory environment (at home, in preschool, school but also outside); the freedom to discover the surroundings freely; the presence of parents that can be consulted when children have questions.

10 Hannaford 1995, p. 48

expression in movement, co-ordination of movement with language and singing, synchronisation of the movements within the group and many other elements are essential to this learning process which is supported by an enriched sensory environment[11].

In this context Verden-Zöller quotes five modes of physical experience that constitute basic processes and structures: rhythm, balance, physical movement, establishing elemental signs or symbols, establishing space and time[12]. When creating play-songs the sensory environment as well as the modes of physical experience can be taken into consideration and integrated.

In both music education and music therapy songs in general as well as specific play-songs should be adapted, altered and re-written according to the particular setting. Every play-song is used somewhat differently in different groups depending on the requirements and abilities within the group in question. In music education, in remedial and inclusive education, in special education as well as in music therapy composed songs play a justified role. *Situational songs* are also used referring to the current situation, which usually leads to their quite spontaneous creation – *for* a child/group, *with* a child/group or *by* a child/group[13]. Songs that develop as the result of a certain situation are reactions and answers to children and can lead to further playing, improvisation, reflection and discussion. They can accompany children in their actions, they can create atmospheres and help to improve understanding, interpretation and creative work with certain experiences. Situational songs are important for all children, but particularly valuable to those who do not speak, those who are hard-of-hearing or those with contact behaviour difficulties[14].

Songs can be inspired by playing, by movement games or by role games in which the activity of playing at the same time provides the motivation for the song text. Well-known children's songs, play- or pop songs can be re-written so that they reflect current themes that are of interest to the child or the group. Baker and Wigram distinguish between *Songwriting for* clients and *with* clients and list many examples from music therapy in which *Songwriting* is used as a form of therapy[15].

Greeting and Farewell Songs often provide the framework for the sessions. The primary aspect of many play-songs is for the children to enjoy the activity, the elements of play, the ritual as well as the real context that the particular theme in question has

---

11 cf. Hannaford 1995
12 cf. Maturana/Verden-Zöller 1996
13 cf. G. Orff 1980, Plahl/Koch-Temming 2005
14 cf. Schumacher 1994, G. Orff 1980, G. Orff 1984, Keller 1971, Baker/Wigram 2005, Plahl/Koch-Temming 2005
15 cf. Baker/Wigram 2005

to offer. Paul Nordoff and Clive Robbins, who towards the end of the 1950s began to develop Creative Music Therapy, composed many play-songs with themes from everyday settings such as: arriving, names of the children in the group, the days of the week, the weather. These songs were especially used for activating and motivating children with cognitive disabilities when they were to sing and play in a group[16].

Play-Songs – Specific Uses

Play-songs not only provide musical experiences, but also experiences on various other levels. Due to the individual's potential in the cognitive, motor, emotional, social, linguistic and perceptive domains, play-songs can supply *special support in certain learning phases*. To Wilhelm Keller the play-song is of particular significance in the process of making contact: "The play-song is [...] especially important in social and remedial pedagogic work with all kinds of 'problem children', for whom it is sometimes indeed the only way of making the first contact."[17] This also becomes clear in the music therapeutic work by Karin Schumacher: "All early mother-child games are elemental music, movement and language games that connect to prenatal experiences. They represent a *multi-sensory* option, which has an effect on the child through the mother's *emotional participation*. The lullaby, the cradle- and rocking song, the clapping game and knee rides all offer sensory-emotional stimulation. They support the child's emotional and cognitive abilities that are a basic necessity for establishing a relationship to the environment. The senses of balance, touch, of hearing and seeing (but surely also the olfactory sense) are simultaneously stimulated and in play lead to the establishment of contact and the development of a relationship between mother and child."[18] The child's emotional and cognitive abilities can also be supported in the educational context.

Sherborne's *"Developmental Movement"*[19] is based on the belief that relating to oneself and relating to others is essential for all human development. It recognizes that movement experiences are fundamental to the development of all human beings, but are particularly important to people with special needs who often have difficulty in relating to their own bodies and to other people. This method places great importance on the equal development of both physical abilities and positive relationships with others through shared experiences. The movement activities referred to as 'Relationship Play' have two main objectives: awareness of self and awareness of others. They are divided in to three main groups:

---

16 cf. Nordoff/Robbins 1964. Further ideas for hard-of-hearing children can be found in Robbins/Robbins 1980, Schmid/Friedrich 2001, Estabrooks/Birkenshaw-Fleming 2003, 2006 and Salmon 2007
17 Keller 1970, Introduction
18 Schumacher 1994, p. 28
19 Sherborne 2001, http://www.sherbornemovement.org

1. Caring or "with" relationships
2. Shared relationships
3. "Against" relationships

Although this approach does not in its original form use music, the types of relationship play can be positively used as preparation for or as extensions to play-songs where the emphasis is on the building of relationships. These can be between parents and children or between children of similar age but especially between children of differing age and ability.

Clive and Carol Robbins (1980) recognised the innate musicality of children with hearing loss and in their curriculum[20] tried to address the children by offering them appropriate musical experiences, thus setting free their often hidden musical talents. "Our view was simply that man is so attuned to music – and music to man – that these same sensitivities, predispositions and capacities must be inherent in the hearing impaired child." Since musical experiences can be a source of joy and initiative for personal development, children with hearing loss, too, have a right to gain such experiences. "We saw no reason whatsoever why deaf children should not be offered the enjoyments, satisfactions and learning potential in a suitable music program."[21]

In addition to traditional singing in music education a commonly practised modified form of vocal music in the Anglo-American region is *song signing* for deaf children, which was developed within the deaf community of the USA in the 1930s. Song signing is an enjoyable musical activity for children with hearing loss, but also for those whose hearing is intact; these forms of singing are not only used in hard-of-hearing classes in the USA, but also in mainstream classes (i. e. regular or inclusive classes), thus supporting communal singing of children who can hear together with deaf or hard-of-hearing children. With song signing (also known as sign singing) the song concerned is simultaneously accompanied by gestures. This activity is based on a well-developed rhythmical feeling, manifest in the rhythmical movement of the whole body (swaying). The music and the content of the song are conveyed in a combination of visualisation and auditory-tactile perception[22].

---

20 Clive and Carol Robbins developed a music curriculum for hard-of-hearing children at the New York State school for the Deaf, USA. *Music for the Hearing Impaired* was published in 1980 and contains a wealth of material for music teachers and teachers of deaf and hard-of-hearing children.
21 Robbins/Robbins 1980, p. 25
22 cf. Prause 2001

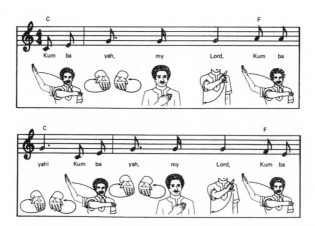

Fig. 1: In: The National Grange 1992

Signed song books, in which the signs are illustrated below the music and song lyrics, have been published in the USA since the 1980s. Usually the grammar remains that of the spoken language and individual sign language signs accompany all or some of the words (e. g. signed English, sign supported English).

In contrast to *silent sign choirs* the importance of singing to deaf and hard-of-hearing children is emphasised in the process of signing the songs[23]. According to Prause (2001) song-signing is an integral part of musical education for all school children with hearing loss in the Anglo-American culture. In European countries this form of singing is only partially practised, not able to look back on a long pedagogic tradition and the choice of literature is scarce.

The use of play-songs with deaf and hard-of-hearing children has various objectives which are often followed simultaneously. Individual songs cannot be categorised according to a specific function and a certain song can either be used with a single child or in a group, in a lesson or in a therapeutic session. The differences in use depend on the children's momentary needs, on the context and the aims, the current educational and therapeutic themes within the group as well as on the methods employed by the teacher or therapist.

Summarising, play-songs can be used to follow one or more of the following aims with deaf and hard-of-hearing children:

• Relaxation, releasing tension, activation
• Sensitisation of the sensory perception

---

23 cf. Prause 2001

- Support of the auditory, visual, kinaesthetic and vestibular perception, memory, concentration
- Support of motor and body perception (e. g. development of body awareness, joint and muscle sense, fine and gross motor control, co-ordination, balance and inner rhythm)
- Initiating and supporting nonverbal and verbal dialogue in spoken or signed language
- Support of voice and language (e. g. development of the ability to use one's voice, to understand the concept of language and to actually speak; introduction of rhythm into spoken language; extension of vocabulary and linguistic concepts; experience, practice and use of phrases and sentence structures; further development of the range of the voice, its quality as well as its melody, timbre, dynamics, prosody)
- Communication (e. g. supporting the establishment of contact and the development of relationships; expression of feelings and needs; inclusion of body language, gestures and pantomime)
- Social learning (e. g. support of self-confidence, independence and self-respect; development and encouragement of a willingness and ability to co-operate)
- Development of personality (e. g. experiencing atmospheres and emotions; focussing attention; activation and emotional expression; coming to terms with emotionally harassing experiences and circumstances; discovery and development of creativity)
- Specific goals in music and dance (e. g. introduction to and experience of various forms of music and dance and their expression; improvisation and creativity; participation in the social and cultural values expressed in the songs, practising of musical, movement and dance skills)[24]

Following the principles of *inclusive education* the use of play-songs should take into account the participation of all children in a group or class.
According to Feuser integration[25] is "co-operative (dialogic, interactive, communicative) activity in the collective", which, from a pedagogical point of view, means for both school and pre-school that
- "all children and pupils (including those children who have severe profound and complex learning difficulties)
- will play, learn, and work together

---

24 cf. Nordoff/Robbins 1971, Robbins/Robbins 1980, Bang 1980, Salmon 2003, Plahl/Koch-Temming 2005
25 "Integration" and "integrative" were used here by Feuser before the term "inclusive" had been widely established. The definition here applies also to "inclusion". The attribute "integrative" merely aids communication: A general approach to pedagogy, in the sense that Feuser has put forward, makes the term "integration" redundant, since on principle it embraces neither pedagogical reductionism of education nor is it of a socially selective and segregating nature.

- at their respective developmental levels (taking into consideration their present levels of competence in perception, cognition and behaviour)
- in co-operation with one another
- within a shared curriculum (project/subject matter/tasks/topic)".[26]

Play-songs can offer a wealth of different forms of activity, which enable *all* children to encounter and deal with the song in an individual way. Certain activities are carried out in a whole group, others in small groups, with a partner or individually. Furthermore various learning situations can and should be offered e. g. communicative learning situations (two partners are focussed on each other), complementary learning situations (one partner helps the other), coexistential learning situations (working side by side), co-operative learning situations (working together). Feuser refers to four factors that are necessary for implementing successful integration: "individualisation", "internal differentiation", "co-operative activity" and the "common object". The common object, though, is not a physical entity here, which becomes an educational subject in the hands of the children and pupils, it much rather represents the central "process".

In every learning process there is the aim to activate each child's abilities in the best possible way. By extending and enhancing the learning environment – and the other children with their diverse competences contribute to this – a positive development is more likely to be achieved than with teaching methods that aim to speed up the learning process based on the deficits diagnosed[27]. Teaching and learning methods which enable the children to make their own experiences are of central interest.

Focal Elements

The following diagram illustrates a network of focal creative elements that can become effective on their own, but frequently also in combination with each other. This diagram can be useful when planning individual lessons, as well as when working on more long-term, interdisciplinary projects. The song and its various aspects can be stimulating and motivating, helping us to find several activities for each creative element. The final choice of activities corresponds with the contents of the song as well as with the current abilities and needs of the children and the group.

---

26 cf. Feuser 1997
27 cf. Athey 1990, p. 76

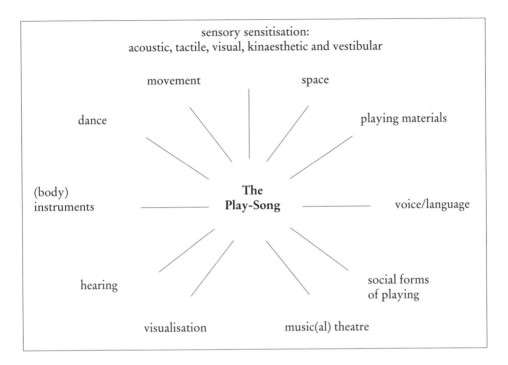

When planning it is useful to consider the following forms of children's participation: perceiving, exploring, experimenting, playing, communicating, recognising, remembering, imitating, choosing, varying, distinguishing, inventing, practising, creating, reflecting and discussing.

To illustrate the wide range of possibilities, a selection of activities is described here which is assignable to one or more fields of the above-mentioned creative elements. Gerda Bächli's song *Jahreszeiten (The Seasons)*[28] serves as the basic reference for all the examples given here. Many of the ideas revolve around the autumn/fall verse in the song, but they can also be adapted for the other seasons.

---

28 In: Bächli, Gerda (2002): *Traumschiffchen. 21 Kinderlieder.* Küsnacht

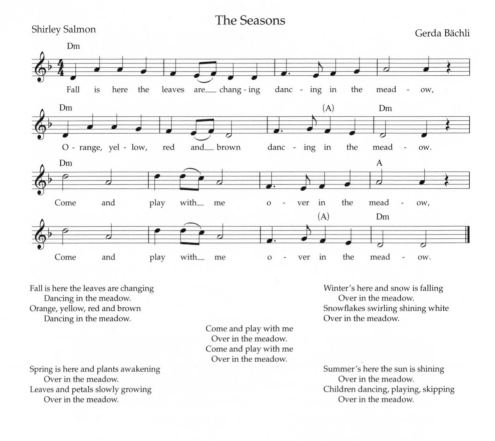

Fall is here the leaves are changing
    Dancing in the meadow.
Orange, yellow, red and brown
    Dancing in the meadow.

                    Come and play with me
                    Over in the meadow.
                    Come and play with me
                    Over in the meadow.

Spring is here and plants awakening
    Over in the meadow.
Leaves and petals slowly growing
    Over in the meadow.

Winter's here and snow is falling
    Over in the meadow.
Snowflakes swirling shining white
    Over in the meadow.

Summer's here the sun is shining
    Over in the meadow.
Children dancing, playing, skipping
    Over in the meadow.

Fig. 2: In: Salmon 2007

Collection of Ideas

The following ideas should stimulate and encourage the reader to create his/her own lessons or projects with children, even though not all creative elements necessarily have to be taken into consideration at the same time. The activities chosen and their creative processes should correspond with the children's maturity, their abilities and interests, the constellation within the group and the situation during the lesson.

Sensory Sensitisation

- Collect autumnal objects and put into groups: e. g. leaves, cones, chestnuts, stones etc., according to their colour, shape etc.
- Discover and experience objects – the quality of their surfaces, their weight, shape, colour, aroma or smell etc.
- Recognise objects by touching or smelling them with eyes closed.
- Explore sounds, noises or movements with a particular object; demonstrating and imitating them.
- Experience objects on and via the body, e. g. feeling, rolling, carrying, balancing, throwing, catching – alone and with a partner.
- Massage the body with the object – alone and with a partner.
- Experience the blowing of the wind, directed at various parts of the body, with eyes closed – the wind can be produced by exhaling breaths of air or by using certain materials such as scarves or pieces of cardboard as fans.
- Balance alone or with a partner on a small area (e. g. a carpet square) in various ways: kneeling, on one foot, with eyes closed.
- Experiment with different positions of the body and assuming different attitudes, e. g. like a leaf, like a chestnut etc.

Fig. 3: Greeting each other with different parts of the body during a "Hello" song

Movement

- Play the wind with gestures and signs, using hands and the whole body in the entire room available for this representation.
- Watch movements closely, imitating them with one's hands or the whole body, as e. g. a falling leaf, a rolling conker, a gradually growing plant.

- Use Rudolf Laban's "Basic Body Activities": locomotion, rotation, elevation, gesture, position to develop and extend movements.
- Take ideas from objects and use them in extending one's own movements.
- Vary the movements under the following aspects: time, dynamics, space, expression.
- Start off with gestures expressing terms such as autumn/fall, leaves, wind, rain, fog and sun, thereby increasing or reducing their range and intensity, so that they no longer take place on the spot, but in the room.
- Develop the gestures (alone or with a partner) into a sequence of movements, while paying attention to the initial and final position.

Fig. 4: Building a snowman

Space

- Each child represents a leaf. The teacher (and later a child) imitates the wind by making movements with a scarf. The leaves move correspondingly and are blown from one place to the other. (Depending on the degree of hearing loss the wind can also be played on an ocean drum or by using a wire brush on a drum.)
- Partner-oriented task: One child plays the leaf, the second takes over the role of the wind. The movements of the wind indicate the force and the direction for the movements of the leaf.
- Experiment with different routes in the room for the whirling leaf: in a straight, in a twisting or zigzag line, circular or spiral. Trying out these routes through the room and retracing them in colour.

- Try out a combination of routes in the room; retracing one line in colour and the other in movement.

Dance

- Initiate a free dancing activity (e. g. whirling leaves, dancing snow flakes) with live accompaniment of the movements or using selected pieces of music.
- Collect the children's ideas and try them out together.
- For the song: trying out walking and skipping steps for the refrain of the song – free in the room as well as within the circle.
- Learn and practise a dance form for the refrain, e. g. skipping eight steps to the right within the circle, followed by eight steps to the left. Alternatively: four steps to the centre, clapping four times, four steps backwards, clapping for four steps and turning at the same time.
- At the beginning of the autumn-verse all leaves start to swirl around and dance (either on the spot or away from it) – the levels and dynamics can vary.
- Spring-verse: Leaves and flowers begin to grow, floating in the wind. Summer-verse: birds flying; winter verse: snow flakes falling and dancing.

Materials

- A great diversity of materials is suitable – e. g. dried leaves tied up in a chiffon scarf; a quarter of a sheet of wrapping tissue in autumnal colours, cut out as a leaf; cloth or crepe streamers in autumnal colours attached to sticks the appropriate size for children.
- A bag made of a scarf filled with nuts, acorns, leaves etc. that can be passed round the circle, held, felt, heard, smelled.
- Experiment with the sheet of paper, a streamer, a scarf (e. g. falling, floating, turning, blowing, gliding).
- Watch your own scarf as it glides to the ground; imitate this movement with your body and/or accompany it with your voice; imitate the shape of the scarf lying on the floor.
- The children let their scarves dance in pairs – various forms of movement are encouraged – also in reference to tempo, dynamics and space. Each pair chooses three sequences of movement which are performed together synchronously.
- In small groups forms of expression to a particular verse of the song are tried out and invented.
- One child after the other moves towards the centre of the circle with their scarf and lays it out artistically without moving the other scarves, thus contributing to the "autumnal picture".

(Body-)Instruments

- Make sounds with objects and simple instruments, e. g. kazoos, wind chimes with nails, nutshell castanets, nutshell rattle, nutshell drum, light bulb rattle, ocean drum.
- Collect additional ideas for each verse, experimenting with traditional and self-made instruments and assigning them to the seasons, e. g. which instruments are to represent snowflakes, whirling autumn leaves, sunshine, and jumping frogs.
- A conductor indicates which season is to be dramatically enacted, and at which volume.
- Perform musical images, possibly also as interludes of the song.
- Accompany the song with musical gestures (clapping, patting, snapping, stamping) e. g. patting the metre, clapping the rhythm of the refrain or playing an ostinato: | | | – or ⁊⁊ ⁊⁊ | – .
- Use the instruments for rhythmical accompaniment, but also for the interpretation of musical images (e. g. autumn weather).
- Accompany the song with a drone or bordun (notes D and A at the beginning of each bar).
- Play the bass line (notes D/A, continuing to play D instead of B flat and F).
- Children already learning to play an instrument should be given their own roles, e. g. playing the melody or an ostinato; improvising over a drone or bordun as an interlude.

Fig. 5: Playing djembes

Voice and Language

- Use one's voice to imitate the falling of a leaf (demonstrated with a real leaf and then with the hand) – experimenting with different vowels and moving correspondingly when doing so.
- Let go of several leaves simultaneously and vocally accompanying them as they float to the ground.
- Produce vocal sounds for certain terms, using them as interludes: e. g. wind, storms, leaves dancing, nuts falling (paying attention to whether the sounds are voiced or unvoiced).
- Vocalise words as ostinati,
  e. g. dancing leaves;   meadow;   come and play with me;
  ⌐⌐ | | – | – | – | – | | | –
- Learn the refrain, speaking rhythmically (possibly with gestures or signs), accompanying with musical pantomime. Depending on the arrangement the text can also be changed, e. g. "… come and dance with me!"
- Together with the children make a collection of terms and ideas describing a particular season – making up new verses and write them down.

Hearing/Listening

- Discover sounds with autumnal objects, experimenting with different modes of play(ing), demonstrating and imitating these.
- Play the sounds as rhythmic accompaniment to the refrain.
- Initiate acoustic perception of autumnal objects such as nuts and chestnuts – dropping them to the ground, on a drumhead etc.
- Cue at particular parts of the song, e. g. "over in the meadow", "play with me".
- Clap or play rhythmical elements in the song, e. g. "come and play with me", "over in the meadow", "Fall is here the leaves are changing" …; recognise these elements, playing and rearranging them.
- Consciously listen to and arrange certain parts of the melody or certain phrases, e. g. making the hands dance like leaves during the autumn verse (on the spot or moving in the room), returning to the circular constellation for the refrain and accompany it with sound gestures.
- Listen attentively to the course of the melody (played on an easily perceivable instrument), show the course of the melody with gestures; later follow the melody written in graphic notation.
- Listen to short excerpts of *Autumn* from Vivaldi's *Four Seasons* (or another piece related to the topic), paying attention to certain musical aspects such as repetition, volume, speed, solo and tutti, types of instruments etc.

Social Forms of Playing

- The children play leaves that are freely dancing through the room without getting in each other's way.
- Partner-oriented task: One child moves as a leaf around the room. The partner follows the first child, imitating his movements. When the pair stops and turns around, the second child takes over the lead.
- Experiment with the roles of the wind and the leaf: The two partners play the wind and the leaf. The wind directs his breath at particular parts of the partner's body that are floating in the air. The leaf can fly around freely in the whole room.
- Each of the small groups decides on a term associated with autumn (e. g. leaves, wind, fog, nuts, chestnuts ...) and chooses the appropriate instruments. The autumn-verse is rewritten, sung and accompanied with the term in question.
- At the end of the verse the small group improvises.

Visualisation

- Rock on the spot in time with the song (standing, sitting, kneeling ...).
- Perceive the rhythm of the song (which can be played on a drum) and visualise the rhythm by "painting" large gestures in the air, by walking in time with the rhythm or by "painting" it with big steps on the ground.
- The rhythm of the song is drawn as large graphic symbols (in due time as notes) – the children follow these drawing movements in the air or on paper.
- Recognise rhythmical elements of the song, e. g. particular phrases.
- Find gestures for the most important terms in the song – practising them phrase by phrase.
- The melody is played on an easily perceivable mallet instrument (e. g. a bass xylophone) or a piano. The children perceive the melody by means of their visual, acoustic and tactile senses and can show the melody or phrases using hand movements.
- Using hand movements the pitch of notes, phrases or the whole melody can be shown.
- The melody, written in notes, is followed.
- The two parts of the song are visualised in the form of a small dance.

Music(al) Theatre

- Terms and ideas associated with the topic of autumn are collected with and by the children.
- Retell or make up an autumn story (in speech and/or in sign language).

- An illustrated book or poem on the topic of autumn is selected and a list of suitable terms/roles is made.
- The children think about how they can express the material selected in terms of movement.
- Various roles are developed – tasks for a whole group (leaves) or for an individual (wind).
- Stage props and other materials for the representation of the roles are collected.
- Use sounds to support the different roles.
- Certain roles can be played using the voice only – e. g. for noises (wind, leaves), but also for language (short texts, rhymes, poems, verses of songs).

Conclusion

Play-songs provide a particularly well-suited basis for a diversity of activities involving music and movement for deaf and hard-of-hearing children, especially in groups of mixed ability. *Several objectives* can be aimed at, focussing on *different creative priorities* with the help of a *diversity of activities*. This work can be interdisciplinary in its concept and inclusive in its realisation providing the topics in question are prepared with the appropriate level of differentiation. The planning results from taking into account the children's individual needs, abilities and interests – a developmental form which is creative and open for adults and children alike. Thus play-songs can be put to use with a creatively stimulating and integrating effect in education, early learning and support as well as therapy especially for children with hearing loss.

Literature

Athey, Chris (2007[2]): *Extending thought in young children. A parent-teacher partnership.* London.

Baker, Felicity/Wigram, Tony (Ed.) (2005): *Songwriting. Methods, Techniques and Clinical Applications for Music Therapy Clinicians, Educators and Students.* London.

Bang, Claus (1980): *A World of Sound & Music.* In: *Journal British Association Teachers of the Deaf*, No. 4.

Benari, Naomi (1995): *Inner Rhythm – Dance Training for the Deaf.* Chur. An accompanying video was also published.

Birkenshaw-Fleming, Lois (2007[2]): *Music for All.* Van Nuys CA.

Birkenshaw-Fleming, Lois (2006[4]) *Music for Fun, Music for Learning.* Gilsum NH.

Brunner-Danuser, Fida (1984): *Mimi Scheiblauer – Musik und Bewegung.* Zurich.

Estabrooks, Warren/Birkenshaw-Fleming, Lois (2006²): *Hear and Listen! Talk and Sing!* Alexander Graham Bell Association for the Deaf and the Hard of Hearing. Washington DC.

Estabrooks, Warren/Birkenshaw-Fleming, Lois (2003): *Songs for Listening! Songs for Life!* Alexander Graham Bell Association for the Deaf and the Hard of Hearing. Washington DC.

Feuser, Georg (1997): *Thesis: Inclusive Education – Education of all Children and young people together in pre-school establishments and schools.* In: *http://bidok.uibk.ac.at/ library/feuser-humanbeing.html*, 01/2008.

Feuser, Georg (1996): *The Relation between the View of the Human Being and Inclusive Education. "There Are No Mentally Handicapped!"* Speech to the members of Nationalrat in the Austrian Parliament on the 29th Oct. 1996 in Vienna. In: *http://bidok. uibk.ac.at/library/feuser-humanbeing.html*, 01/2008.

Hannaford, Carla (1995): *Smart Moves. Why learning is not all in your head.* Arlington, VA, USA.

Haselbach, Barbara/Grüner, Micaela/Salmon, Shirley (Ed.) (2007): *Im Dialog – Elementare Musik- und Tanzpädagogik im Interdisziplinären Kontext. Orff-Schulwerk Symposion Salzburg 2006. In Dialogue – Elemental Music and Dance Education in Interdisciplinary Contexts. Orff-Schulwerk Symposium Salzburg 2006.* Mainz.

Haselbach, Barbara (1978): *Dance Education. Basic principles and models for Nursery and Primary School.* London.

Haselbach, Barbara/Nykrin, Rudolf/Regner, Hermann (1985): *Musik und Tanz für Kinder. Unterrichtswerk zur Früherziehung.* Mainz.

Jungmair, Ulrike (1992): *Das Elementare. Zur Musik- und Bewegungserziehung im Sinne Carl Orffs. Theorie und Praxis.* Mainz.

Keller, Helen (2004): *The World I Live In.* New York, USA.

Keller, Wilhelm (1970): *Ludi Musici 1. Spiellieder.* Boppard/Rhein.

Laborit, Emmanuelle (1999): *The Cry of the Gull.* Washington DC, USA.

Marbacher-Widmer, Pia (1991): *Bewegen und Malen. Zusammenhänge – Psychomotorik – Urformen – Körper- und Raumerfahrung.* Broadstairs, UK.

Maturana, Humberto R./Verden-Zöller, Gerda (1996): *Biology of Love.* Munich/Basle.

Matterson, Elizabeth (Ed.) (1991): *This Little Puffin: Finger Plays and Nursery Games.* London.

Mort, Linda/Morris, Janet (1991): *Starting with Rhyme.* Scholastic publications. UK.

Nordoff, Paul/Robbins, Clive (1964): *The second book of children's play-songs.* Pennsylvania, USA.

Nordoff, Paul/Robbins, Clive (1971): *Therapy in Music for disabled children.* London.

Orff, Carl: *Das Schulwerk – Rückblick und Ausblick.* In: Orff Institute (Ed.) (1964): *Jahrbuch 1963.* Mainz, 13; *Orff-Schulwerk: Past and Future.* In: *Music in Education*, Sep/Oct 1964. Translation: Margaret Murray.

Orff, Carl/Keetmann, Gunild (1950-1954): *Orff-Schulwerk. Musik für Kinder.* Mainz.

Orff, Carl/Keetmann, Gunild: *Music for Children.* English Adaptation by Margaret Murray.

Orff, Carl Orff-Schulwerk: Past and Future, in: Music in Education, Sep/Oct 1964 (Translation: Margaret Murray).

Orff, Gertrud (1980): *The Orff Music Therapy.* Translation: Margaret Murray. London.

Orff, Gertrud (1984): *Key Concepts in the Orff Music Therapy.* Translation: Jeremy Day and Shirley Salmon. London.

Plahl, Christine/Koch-Temming, Hedwig (Ed.) (2005): *Musiktherapie mit Kindern. Grundlagen – Methoden – Praxisfelder.* Bern.

Prause, Manuela-Carmen: *Musik und Gehörlosigkeit. Therapeutische und pädagogische Aspekte der Verwendung von Musik bei gehörlosen Menschen unter besonderer Berücksichtigung des anglo-amerikanischen Forschungsgebietes.* In: Priel, Walter (Ed.) (2001): *Kölner Studien zur Musik in Erziehung und Therapie,* Vol. V. Cologne/ Reinkassel.

Robbins, Carol/Robbins, Clive (1980): *Music for the hearing impaired* & *other special groups. A resource manual and curriculum guide.* Saint-Louis MO, USA.

Sacks, Oliver (2000): *Seeing Voices. A Journey into the World of the Deaf.*

Salmon, Shirley (2007): *Hello Children. A collection of songs and related activities for children aged 4-9.*

Salmon, Shirley (1992): *Musik und Bewegung mit schwerhörigen Kindern in Kooperationsklassen.* In: Orff Institute (Ed.): *Orff-Schulwerk Informationen,* Nr. 50. Salzburg; and in: *http://bidok.uibk.ac.at/library/salmon-musik.html,* 01/2008.

Salmon, Shirley (1999): *Music for Everyone. The challenge of people with special needs.* Lecture at the "1st International Symposium Music Education and Music Therapy" in Guadalajara, Mexico, February 1999. In: *http://bidok.uibk.ac.at/library/salmon-everyone-e.html,* 01/2008.

Salmon, Shirley/Schumacher, Karin (Ed.) (2001): *Symposion Musikalische Lebenshilfe. Die Bedeutung des Orff-Schulwerks für Musiktherapie, Sozial- und Integrationspädagogik.* Hamburg.

Salmon, Shirley (2003): *Spiellieder in der multi-sensorischen Förderung von Kindern mit Hörbeeinträchtigungen.* Diplomarbeit zur Erlangung des Magistergrades der Philosophie an der Geisteswissenschaftlichen Fakultät der Leopold-Franzens-Universität Innsbruck 2003. In: *http://bidok.uibk.ac.at/library/salmon-dipl-hoerbeeintraechtigung. html,* 01/2008.

Schmid, Bärbel/Friedrich, Wolfgang (2001): *Momel singt Lieder in einfacher Sprache. Ein Liederbuch für die Förder- und Grundschule mit vielen Kopiervorlagen.* Donauwörth.

Schumacher, Karin (2001): *Ammenscherze und Sprachentwicklung. Entwicklungspsychologische Erkenntnisse für die Arbeit mit noch nicht sprechenden und sprachgestörten Kindern.* In: Orff Institute (Ed.): *Orff-Schulwerk* Informationen, Nr. 66. Salzburg.

Schumacher, Karin (2003): *Frühe Mutter-Kind-Spiele und ihre Bedeutung für die zwischenmenschliche Beziehungsfähigkeit.* In: *Der Vierzeiler. Zeitschrift für Musik. Kultur und Volksleben,* 23. Graz.

Schumacher, Karin (1994): *Musiktherapie mit autistischen Kindern.* In: *Praxis der Musiktherapie,* Vol. XII. Stuttgart et al.

Sherborne, Veronica (2001): *Developmental Movement for Children: Mainstream, special needs and pre-school.* UK.

The National Grange (1992): *Lift up your hands. Popular songs in Sign Language.* Washington D.C., USA.

Tischler, Björn/Moroder-Tischler, Ruth (1990): *Musik aktiv erleben. Musikalische Spielideen für die pädagogische, sonderpädagogische und therapeutische Praxis.* Frankfurt/Main.

The Emerging "Musical Self" –
the Role of the Nordoff-Robbins Music Therapy Approach
for Teenagers at the Mary Hare Schools for the Deaf

Christine Rocca

Two schools make up the Mary Hare Schools for the Deaf: a primary school, catering for severely and profoundly deaf children, aged 4–10, and a secondary school and sixth form with students aged 11–18 years. Of the 250 students at the secondary and sixth form, the majority are profoundly deaf, the remainder severely deaf. Both sites are located in Newbury, Berkshire, UK.

Currently 80 % of the 250 students study an individual instrument in addition to their class based music lesson. They take the Royal Schools of Music examinations, ranging from grade 1 to grade 8. The full orchestral range of instruments is studied. The most popular being the flute, which is played mainly by profoundly deaf students. Students study music at national examination level for GCSE[1] and A-level[2], with an increasing number of students continuing their musical studies at university and music colleges.

Since 1986, musical life for teenagers at the Mary Hare secondary school and sixth form has been influenced by the music therapy approach developed by Paul Nordoff and Clive Robbins. Nordoff and Robbins developed their own approach to music therapy during the 1960s and 70s and founded the Nordoff-Robbins Music Therapy Centre in 1977. The concept of the presence of an inner musical self as part of our earliest living experience, expressed through rhythm, tempo, and pitch is a founding concept. Deaf children possess this innate musicality, and how we access this, is the key to their musical expression and development. A deaf child requires us to listen in a different way. Initially there can seem an apparent un-musicality and lack of rhythmic perception. However, if we consider their deafness as a kind of veil drawn over their inner musical self, we can begin to listen to the implicit musical persona.

The Nordoff-Robbins approach encourages individuals to express themselves through improvisation. Initially this is done using percussive instruments, supported by the therapist at the piano. This technique encourages confidence in making sounds, and broadens musical experience and understanding. It can provide

---

1   The General Certificate of Education (GCSE) is a set of British qualifications usually taken by secondary school students between the ages of 14 and 16.
2   A-level is short for 'Advanced Level' – a General Certificate of Education qualification usually taken by students in the sixth form – the final two years of secondary school after they have completed their GCE exams.

opportunities for individuals to discover and nurture their musical self, to consider themselves musical and to embark on a discovery of sound, both internal and external. The child centred approach by Nordoff-Robbins has existed as the underlining premise from which the work at Mary Hare has grown.

Nordoff and Robbins recorded and documented individual music therapy sessions, group music therapy sessions, rehearsal groups and performances. These stages, whilst distinctive are viewed as inter-connected within the context of Mary Hare. The development of individual musical work, group work leading to performances is a fundamental aspect of the integrated musical experience.

The work of Clive and Carol Robbins at the Rochester State School for the Deaf, USA, has also played a significant part in the foundation of the strategies used at Mary Hare. They described their work not in music therapy terms, rather as a musical process. Until their work, music with deaf children traditionally emphasised speech, language acquisition and discrimination exercises. Carol included broader developments of cognition and the exploration of musicality and used it as a model for developing a positive musical experience for deaf children.

Carol, a teacher of the Deaf and a music therapist, was the first person to set auditory discrimination within a musical context. Her sessions involved a strong sense of the music used, and the role music plays in the development of auditory skills was recognised. The music she used was highly structured and centred in a narrow key framework, so that the musical intention was always very clear. This allowed a child to feel confident, to enjoy the challenges of playing and to support others in a group. The use of such structured musical experiences centred in a narrow key framework has been integrated into the approach at Mary Hare. It has been developed further to encompass a more individual improvisational element reflecting music therapy techniques, yet centred in an educational context. The focus goes beyond auditory discrimination to explore the emotional and expressive aspects of the individual as expressed through improvisational and structured music. At Mary Hare the main essence within the musical curriculum is to develop child centred musicality, both individually and within group contexts.

This is not intended to suggest that all deaf children within Mary Hare require 'therapy'. The term in this context refers to the concept of 'change' and is an acknowledgement of the influence of the Nordoff-Robbins music therapy approach.

The work at Mary Hare is carried out within an educational context. Students must also cover all aspects of the National Music Curriculum. However, the approach combines themes from education, music therapy and community music. The sharing and interlocking of ideas is a core feature of the work, they enrich and influence each other and form a basis for musical opportunity and personal growth.

Cochlear Implants

Two new technologies, digital hearing aids and cochlear implants, have had a major effect on the way deaf people perceive sound and music. As the majority of young, profoundly deaf children are now receiving cochlear implants, and the majority of pupils in the entry years at Mary Hare have implants, it was necessary to consider how this would affect the musical approach within the school.

Some of the older Mary Hare students, aged 15–18, were implanted when they were three, and were among the first children in the country to receive implants. Many in this group are currently being re-implanted with technically improved equipment, and are learning to adjust to new hearing equipment for a second time. A smaller percentage of our student population were implanted as teenagers.

The first generation of cochlear implants, in the 1990s, were poorly optimised for music. Quotations such as "works well for speech and less well for music" and "the currently used CI coding strategies are primarily optimised for speech perception rather than for listening to music, and CI recipients are not satisfied with the way music is processed and presented" were commonplace, and reflected doubts that many professionals who worked with implanted teenagers were having.

At Mary Hare we were concerned at what we felt was restricting the musicality of implanted teenagers. The students showed a distinct lack of flexibility and sensitivity when playing in groups and as soloists; they did not seem to perceive the pulse; although they were able to imitate the correct number of sounds in a rhythmic imitation exercise, they were unable to imitate the rhythmic pattern; and they were unable to tell if one pitch was higher or lower than another, and would often invert pitches.

In 2002, at the World Congress on Music Therapy, we presented a paper that demonstrated these difficulties. We hoped the paper would encourage companies to improve the technology for musical perception. We also considered how a music therapy approach would assist in the development of a better musical experience for the newly implanted teenagers. We decided to focus on individual improvisation, as this allows us to go beyond discriminatory listening exercises, and explore a broader kinaesthetic and holistic context.

Implants today are optimised to work best within the range of frequencies of speech. Instruments that sound mostly around 250 Hz are difficult for students to hear; whereas high frequency instruments, such as wind chimes, triangles, metallophones and the upper registers of the piano are easy to hear. Following implantation, students needed time to explore the sounds and readjust their perception of instrumental sounds.

Young deaf children explore their musicality by playing, improvising, dancing, acting and singing, all in a free uninhibited manner. This is not generally true for adolescents. It would have been a mistake to make our newly implanted teenagers start
at the beginning of the musical process with simple exercises on percussion instruments. Many of these older students have had years of percussion. So we decided
to let each student explore their new music and sound world with whatever instrument they wanted to, focussing more on orchestral instruments. Many students
choose one of the following: the flute, the clarinet, the piano or the keyboard. The
choice indicates a preference for instruments that are strong in the higher frequency ranges, and the flute has become the most popular instrument in the school.

Fig. 1: Flute concert

One positive result of implantation is that teenagers say they find song lyrics easier
to hear. Playing pre-composed music has unlocked a whole world of musical experience for implanted teenagers. Because they can hear the lyrics better, they are able
to understand the lyrics in relation to the melody and have a more complete picture
of the meaning of a piece. In a sense, the lyrics and melody have come to life.

This has had the knock-on effect of making it easier for many to play in a group,
by enabling them to maintain tempo and rhythm. We have found that the most advantageous music to introduce to groups uses strong repetitive beats, strong bass
lines, predictable harmonic sequences, clear structure and melodic phrasing. Playing music like this fosters group awareness, and promotes confidence in individual
players and the group as a whole. It also gives individuals a strong starting point
for their own compositions and improvisations, from which they can develop their
musicality and self-expression.

Both the students and the teachers determine the musical styles our groups play.
Students often have very specific reasons for wanting to play a particular piece;

it may hold a special significance for them or their families, or they may want to know how it works or how the words fit. The lyrics are centred on the strength and security of the rhythmic framework. The holding potential of the bass draws the group together, as they play and move within its anchor. Students often talk about the relationship to movement as part of their musical experience. I have rarely seen children who do not move whilst playing and many extend their musical experiences into dance.

The benefits of playing in a group are: the unifying element of the clarity of the lyrics, the development of a strong discriminatory skill in relation to a variety of instruments, heightened auditory perception and a positive social experience.

Fig. 2: Dancing together

Instrumental Playing in Ensembles

Studying an instrument is an important part of the work at Mary Hare. The individual learning experience becomes a fundamental part of the process in educational and therapeutic terms. The intense sensation of experiencing the sound, vibration and emotional quality of an instrument can help teenagers to find their musical strengths and to focus on the essence of sound from a starting point of their choice. They can develop a secure understanding of their own sound. One student frequently discussed her experience of music as she played in relation to resonance through her hair and body.

Deafness can be isolating, especially for young children in the early stages of communication. A group experiencing music together fosters interaction and communication through playing. It encourages self-expression and leads to increased levels of confidence. The advantages of developing cognitive, physical and musical skills are self-evident. Deaf children face considerable challenges however when playing in a music group. While their experience of music is just developing they must learn to cope with varying levels of sound quality whilst combining listening, lip-reading and following the music. If there is a fundamental lack of confidence in their own sound and experience of sound, then it is hard for teenagers to improvise or play within a group. They are often anxious about how they will sound to others, and have the misconception that all hearing people will know if they have gone wrong.

It's important within a group to emphasise points of musical structure and sections of improvisation within a session. The clarity of the structure provides a clear experience and expectation within the music, aids confidence and encourages the exploration of sound as a means of musical expression. The positioning of a group should also be considered. Groups might be placed in a semi-circle and in an acoustically favourable area. Some players like to stand while lip reading songs or put one foot against that of another player.

Composition

Once secure within their own sound and musicality, many deaf children are ready to extend their experiences individually or within a group situation towards composition. Therapy and education must continue to work in synthesis if students are to be led towards their own musical identity. For example, one young deaf man explores his voice through scat singing, showing freedom to explore and the confidence of his own sound to improvise. He is able to subdivide the beat through syncopation and cross rhythmic effects. The intonation within the voice rises and falls in a natural musical expression with dynamic contrast. Another profoundly deaf singer composes her own melodies to her lyrics. She records these on a tape in order to notate them, and then adds the harmonic framework.

Composing is a wonderful way for students to hear and visualise their ideas. It often strengthens their perception of the music and is the first step towards using improvisation to help express their emotional and life experiences, for example a young man from Northern Ireland desperately wanted to play his cornet in the local brass band. *He* wanted to play within his hearing band, something many find difficult as they feel judged and experience difficulties in following conductors. This young man composed a series of movements based on the theme *A day in the life of a deaf man,* in essence to play musically with his friends within his world, for them to experience from his perspective and for him to be in a strong leading position. He knew every detail of his composition and found it an amazing experience to hear it coming to life with the bass pedal note, a holding secure basis from which he could write and explore his musical ideas.

By comparison two twins from Oxfordshire with cochlear implants both play the piano and the flute. Having developed a technique of writing using sequences of harmonic progression such as the cycle of fifths, they explore their own compositional dimensions within the security of this framework.

Composing reflects a similar process as performing in terms of developing with a balance between structural and improvisational elements. The culmination of the two is performance.

Performance

The Nordoff-Robbins approach encouraged the development of performance in part of some of their work with children. Historically, the area of performance has not been included within the therapeutic process, and has generally not been considered appropriate or valuable. Yet within the context of a school the underlying elements of performance are highly relevant. Performance at Mary Hare is an integral part of the musical life for many teenagers. They instigate ideas and themes and develop them into performance pieces worked out in small groups through improvisatory sessions or presentations.

Performances within the school have greatly developed in complexity over the years and reflect the creative talents of the students. These have resulted in individual and group benefits, with up to 70 pupils being involved at one time in annual productions. Often a popular musical is used as the vehicle for the work, and adapted by the students to reflect more of their cultural identity and performance intention The choice and mode of the performance is guided by the students, they decide individually if they want to sing, play, dance or act, in any combination or all of the art forms.

The following productions are representative of many of the works.

Toad of Toad Hall presented in the style of 'rap'. The rhythmic impetus and repetitive rhythmic sequences of rap, used for both solo and chorus numbers, enabled many pupils to deliver ideas through a controlled basic beat framework. This internal recognition of the basic beat or pulse within music is a fundamental facet of the Nordoff-Robbins approach, namely "the underlying time base of coherent musical activity and experience"[3].

Whilst the aural and physical experience of a basic beat or pulse can be achieved easily with young deaf children, it is necessary to present it to teenagers in a way in

---

3   Nordoff, Paul/Robbins, Clive (1980): *Therapy in Music*, p. 22

which they are positively engaging with the rhythmic, timbral and dynamic qualities of the beat, in a confident manner. The style of rap uses a strong basic beat, which provides a structural framework and gives a sense of security, yet it also allows for an improvisational element to extend the musical development.

Cultural influences are strongly reflected within performances. They often include physicality and gestural sections featuring strong mime and facial expressive elements. These sections are typically developed through improvisational dance sessions based around a stimulus. Here the unity between musical experience and movement is evident. All children move as they play music and this natural expression of musical experience can be extended into dance/movement. The influence of structural and improvisational elements forms a similar development process.

Cultural influences also inform the development and presentation of performance works. A recent performance of *Lower East Side* combined a hip-hop funky group, contrasting with a salsa, samba influence. The rhythmic impulse inspired the ensembles both in their instrumental presentation and choreographed dance numbers.

Large chorus ensembles of over 60 teenagers provide a sense of unity and strength. For this a consistent basic beat is essential to maintain confidence for the performers. Often floor based amplifiers and fold-back monitors have enabled dances of over 10 minutes to be achieved. The synthesis of movement creates an intensity and fluidity of its own making.

Summary

The boundaries which exist between Music Therapy, Music Education and Community Music are distinctive, yet there are certain contexts within which an interchange of forms is professionally possible and appropriate. As Mercédès Pavlicevic suggests in *Music Therapy in Context. Music, Meaning and Relationship*, there are "aspects of group work that belong exclusively to music therapy, and those that are shareable and open to being inspired and informed by other, adjacent practices".

All groups are unique and how we engage with them individually and as a group will also be very distinctive. There are however common features, definite areas of structure, style and instrumentation. How we use these elements through structured and improvised forms will inform the development of the group. The strategies used with implanted children and effective methods of working are based on an underlying music therapy principle, combined with educational goals.

Music and performance is a natural part of the lives of teenagers at Mary Hare. Some may follow up these experiences through an academic route. But for the majority it is a personal, private and individual experience that they either choose to share or to explore individually.

The music therapy approach of Nordoff and Robbins has played a significant part in the development of a teaching style at the Mary Hare schools, and illustrates that "Music therapy theory and practice does and must offer something rich, complex and acutely inspired to group music making across the boundaries of healing, teaching, learning, relaxing, performing and simply living in music"[4].

---

4   Pavlicevic, Mercédès (2000): *Music Therapy in Context. Music, Meaning and Relationship*, p. 34

Inclusive Dance Theatre

Wolfgang Stange

I had my first dance lesson at the age of 23 at the Hilde Holger School of Contemporary Dance in Camden Town in London. There was always singing and music making in my working class family background, but it was kept very much a family endeavour. My love was the theatre, but my parents did not have the means to support my longings and so I became a chef in the hope to travel, learn languages and then return to the theatre through the back door by translating plays. It all changed when my friend Karola took me to Hilde Holger. When questioned by Hilde Holger about my intentions, I grew nervous and said "I love to dance, but feel I am too old". "If you think you are too old, don't waste my time. You are never too old if you really want to do something. Do you, or don't you?" Hilde Holger questioned me. And of course I wanted to and she asked me to get ready for the class. My fate was sealed there and then. It was this "You are never …" that stuck with me when I decided to give people a chance to take part in the performing arts, if they really wanted, and so my work took me to explore avenues, to make the world of music and dance and the performing arts accessible to people of different backgrounds and different abilities.

I soon realised that as individuals we all have to experience the subject matter on our terms. It means there have to be different approaches without losing or diluting the source, the soul of what we are teaching. The essence has to be experiencing the art form. Allowing people to have the experience of music and dance. Our development is based on learning from and through experiences. So because some people cannot lift an instrument with two hands because they do not have two hands, they should not be withheld the experience of creating sound with this particular instrument. *Dance Dynamics* for all.

AMICI Dance Theatre Company[1], which I founded, was not born out of a political initiative, but evolved from a progression of work with different groups in the community – dance being the focal point. As I taught and choreographed I felt that there was a lot we could learn from each other and this conclusion prompted me to invite three different community groups who shared a love for dancing to work on a dance drama piece together. This was in 1980 and involved non-sighted dancers, sighted dancers, dancers with learning difficulties and an actress called Judy Fairclough who was a wheelchair user – and also wrote the script for our first performance called *I am not yet dead*.

---

1   http://www.amicidance.org

There is always a way to include people of different abilities as the focus should be on their ability and how to develop their artistic potential rather than their disability. The essence of dance has to be explored and developed. If we focus on the expression in dance, then surely a different movement vocabulary that is complementary to the individual to express his or her ideas or feelings is necessary. If we believe in individual expression, then there are no difficulties in implementing this within the choreography.

If the focus is on learning a technique to extend the body's movement capabilities, then it is possible for instance to teach ballet to physically or mentally different individuals. This can only be successfully achieved, if we once again work on or with the essence.

What is the essence of a *plié*? Is it to bend one's knees in the five positions only, or is it to establish the feeling of a counter pull in the body with a straight back. Both are important, but if the individual has no means of bending the knees, is the feeling of counter pull and straight back at that moment more important?

Is a *tendu* only the extension of a pointed foot in time to music in three directions? It also involves the isolation of one foot. For a wheelchair user with limited or no movement in the legs and feet, it is focussing on that leg and foot, sending energy into this area that matters. Integration is possible if we focus on the individual and help them to be part of the experience that the different dance forms have to offer.

I had the privilege to hold workshops and be generally involved in work for a public performance with Tsunami survivors and young people from a Special Needs School in the South of Sri Lanka. The majority of the school's pupils were profoundly deaf or hard-of-hearing, some others had Down's syndrome. From the very beginning I was astonished by the apparent musicality of those who were referred to as deaf or hard-of-hearing.

Fig. 1

I started the morning class with the whole group standing in a circle holding hands. The Sri Lankan greeting of Ayubowan is done by putting both palms together and bowing to a person or group. The deaf students then showed us their good morning greeting, by presenting their thumb and then opening the whole hand, which signifies the opening of the flower in the morning. We then proceeded with running hand in hand on the spot (with linked hands). Basic exercises by turning the head and stretching the arms and others to warm up the body were then demonstrated by me and followed by the group. No translation was needed as no language was used. Just the observation. The first part was done without any music or any verbal instructions and developed a sense of learning together.

The second part involved the random choice of music, in which a group member is chosen by the turning of a pen to take up the centre to create his or her own dance, which the group has to follow. Sri Lankan dancing which is based on old rituals is very different from the refined Indian hand and finger movements, it is rather boisterous and extremely vigorous. It seems Sri Lankans are born with this physical expression and it is not different for people who are born without hearing. I was amazed with which confidence the deaf youngsters took to the centre stage and exhibited not only a terrific sense of rhythm, but also executed the steps with amazing precision.

Fig. 2

In the group improvisation they showed great sensitivity, observing the others, sensing the pulse of the music and developing real artistic short dance pieces. I realised that their contribution to the performance would be immense. And I was proved right. We all learned from one another. Soon everybody, whether the student with Down's syndrome or the Tsunami affected youngsters, would sign to each other picking up the basics signs in order to communicate. In fact for me not being a native speaker, it was advantageous as I would demonstrate my points physically when I had difficulties with my Sinhalese. We also had young Tamils from the East coast in the group, so the signing helped throughout. Naturally, the piece, which reflected the real life experience of the Tsunami survivors, developed simultaneously in four languages, Sinhalese, Tamil, English and sign language. All four languages are part of Sri Lanka and so it was only right the show should be presented in these languages.

Fig. 3

The opening scene of life before the Tsunami showed a fishermen dance where the majority of dancers were deaf. Their natural feel for movements and their inborn sense of rhythm made them on par with the professional dancers in this dance. *Memories of a Monkey Boy*, the title of the dance drama, had a young Tamil and a deaf performer in the major roles. Both being of a minority group within Sri Lanka. It showed us that working together, learning from one another, respecting one another, is the only way forward. Every single person with their difference is contributing positively towards the whole without losing their identity. The words hearing, seeing, speaking have been interpreted only one way, not taking into account that they are linked to receiving and passing on information. Information can be received in many different forms through vibration, touch, and smell. We can talk with our voice, hands or eyes, we can see through touch, smell or voice and we can hear with our eyes and through vibrations.

Fig. 4

The richness of a diverse group like this is very powerful as they are all present-ing themselves as they are. There is no fudging the issues, not trying to hide the differences, but celebrating them. *Memories of a Monkey Boy* was performed for seven nights in the Sri Lanka capital Colombo and left a mark on the audience. It not only left a mark on the audience, but also on the cast as they learnt that every-body has a cross to bear and that it is easier to do so, if we share the burden. Our monkey boy who was treated as an outcast was helped and supported by a deaf young man. There was no communication problem between them. Spoken lan-guage was not necessary. We often create barriers were there are none. If we allow ourselves to be more open and realise there are different ways of experiencing the same thing, we may be able to help ourselves in the process of unlocking our deep seated prejudices.

For me it was equally a learning process to see the apparently deaf exhibiting a high standard of musicality and performing skills. I am grateful to my deaf friends from the Rohana School in Matara in the South of Sri Lanka.

Contributors

Claus Bang

Music therapist and audio speech therapist born 1938. Trained in Music Education and Music Therapy in Germany, Austria, the Netherlands, Great Britain and the United States. Head of the Music Therapy Programme at the Aalborg School and Guidance Centre for Deaf, Hearing-Impaired and Deaf-Blind Children and Adolescents, Denmark 1961–1998. 1969 co-founder of the Danish Society of Music Therapy and member of the Board 1969–1979. Head of Music Therapy Training at the Royal Danish College of Educational Studies 1973–1976. Initiator and member of the planning group for the Music Therapy Institute at Aalborg University 1977–1982. Since 1976 instructor and member of the Board of the International Society for further Training in Music Education (IGMF), Germany, and since 2004 honorary member. Vice-president and instructor for The Beethoven Fund for Deaf Children, Great Britain since 1981. Presentations and demonstrations of music therapy in 42 countries. Free-lance instructor, project leader and pensioner since 1998. Founder and chairman of The Music Therapy Foundation "A World of Sound and Music" for Deaf, Hearing Impaired and Multi-Handicapped Children and Adolescents, Denmark in 2000. Published the multimedia production (3 dual-layer DVD+Rs) *A World of Sound & Music – Music Therapy for Deaf, Hearing Impaired and Multi-Handicapped Children and Adolescents*, material for treatment, education, training and research in 2005.

Address: Söndergade 61, 9480 Løkken, Denmark
Tel.: +45 9899 1699; Fax: +45 9899 1698
E-mail: mail@clausbang.com; Homepage: www.clausbang.com

Elke Bartlmä, Dipl. Päd.

Trained as a special school teacher at the college of education in Klagenfurt, Austria and as an audio-pedagogical teacher for deaf and hard-of-hearing children. Works as a supporting teacher for hard-of-hearing children integrated in primary and secondary schools in Carinthia, Austria.

Address: Rosentalerstr. 48, 9020 Klagenfurt, Austria
E-mail: elvebar@hotmail.com

Naomi Benari, MA

Danced with Ballet Rambert and has an MA in Dance Studies. She created "Dance for Everyone", the first dance company to be set up in Great Britain solely for work in education. The company gave performances and dance workshops in schools for many years. She taught dance to profoundly deaf children in a number of schools and units using Inner Rhythm, and also gave therapeutic dance sessions to children with learning difficulties, often employing Inner Rhythm techniques. She has written and lectured widely on her work with deaf children.

E-mail: benari@toucansurf.com

Lois Birkenshaw-Fleming

Was for many years the director of the Orff Music Program for the Toronto Board of Education in Canada. She also directed the Orff Teacher Training courses at the Royal Conservatory of Music and York University, Canada as well as teaching courses in Special Education through Music. She has given workshops and courses throughout Canada and the USA and in many parts of Europe and South Africa. Lois Birkenshaw-Fleming has authored many articles and books on the subject of music education, including *Music for Fun, Music for Learning, Come On Everybody, Let's Sing, Music for All* and she edited *An Orff Mosaic From Canada, Orff au Canada: une mosaïque. Songs for Listening, Songs for Life!, Hear and Listen! Talk and Sing!* and *The Goat with the Bright Red Socks.*

Address: 67 Heath St. West, Toronto, Ontario, Canada
E-mail: loisfleming@sympatico.ca

Giulia Cremaschi Trovesi

Pianist, composer, music teacher (piano and composition), music therapist, trainer and supervisor. Taught music in secondary schools, was responsible for music therapy from 1981 to 1997 at the Institute of Audiology of the University of Milan, Italy and taught on the four-year music therapy course in Assisi from 1981–2000 as well as on music therapy courses in other countries. Founded the APMM 'Giulia Cremaschi Trovesi' (Musical Pedagogy and Music Therapy Association) centre of Humanistic Music Therapy in 1991, president of the APMM. Founded the I.F.M. (Italian Federation of Music Therapists) in 1998 together with a group of professionals. President to the European and world-wide Conferences of Music therapy. Has researched in the fields of communication, music therapy, music pedagogy, LD (learning disorders), ADD (Attention Deficit Disorder) and ADHD (Attention Deficit, Hyperactivity Disorder). She received the national prize "Motta" in December 1989 for her work with deaf children, was awarded the prize at the 3rd International Video Congress "The New Born and the Sound", conference for Infantile Neuro-Psychiatrists and Neonatal Pathologists and received the "Certificate of Civic Merit" in 1996 from the Mayor of Bergamo, Italy. She has published widely on her research.

Address: via Rosciano, 15, 24010 Ponteranica (BG), Italy
E-mail: giulia.cremaschi@musicoterapia.it
Homepage: www.musicoterapia.it

Katharina Ferner, Dipl. Päd.

Trained as a special school teacher and speech therapist, qualified in the education of deaf and hard-of-hearing children, trained in Montessori Pedagogy. She is currently teaching in an inclusive class, running projects on singing and learning songs, organizing playgrounds for all the senses, teaching rhythmic-musical education and music to deaf children as well as running project weeks for families with hard-of-hearing children in Salzburg.

Address: Bahnhofstr. 17, 5580 Tamsweg, Austria
E-mail: freieslesen@yahoo.de

Georg Feuser, Prof. Dr. phil.

Trained as teacher for primary, secondary, grammar schools and special schools. Professor for "Special Education, Didactics, Therapy and Integration of children/people with cognitive disabilities and severe developmental problems" at the University of Bremen, Germany since 1978. Guest professor at the Institute for Special Education, University of Zurich, Switzerland since 2005. Developed and put into practice among other projects "Universal Pedagogy and Developmentally Logical Didactics" as well as "Inclusive Education in Intercultural Contexts". Has published widely and was guest professor at Innsbruck, Klagenfurt and Vienna universities, Austria.

Address: Institute for Special Education, University of Zurich, Hirschengraben 48,
8001 Zürich, Switzerland
E-mail: feuser@isp.uzh.ch

Wolfgang Friedrich

Studied Special Education at Würzburg University, Germany. After further studies he acquired his diploma as musical therapist from the Music Academy in Würzburg. He has been working as a special school teacher at the Dr.-Karl-Kroiß school for deaf and hard-of-hearing children in Würzburg since 1987, at present working with emphasis on hearing. Since 1993 he has lectured on the subject of rhythmic musical education for children with hearing loss at Munich University, Germany, Department for the Education of Deaf and Hearing Impaired Children. He has worked on the committee for developing the school curriculum, teaches on advanced training courses in German speaking countries and his work has lead him among other things to Ethiopia (Alpha-School in Addis Abeba). Initiator of the EU project "SiLaSo – Sign Language and Song".

Address: Förderzentrum Hören, Berner Straße 14–16, 97084 Würzburg, Germany
E-mail: wolfgangfriedrich@t-online.de

Marion Honka

Studied pedagogy for the Deaf, trained as a special school teacher and completed a Master's degree at the Ludwig-Maximilian University in Munich, Germany. Further training in pedagogy for behaviourally disturbed children. Studied for one term at the University of Northumbria (Newcastle upon Tyne), Great Britain, in preparation for her final paper entitled "Benefits and Challenges of the Unit System for Hearing Impaired Children". Started teaching in 2000 as a special school teacher at the Dr.-Karl-Kroiß school for deaf and hard-of-hearing children in Würzburg, Germany (centre with an emphasis on hearing). Teaches in classes with students of differing abilities in hearing and speaking. Director of the mobile special educational support (MSD) which advises and accompanies children with hearing loss who are in regular primary and secondary schools. Participant in the school Comenius projects.

Address: Förderzentrum Hören, Berner Straße 14–16, 97084 Würzburg, Germany
E-mail: m.honka@web.de

Kent Lykke Jensen, MA, RMT

Music therapist, member of LAM (Danisch association of trained music therapists). Worked at the Institution for the Deaf Blind in Aalborg, Denmark from 1993–1998. Studied music therapy at the University of Aalborg. Worked since 1998 at the Aalborgskolen (school for deaf children, children with special needs and children with autism). Extended his studies 2001–2003 and acquired an MA in Music Therapy from the University of Aalborg. Board member of Claus Bang's music therapy foundation "Musikterapiforeningen" (www.clausbang.com). Founded the Tranum Music Therapy Centre where he works with brain damaged adults and refugees in music therapy and also teaches music. He plays piano, drums, guitar, bass percussion, church organ, sings and is jazz pianist in the JaDa Band.

Address: Tranum-Musik-Terapi Center, Fuglevaenget 1, Tranum, 9460 Brovst, Denmark
Tel.: +45 2396 3123
E-mail: kent@tmtc.dk

Christine Kiffmann-Duller

Teacher for pre-school children with and without disabilities, audio pedagogical pre-school teacher, teacher, supervisor, qualification in didactics. Has worked in Austria for 30 years in early learning, with children with hearing loss, in kindergartens for children with and without disabilities as well as on training courses and in further education. Her main areas are: integration/inclusion, co-operative education, education in co-operation with parents, interdisciplinary projects.

Address: Audiopädagogische Frühförderung und Familienbegleitung, Chance B, Franz-Josef-Straße 3, 8200 Gleisdorf, Austria
E-mail: christine.kiffmann@chanceb.at

Sigrid Köck-Hatzmann, Dr. phil.

Studied Music, Psychology and Education at Graz University, Austria, Rhythmic Musical Education in Vienna, Austria, and Munich, Germany, and Educational Science in Innsbruck, Austria. She has over 30 years experience in a wide range of institutions (kindergartens, schools, teacher training establishments and universities) with people with and without disabilities.

Address: Birkenhang 10, 8010 Graz, Austria
E-mail: sigrid.koeckhatzmann@gmail.com

Helga Neira Zugasti

Special school teacher for children with multiple limitations. Teacher of rhythmic musical education, lecturer on Didactics and Practice of Rhythmic Musical Education in Special Education at the University of Music and Performing Arts Vienna, Austria. Director of the research project "Rhythmic musical education as catalyst for the development of cognitive functions". Active in the further education of teachers within the special area "Rhythmic musical education as the basic method of inclusive education". Publications in specialist journals. Handbook *Rhythmik als Unterrichtshilfe bei behinderten Kindern*, Wien, 1989.

Address: Sieveringerstraße 79b/2/1, 1190 Wien, Austria
E-mail: hneira2002@yahoo.de

Regina Neuhäusel

Diploma in Music Therapy (University of Applied Sciences), has worked at the Children's Centre (Kinderzentrum) in Munich, Germany since 2001. Lecturer on further training courses and in the in-service training course in Orff Music Therapy.

Address: Kinderzentrum München, Heiglhofstr. 63, 81377 München, Germany
E-mail: r.neuhaeusel@freenet.de

Christine Rocca

Teacher of the Deaf and music therapist at the Mary Hare Schools for the Deaf in Berkshire, Great Britain. Director of the Nordoff-Robbins/Mary Hare Unit at the PACE centre in Newbury, Great Britain. She has worked with a wide range of children and adults in schools for the Deaf and inclusive settings, including those with additional needs, autism and multiple sensory impairments. She presents papers and workshops internationally on areas of the Performing Arts and Music Therapy. Publications include the DVD *Music Time*, a resource for those working with deaf pre-school children.

Address: Mary Hare School, Arlington Manor, Snelsmore Common, Newbury, Berkshire, Great Britain
E-mail: c.rocca@maryhare.org.uk
Homepage: http://www.earfoundation.org.uk

Shirley Salmon, BA (Hons), PGCE, MPhil.

Studied music at York University, Great Britain and trained as a kindergarten and primary school teacher at the Froebel Institute, London. After moving to Austria she took further training in music and movement education, music therapy, sign language and integrative education and studied Educational Science at the University of Innsbruck, Austria where she acquired her master's degree. She has worked with infants, children, teenagers and adults of different abilities in mainstream classes, in groups of mixed ability, in residential homes, kindergartens and schools for 30 years. From 1979–2000 she was employed by the county of Styria using music and movement in homes for behaviourally disturbed children and teenagers and with deaf and hard-of-hearing children while also working free-lance for kindergartens and schools and with families. She has been a lecturer at the Orff Institute, Mozarteum University, Salzburg since 1984 teaching classes in Didactics, Practice Teaching, Theory and Practice of Music and Dance in Integrative Education and in Community Work. She co-ordinates the elective and in-service course "Music and Dance in the Community and in Integrative Pedagogy", co-directs summer courses at the Orff Institute and has been director of the postgraduate university course "Advanced Studies in Music and Dance Education – Orff-Schulwerk" since 2006. She has published numerous articles in journals and has given courses, workshops and lectures in Austria, Germany, Spain, Italy, USA, Japan, Mexico, Hungary, Denmark, Japan, Turkey and Hong Kong.

Address: Department for Music and Dance Education – Orff Institute, Mozarteum University, Frohnburgweg 55, 5020 Salzburg, Austria
E-mail: shirley.salmon@moz.ac.at
Homepage: http://www.moz.ac.at/people.php?penr=50199&lang=2

Wolfgang Stange

Founded AMICI Dance Company and is its director and principle choreographer. He was born in Berlin, Germany and came to Great Britain almost 33 years ago to train at the London Contemporary Dance School. At this time he worked with the distinguished dance expressionist Hilde Holger who became his mentor. He first appreciated the possibilities of dance as a therapeutic force whilst in Sri Lanka. After successful work with people with learning difficulties at Normansfield Hospital, Great Britain he was soon teaching classes to groups with learning and/or physical difficulties in a range of venues, sometimes including aspiring dancers without obvious disabilities. In 1980 AMICI made its groundbreaking debut at the London Roof Top Theatre. Wolfgang Stange is now known internationally for his teaching methods which stress the need to share and acknowledge each other's abilities, whether disabled or not.

E-mail: wolfamici@talktalk.net;
Homepage: http://www.amicidance.org

Ulrike Stelzhammer-Reichhardt, MA, Dr. rer. nat.

Teacher of Music and Dance Education. Studied Music and Dance Education at the University of Music and Performing Arts Vienna and at the Mozarteum University in Salzburg, Austria. She has worked with deaf and hard-of-hearing children and adults, including their families, since 1992 and was involved in the rehabilitation phase for children after cochlear implantation from 1992–1996. From 1997–2002 she co-organized and ran weekly summer camps using music as therapy and education for families with hard-of-hearing children. She completed her Ph.D. on the topic of Music Perception for the Deaf and Hard-of-Hearing at the Mozarteum University, Salzburg. Other focuses include consulting and lecturing on elemental music education, as well as writing articles.

Address: Neutorstraße 21, 5020 Salzburg, Austria
E-mail: ulrike@stelzhammer.eu
Homepage: www.stelzhammer.eu

Ursula Sutter

Diploma in Social Pedagogy (University of Applied Sciences), Orff music therapist, psychotherapist for children and adolescents. Has worked at the Children's Centre (Kinderzentrum) in Munich, Germany since 1992. Works as a music therapist in an inclusive kindergarten and in a centre for children with speech development difficulties, gives lectures and seminars and teaches on the in-service training course in Orff Music Therapy.

Address: Kinderzentrum München, Heiglhofstr. 63, 81377 München, Germany
E-mail: u.sutter@kinderzentrum-muenchen.de

Insa Tjarks

Diploma in Music Therapy (University of Applied Sciences), psychotherapist (HPG). Has worked in the Children's Centre (Kinderzentrum) in Munich, Germany since 1999. Also works as a music therapist in an inclusive kindergarten and in a centre for children with speech development difficulties. Gives lectures and seminars and teaches on the in-service training course in Orff Music Therapy.

Address: Kinderzentrum München, Heiglhofstr. 63, 81377 München, Germany
E-mail: i.tjarks@web.de

Paul Whittaker, D. Litt., MA (Oxon), DipAdvStudMus (Perf), ARCO, ALCM

Born in 1964 with a hearing loss, profoundly deaf since the age of 8. After gaining a music degree from Wadham College, Oxford, Great Britain he founded "Music and the Deaf" a registered charity that helps deaf people – and those who live and work with them – access music and the performing arts. An organist and pianist, he is also much in demand as a speaker, workshop leader and sign language theatre interpreter.

Address: "Music and the Deaf", The Media Centre, 7 Northumberland Street, Huddersfield, West Yorkshire, HD1 1Rl, Great Britain
Tel.: +44 1484 483115; Fax: +44 1484 483116; Minicom: 01484 483117
E-mail: info@matd.org.uk
Homepage: www.matd.org.uk

Helga Wilberg

Trained teacher with practical experience working with children and adolescents with physical disabilities. Further training and diploma in Music and Dance Education from the Orff Institute, Mozarteum University, Salzburg, Austria. Music teacher in the secondary school in Straubing, Germany with special responsibility for interdisciplinary projects, hands-on learning, music and dance performances, choir and ensemble. Member of the teachers' quartet and teachers' band.

Address: Mädchenrealschule der Ursulinen-Schulstiftung, Burggasse 9, 94315 Straubing, Germany
E-mail: w_helga@web.de